TEACHING EVOLVED

Partnership Strategies
for an Equitable, Inclusive,
& Tech-Powered Classroom

**Matthew Rhoads
Belinda Dunnick Karge**

Solution Tree | Press

Copyright © 2025 by Solution Tree Press

Materials appearing here are copyrighted. With one exception, all rights are reserved. Readers may reproduce only those pages marked "Reproducible." Otherwise, no part of this book may be reproduced or transmitted in any form or by any means (electronic, photocopying, recording, or otherwise) without prior written permission of the publisher.

555 North Morton Street
Bloomington, IN 47404
800.733.6786 (toll free) / 812.336.7700
FAX: 812.336.7790

email: info@SolutionTree.com
SolutionTree.com

Visit **go.SolutionTree.com/instruction** to download the free reproducibles in this book.

Printed in the United States of America

Library of Congress Cataloging-in-Publication Data

Names: Rhoads, Matthew, 1990- author. | Karge, Belinda Dunnick, author.
Title: Co-teaching evolved : partnership strategies for an equitable, inclusive, and tech-powered classroom / Matthew Rhoads, Belinda Dunnick Karge.
Description: Bloomington, IN : Solution Tree Press, 2025. | Includes bibliographical references and index. | Summary: "Co-teaching has been practiced in schools for years. But as the world becomes more globalized and digitized, and concerns shift and evolve, co-teaching approaches should be revisited and updated to meet current needs. In Co-Teaching Evolved: Partnership Strategies for an Equitable, Inclusive, and Tech-Powered Classroom, Matthew Rhoads and Belinda Dunnick Karge offer a revived approach to co-teaching that accounts for pressing topics in today's classroom, like ed tech and artificial intelligence. PreK-12 teachers will learn to create collaborative co-teaching partnerships and navigate key co-teaching components-such as lesson design, conflict resolution, and communication with stakeholders-with research-backed tools and strategies"-- Provided by publisher.
Identifiers: LCCN 2024032921 (print) | LCCN 2024032922 (ebook) | ISBN 9781960574824 (paperback) | ISBN 9781960574831 (ebook)
Subjects: LCSH: Teaching teams. | Education--Effect of technological innovations on.
Classification: LCC LB1029.T4 R46 2025 (print) | LCC LB1029.T4 (ebook) | DDC 371.14/8--dc23/eng/20240821
LC record available at https://lccn.loc.gov/2024032921
LC ebook record available at https://lccn.loc.gov/2024032922

Solution Tree
Jeffrey C. Jones, CEO
Edmund M. Ackerman, President

Solution Tree Press
President and Publisher: Douglas M. Rife
Associate Publishers: Todd Brakke and Kendra Slayton
Editorial Director: Laurel Hecker
Art Director: Rian Anderson
Copy Chief: Jessi Finn
Senior Production Editor: Miranda Addonizio
Copy Editor: Charlotte Jones
Cover Designer: Abigail Bowen
Text Designer: Fabiana Cochran
Acquisitions Editors: Carol Collins and Hilary Goff
Content Development Specialist: Amy Rubenstein
Associate Editors: Sarah Ludwig and Elijah Oates
Editorial Assistant: Anne Marie Watkins

ACKNOWLEDGMENTS

This book is dedicated to the many teachers who believe in the power of co-teaching with a colleague to strengthen student outcomes.

Solution Tree Press would like to thank the following reviewers:

Louis Lim
　Principal
　Bur Oak Secondary School
　Markham, Ontario, Canada

Paula Mathews
　STEM Instructional Coach
　Dripping Springs ISD
　Dripping Springs, Texas

Bo Ryan
　Principal/Solution Tree and Marzano Associate/Author
　Ana Grace Academy of the Arts Middle School
　Bloomfield, CT

Dianne Yee
　Assistant Professor
　Western University
　London, Ontario, Canada

Visit **go.SolutionTree.com/instruction** to download the free reproducibles in this book.

TABLE OF CONTENTS

Reproducible pages are in italics.

About the Authors		ix
Introduction		1
	Underlying Themes of Co-Teaching in Changing Classrooms	3
	A Guide to Reading This Book	9
	A Model That Can Work for Every Teacher	13
Chapter 1	**Navigating Co-Teaching Partnerships**	15
	A Dynamic Co-Teaching Classroom Environment	17
	Co-Teaching Partnerships	18
	Types of Co-Teaching Partnerships	18
	Hidden Potential of Prospective Co-Teachers	19
	Basic Elements and Examples of Co-Teaching Partnerships	22
	Conclusion	26
	Reflection and Action: Next Steps	27
Chapter 2	**Introducing Co-Teaching Strategies**	29
	A Three-Stage Co-Teaching Strategy Sequence	30
	The Eleven Co-Teaching Strategies	32
	The Role of Collaboration	42
	Conclusion	43
	Reflection and Action: I Noticed, I Wondered	45

Chapter 3 Building and Maintaining
Co-Teaching Relationships 47
  Fourteen Suggestions for Building and Maintaining
    Co-Teaching Relationships 49
  Strong Partnerships for Better Student Outcomes 53
  Conclusion 55
    Reflection and Action: I Used to Think *Versus* Now I Think 57

Chapter 4 Synthesizing Efficacy, Attitude, and
Essential Agreements 59
  Efficacy and Mindset 60
  Elements of Co-Teaching That Maximize Co-Teacher Efficacy 62
  Essential Agreements for Greater Co-Teacher Efficacy 67
  Conclusion 78
    Reflection and Action: Agree, Argue, and Inspired 79

Chapter 5 Planning and Designing Lessons 81
  Long- and Short-Term Planning With Workflow in Mind 82
  Shared Teaching Philosophies and Integration Into
    Classroom Instruction 88
  Roles and Responsibilities in Planning and Workflow 90
  Instructional and Co-Teaching Strategy and Routine
    Incorporation Into Lessons 92
  Conclusion 97
    Reflection and Action: 3-2-1 Format 99

Chapter 6 Integrating Instructional Strategies With
Co-Teaching Strategies 101
  Review of Co-Teaching Strategies 103
  Guided Instruction and Gradual Release of Responsibility 103
  Instructional Strategies and Instructional Design 104
  Instructional Strategies in Action: Putting Strategies
    Together With Co-Teaching 111
  Conclusion 115
    Reflection and Action: Square, Circle, and Triangle 117

Chapter 7 Co-Teaching in Classrooms Without Boundaries 119
  Instruction Without Boundaries 120
  Co-Teaching With Formative Assessment to Support
    Differentiation and Equity in Physical and Digital Realms 127
  Generative AI and Ed Tech Support in Classrooms
    Without Boundaries 131
  Conclusion 134
    Reflection and Action: Pause, Ponder, and Wonder 135

Chapter 8 Integrating Specialists Into Co-Teaching 137
    Special Education and General Education Co-Teaching 138
    Dual-Immersion Bilingual Education Co-Teaching 143
    Co-Teaching With Speech and Language Pathologists
       and Other Related Services Personnel 145
    AI Copilots and Ed Tech Tools for Specialists 145
    A Case Study 147
    Conclusion 148
       Reflection and Action: Reflection and Goal Setting 149

Chapter 9 Co-Teaching in PreK and Early Childhood Settings 151
    Inclusion in Early Childhood Programs 153
    Adults With Different Expertise 154
    Lessons Based on Observation 155
    Creative Systems of Inclusive Support 158
    Conclusion 161
       Reflection and Action: Challenge 163

Chapter 10 Cultivating a Culture of Co-Teaching 165
    Leaders at Every Level to Build School Culture 166
    The Coherence Framework for Cultural Change 167
    Leadership for Building and Sustaining the Best
       Co-Teaching Programs 178
    Conclusion 180
       Reflection and Action: Develop an Action Plan 181

Epilogue: Moving Forward as a Co-Teacher 183
    Key Takeaways 184
    The Rewards 187
       Reflection and Action: Key Takeaways and Action Steps 190
References and Resources 191
Index 207

ABOUT THE AUTHORS

Matthew Rhoads, EdD, is an expert and innovator in educational technology and instructional strategy integration within online, blended, and traditional in-person classroom settings. With a special education background, Dr. Rhoads co-taught for many years at the high school level in the areas of English, mathematics, and social sciences. He continues to co-teach regularly while coaching teachers and presenting professional development.

As a practicing technology and instructional leader, trainer, integrationist, and coach in adult education, K–12, and higher education, he develops instructional integrations of ed tech tools with research-based strategies to drive instruction. He is a coach and professional learning specialist for new and experienced teachers for the Education to Career Network of North San Diego County, San Diego State University, and Concordia University Irvine. Dr. Rhoads is also a doctoral dissertation chair who coaches doctoral students to conduct their research, write, and defend their dissertations. Dr. Rhoads's eight books focus on integrating instructional strategies with ed tech and AI tools to amplify student learning within in-person, online, and blended learning classrooms. His latest books include *Crush It From the Start: 50 Tips for New Teachers*, *Instruction Without Boundaries: Enhance Your Teaching Strategies With Technology Tools in Any Setting*, the *Amplify Learning: A Global Collaborative* series, and *Navigating the Toggled Term: A Guide for K–12 Classroom and School Leaders*. He also has his podcast, *Navigating Education*, which discusses all topics related to education and instruction.

Dr. Rhoads obtained his bachelor's degree in political science, single-subject English and social science credentials, special education mild/moderate teaching credentials, and master's degree in teaching from Point Loma Nazarene University in San Diego, California. Additionally, he earned his doctorate in educational leadership from Concordia University Irvine in California.

Visit https://coteachingevolved.com and www.matthewrhoads.com for more information on Dr. Rhoads and his work.

**Belinda Dunnick Karge, PhD,** is a professor in the doctoral studies program at Concordia University Irvine and a professor emeritus at California State University, Fullerton. She taught both general education and special education and served in administrative roles in elementary and high school prior to teaching in higher education. Her interest in co-teaching began when she was originally in the classroom; she has co-taught at several levels.

Dr. Karge's professional record demonstrates a consistent pattern of research publications; she has produced five textbooks, five curriculum texts, four book chapters, several educational tools, and more than 150 articles. Her latest book is *Watch, Listen, Ask, Learn: How School Leaders Can Create an Inclusive Environment for Students With Disabilities.* She has made numerous presentations to international, state, and local groups of school district employees and has keynoted several conferences. She serves as a consultant for the U.S. Department of State's Office of Overseas Schools and travels extensively around the world. Research-based instructional strategies, schoolwide change, co-teaching, and inclusive practices are a few areas on which she consults.

Dr. Karge received the Council for Exceptional Children's Susan Phillips Gorin Award. She was also honored with the Council for Learning Disabilities' Floyd G. Hudson Outstanding Service Award and the Association for Childhood Education International service award.

Dr. Karge's PhD is in quantitative methods, special education, and educational psychology, and her master's degree is in special education and reading. She received both from the University of California, Riverside.

Visit https://coteachingevolved.com and www.cui.edu/academicprograms/graduate/edd/leadership/faculty and follow her on X, formerly known as Twitter, @dr_karge and on LinkedIn at www.linkedin.com/in/belinda-karge-024b3a30 to learn more about Dr. Karge's work.

To book Matthew Rhoads or Belinda Dunnick Karge for professional development, contact pd@SolutionTree.com.

INTRODUCTION

Co-teaching is a harmonious partnership where educators blend their unique strengths, creating an enriched environment that not only fosters collaboration but also cultivates diverse learning experiences. In this shared journey, teachers find inspiration in each other, and students blossom, as together they build connections to understanding and nurturing lifelong learning.

—M. Leftwich, co-teaching expert and vice president at 2Teach Global, personal communication, February 1, 2024

As the world changes, the classrooms and experiences of our students look immensely different than they once did. Classrooms are much more inclusive of students' differences and embrace equity. Additionally, the complexities of an interconnected world bring challenges such as climate change, a global economy, and new technologies like artificial intelligence (AI) that are changing the landscape of work and everyday life. Exciting advancements also foster opportunities; students can travel and work anywhere on the planet with the potential to have local and global impact. Consequently, teachers must provide students an equitable, inclusive environment in which to learn the content and skills they need to be resilient, flexible, lifelong learners who are ready to navigate an ever-changing world and take on collective problems. Co-teaching is a sustainable and effective way to achieve this goal.

Co-teaching is not new. Teachers have used it for years, and research reveals that it produces higher degrees of student academic achievement and teacher efficacy (Hill, 2020; Hoover, 2007; Karge, 2023b; Little & Theker, 2009; Murawski & Lochner, 2018; Murawski & Spencer, 2011; Villa, Thousand, & Nevin, 2013). It also means a higher probability for sustained partnerships and retention of teachers (Donohoo, Hattie, & Eells, 2018). *Co-teaching* describes a situation where two educators collectively plan, organize, deliver, assess, and reflect on instruction (Friend & Barron, 2016). Co-teaching, in theory and design, provides an inclusive space where teachers build students' content knowledge and skills to navigate and succeed in a changing landscape.

Access a video introduction to co-teaching:

https://bit.ly/3wizD12

Co-teaching is not easy. Teachers who embark on this journey, however, improve their practice because co-teaching gives them the opportunity to collaborate daily and receive regular feedback on their teaching. Co-teachers get the chance to reflect on their practice more than they would as individual practitioners, since the nature of collaboration and teaching together requires constant reflection on their individual and collective practice (Jenkins & Murawski, 2024).

Lynn Cook and Marilyn Friend originally introduced six strategies for co-teaching between general education and special education in their seminal text in 1995. Since that time, many journal articles and dissertations have discussed the process. The co-teaching strategies may have changed; however, the qualities of effective co-teaching remain consistent for both co-teacher and student effectiveness (DeVoss, 2023). The literature on co-teaching has also expanded to the fields of gifted education (Mofield, 2020), dual-immersion bilingual education (Daley, 2021), related services such as designated English language development, and others (Karge, 2023b). Knowing the evidence is so strong and having experienced the value of co-teaching, our goal is to extend the work and enhance the practice for you.

We believe co-teaching and teaching in general since the mid-2010s have become much more complex and interdimensional, requiring planning, attention to interpersonal sensitivities, open communication, collaboration, interdependence, experience, and willingness to take instructional risks to create a wide array of opportunities for all students. Co-teaching must evolve to meet changing classrooms and prepare students for the challenges they will navigate. Using a foundation of research-based co-teaching strategies that incorporate instructional strategies to meet their students' diverse needs, co-teachers must integrate educational technology to a high degree to make learning not only accessible but also differentiated and personalized. AI is a key part of this evolution and will change the nature of how teachers provide instruction to their students. As a result, each co-teacher must learn how to effectively use AI as a copilot to support them in planning, creating content, and delivering instruction.

In this introduction, we discuss some underlying themes of co-teaching in changing classrooms, including some overarching frameworks that we'll turn to throughout the book and a guide to reading this book, including a preview of its structure. Then, as we embark on this journey, we will argue that every teacher can become a seasoned co-teacher who will greatly impact the lives of the students they serve.

Underlying Themes of Co-Teaching in Changing Classrooms

The underlying themes we acknowledge here are foundational to what we outline in this book: principles that nurture the classroom environment from an instructional standpoint whether you are co-teaching for the first time or have years of experience. We will first discuss the great impact of relationships and partnerships in co-teaching, followed by major instructional principles to support teaching and learning in changing classrooms: Universal Design for Learning (UDL), Technological Pedagogical Content Knowledge (TPACK), and the advent of generative AI.

Relationships and Partnerships for Teachers and Students Alike

Relationships matter. The relationships teachers have with their co-teaching partners can make or break the school year. Similarly, the relationships teachers have with their students can be the difference between a great or challenging year. Establishing and maintaining relationships as well as cultivating a positive classroom culture and environment are essential. Teachers who work together positively have a higher degree of collective efficacy (Goddard, Skrla, & Salloum, 2017). Also, teachers who cultivate positive classroom environments and maintain positive teacher-student relationships put their students in a better position to achieve higher academic gains in class content and skills (Roorda, Koomen, Spilt, & Oort, 2011).

To help nurture relationships between co-teachers, each partner needs to research and understand what teaching looks like in their particular classroom and teaching setting. This means that general education teachers should have an idea of the role of a special education teacher on campus. A general education teacher might collaborate with a special education teacher to support students who require additional instruction to meet their individualized education program (IEP) goals. Another option is collaborating with special education teachers during the IEP drafting and monitoring processes. Conversely, special education teachers should understand how general education teachers provide instruction within the school's context, including the instructional strategies they use and classroom and school policies around assessment, homework, and grading. Co-teacher understanding of each other's varied roles not only fosters mutual respect but also builds a seamless and effective collaborative environment where each co-teacher can better support the unique needs of all students. It also means that co-teaching partners are well prepared to adapt and thrive together in their shared classroom setting.

This book focuses not only on building relationships but also on creating accord between co-teachers within a co-teaching partnership. We agree with the research showing that strong co-teaching partners produce greater student achievement, teacher efficacy, and teacher retention. Therefore, as you read, we want you to focus on the relationships you have with your co-teaching partner and students. As you self-evaluate, reflect on the daily interactions and conversations you have with both co-teaching partner and students. Consistent reflection on these relationships is key to successful co-teaching classrooms.

Universal Design for Learning and Co-Teaching

As we discuss the various co-teaching strategies and instructional strategies throughout this book, we will consider them through the lens and scope of the UDL framework. This overarching instructional theory provides a wide variety of opportunities for teachers to teach content and skills because it gives the *why*, *what*, and *how* of learning that teachers can integrate and sequence into any lesson (Center for Applied Specialized Technology [CAST], 2011). The *UDL framework* advocates for teachers to create learning environments that accommodate the diverse needs of students with multiple means of representation, expression, and engagement, thereby ensuring that every learner can access and participate in meaningful learning experiences in an equitable and inclusive manner (CAST, 2011). Ultimately, UDL in action looks like purposeful teachers who motivate students through engaging tasks while providing a wide variety of modalities to present information. Then, when students demonstrate what they know, UDL provides a multitude of opportunities for expression of the content and skills they are learning. This, in turn, means students can show what they have learned in a strengths-based approach, which allows teachers to truly differentiate for students to meet their own learning needs and goals.

Co-teaching provides an enriching opportunity to implement the UDL framework. By nature, it integrates two educators with potentially diverse instructional approaches, catering to a broad range of learners in an inclusive co-teaching classroom. Let's now delve deeper into how co-teachers can harness principles of UDL to amplify the benefits of a co-teaching strategy by providing several examples of each major element in play: engagement, representation, and action and expression.

ENGAGEMENT

UDL's principle of *engagement* aims at immersing learners through relevance, choice, goals, feedback, expectations, self-assessment, and coping skills. When integrated with co-teaching, however, engagement takes a multidimensional form. Two co-teaching partners teaching together and drawing on each other's strengths can jointly craft learning experiences that cater to diverse student needs (Murawski & Scott, 2017). For instance, while one teacher introduces objectives and the relevance of the lesson, the other can weave in real-life examples, stories, or immersive experiences with the help of ed tech to make them more relatable to their students. As the lesson progresses, both teachers can share the responsibility of offering mastery-oriented feedback to the whole class and individuals, setting clear expectations, and guiding students in self-assessment and reflection at various junctures throughout a lesson and unit.

REPRESENTATION

The principle of *representation* in UDL emphasizes diverse ways of presenting information to students. Representation is amplified by dual facilitation during co-teaching because two teachers can use their various instructional strengths and expertise. For example, let's visualize a reading lesson with a group of third-grade students in a co-taught classroom (note this set of strategies can work at any level or content area). One teacher might introduce vocabulary, while the other plays a short video clip elucidating the story's themes. The teachers use a co-teaching strategy called parallel teaching. As students indulge in a notice-and-wonder thinking routine at the beginning of the lesson, co-teaching partners can spark rich discussions by offering varied perspectives or addressing different student questions.

As another example, during an eleventh-grade English Socratic seminar, two teachers can conduct two distinct seminars simultaneously on the same topic and then come together. When it comes to modeling, two teachers can also enable real-time differentiated instruction—one might guide the class, while the other supports students needing extra attention and support or an alternative approach such as reteaching, using another worked example in addition to what the whole class has already gone through. Co-teachers can seamlessly integrate tools like interactive slides or immersive readers, with one educator guiding their use and the other focusing on instant formative assessments to make real-time, data-driven decisions.

ACTION AND EXPRESSION

UDL's principle of offering students multiple means of action and expression magnifies under the co-teaching model. Choices are not just about the modes of demonstrating understanding but also about harnessing the complementary strengths of both teachers. Extending the third-grade reading lesson example, after students complete their reading, co-teachers might offer varied ways to express their understanding, from summaries to podcasts to comic book creation. Teachers can use the same strategy at the end of many lessons where students receive a similar set of choices to express what they have taken away from the lesson or unit. What's essential here is the collaborative nature of choice in a co-teaching environment. The two teachers can bring to the table diverse modalities of expression, ensuring that the options cater to a wider range of learners. They can use a variety of summative choice opportunities and be creative in differentiating them. For example, while traditional methods such as direct instruction and guided practice take place, co-teachers can jointly scaffold choice in the work products student create, ensuring that as students pick their preferred mode, they are well equipped with the routines, expectations, and ed tech tools they may need to succeed.

The three components of UDL and examples of their co-teaching applications are summarized in table I.1 (page 6).

TABLE I.1: UDL Component Definitions and Co-Teaching Applications

UDL Component	Definition	Co-Teaching Application of the Components of UDL in Action
Engagement	Capturing interest and motivating students in the content and skills being taught	In a kindergarten classroom, one co-teacher introduces the lesson by reading an engaging story aloud. After the initial reading of the story, the other integrates augmented reality on students' tablets of various characters and places related to the story to bring the story to life.
Representation	Delivering information relating to the content and skills students are learning about in different formats	During a science lesson, one teacher explains concepts verbally, while the other uses the document camera and models, draws, and labels the concepts on a mind map.
Action and Expression	Providing multiple ways and opportunities for students to express their understanding that can be measured	In a high school history class, students can choose to write an essay, create a digital presentation, or role-play. All three work products are assessed for key ideas and themes related to their unit of study. Both co-teachers guide each work product according to their strengths and preferences during the time they planned the lesson.

Source for definitions: CAST, 2011.

Technology and Co-Teaching Classrooms Without Instructional Boundaries

Underpinning UDL in our modern classrooms is *technological pedagogical content knowledge* (TPACK), what all teachers must know to successfully integrate technology in their classrooms. This is no different in co-taught classrooms, as co-teachers can synthesize the integration of research-based instructional strategies with ed tech tools to amplify opportunities for students to demonstrate their learning, offer accessibility, and provide one-on-one support and assessment. TPACK focuses on the technology, pedagogy, and content knowledge of teachers who are able to interrelate their knowledge and experience within each of these domains to integrate technology (Koehler & Mishra, 2009). In other words, teachers know how various instructional strategies can integrate with technology tools to help them effectively teach the content and skills in their lessons.

For example, when teaching a reading lesson, co-teachers may provide prereading formative assessment and guided reading on interactive slides, employing a tool such as Pear Deck or Nearpod and using co-teaching strategies such as team teaching; one teach, one observe; and one teach, one support (see chapter 2, page 29, which discusses co-teaching strategies in detail). Teachers often move between various co-teaching strategies. In this example, think about how co-teaching ebbs and flows in an instructional sequence. As the co-teachers guide students through part of the text they are using for the lesson, they ask them to paraphrase and answer formative assessment questions. Each co-teacher can see which students may need additional support because the interactive slides act as mini whiteboards that update the students' thinking as they paraphrase, annotate, and answer comprehension questions. After the initial guided reading, the co-teachers can develop differentiated groups based on student performance data and then lead and monitor as groups review another part of the text while receiving just-in-time direct instruction and modeling.

This is TPACK in motion; the co-teachers directly use their content, pedagogy, and technology know-how for this lesson, which they integrate and sequence together. Table I.2 further lays out each component of the TPACK, defining each component and providing an example of what each component may look like in action within a co-taught classroom. Focus on the actions of each co-teacher in the examples, because much of what we discuss in this book relates to co-teaching strategies they integrate through their actions to support student learning in these classroom environments.

TABLE I.2: TPACK in Action for Co-Teachers

TPACK Component	Definition of Component	Co-Teaching Application of the Components of TPACK in Action
Content Knowledge	Deep understanding of the actual subject matter that students are learning	Co-teachers divide topics based on expertise. For example, in an English class, one co-teacher may have expertise in teaching the novel while the other excels at connecting events in the novel to current events and pop culture.
Pedagogical Knowledge	Knowledge about the processes and methods of teaching and learning	Co-teachers collaborate on lessons in which each teacher may allocate their strengths to different parts of the lesson. For example, one co-teacher may be best at providing direct instruction and modeling during team teaching, and their partner has more experience in developing and implementing student cooperative learning strategies such as think, pair, share.
Technological Knowledge	Knowledge about standard technologies (such as books or whiteboards) and advanced technologies (such as the internet or digital video)	Co-teachers integrate tools like interactive slideshows and whiteboards or educational apps to enhance student engagement and interaction during a lesson. For example, in a mathematics lesson, as one co-teacher provides and models a new problem, the other co-teacher monitors students' solutions within an interactive slideshow to determine student trends. Based on these trends, the monitoring co-teacher models a common error, gathering whole-class feedback before moving on to the next problem.
Pedagogical Content Knowledge	Knowledge about how to effectively teach a particular pedagogy along with content, including the best instructional strategies for presenting specific topics or content	Co-teachers collaborate to use their pedagogical strengths to best meet the needs of the learners in their classrooms. For example, while teaching a science lesson, one co-teacher explains a concept like gravity through modeling and direct instruction, while the other demonstrates the concept by dropping an object on the floor.

continued ▶

TPACK Component	Definition of Component	Co-Teaching Application of the Components of TPACK in Action
Technological Content Knowledge	Knowledge about how to effectively teach content with technology, including integrating the most appropriate ed tech tools for presenting specific topics or content	Teachers can apply technical knowledge of an ed tech tool to how they want students to interact with the content they will present in the lesson. In a history lesson about the Roman Empire's expansion, for example, co-teachers design a lesson using virtual reality on Google Earth to explore various historical sites, battle locations, and expansion cities of the Roman Empire. During the virtual field trip, students complete a graphic organizer on how each historical site and event relate to one another as well as how each impacted the Roman Empire's expansion.
Technological Pedagogical Knowledge	Knowledge about how teaching and learning change when using particular technologies	The co-teaching partnership uses ed tech tools and resources in concert with their expertise. One example is co-teachers implementing elements of a flipped classroom model, which front-loads concepts and content online at home; they use station rotation as an opportunity for students to apply and practice knowledge in class.
Technological Pedagogical Content Knowledge (TPACK)	Knowledge about how teaching and learning change when using particular technologies, content, and pedagogy	Co-teachers use technology effectively for student engagement and assessment with pedagogically sound targets and by embedding instructional strategies like formative assessment and guided practice. For example, co-teachers collaboratively develop an interactive slideshow that aligns with the curriculum standards on adding basic fractions. However, if the slides themselves are not interactive, co-teachers will use them differently by incorporating a different set of pedagogical strategies, such as direct instruction and modeling, to convey the information to students.

Source for definitions: Koehler & Mishra, 2009.

Co-Teachers and Generative AI Copilots

Integrating generative AI, such as ChatGPT, Gemini, Claude, or other tools, as a co-teaching copilot within the frameworks of UDL and TPACK transforms the modern classroom, providing dynamic support in lesson planning, content creation, differentiation, communication, report writing, data analysis, and developing student feedback. For example, one or both co-teachers can prompt an AI tool to create classroom content and assignments during planning, provide feedback on student work, refine or recreate an assessment for student retakes, and differentiate content based on the diverse needs of students as well as how the lesson or unit unfolds in the classroom. Co-teachers can accomplish each of these tasks much more quickly and efficiently with the help of the AI copilot, which allows for more time supporting students as well as creating a more sustainable teaching practice.

With the help of generative AI tools they can prompt to support these tasks, co-teachers must also be aware AI is already integrated into many of our favorite ed tech tools to assist in data analysis, content creation and curation, and designing lessons. Throughout the book, we provide examples of how you can use generative AI along with co-teaching strategies within the lens of UDL and TPACK. As you learn the various co-teaching strategies, instructional strategies, and ed tech tool integrations, think back to this theme, as it will help your ideation of how everything comes together when designing and implementing lessons with your co-teaching partner.

Let's focus for a moment on the promise of generative AI when it comes to differentiating instruction and content creation. Differentiating instruction becomes more efficient, as AI can generate content tailored to diverse learner needs from assessment scores. This supports strategies like parallel teaching, in which co-teachers simultaneously instruct different small groups of students with AI-generated materials suited to each group's level. For example, say you need to differentiate reading levels for students practicing reading comprehension and fluency. Co-teachers can prompt the AI to generate reading materials from an original text at varying difficulty levels. For example, they might input, "Using the text I have copied and pasted below, create differentiated levels of it at the third-, fifth-, and seventh-grade level. [Insert text]" The AI then produces texts geared toward these specifications. Co-teachers should review these outputs and perhaps use further prompts for revision and refinement. Once the texts are ready, co-teachers can assign them based on individual student needs. This allows for more personalized learning by grouping students into reading groups with texts about the same themes and concepts that meet students' diverse reading abilities where they are.

In a similar manner, co-teachers can create class content such as assignments, slideshow presentations, graphic organizers, and rubrics using generative AI tools. However, we emphasize that throughout the process of generating this content, teachers must evaluate and revise what AI provides for accuracy and what they want to use the content for in their lessons before moving it over to their ed tech applications, learning management systems (LMSs), and papers they print out for students. Generating content for students to interact with can be a quick process, but it requires many elements of instructional design with research-based strategies at the forefront.

Generative AI is here to stay. Throughout this book, and more specifically in chapter 8 (page 137), we focus on how teachers can use these tools to support co-teaching classrooms. Co-teachers navigating modern classroom environments have another set of hands to support them in the myriad instructional and administrative tasks they must accomplish daily. As you progress throughout this book, we recommend practicing with AI tools to build your capacity to use them. Ultimately, we believe it will make you more efficient, which will leave more time to work with students to support them in their learning.

A Guide to Reading This Book

This book is structured such that new and seasoned co-teachers, coaches, and leaders can navigate its content in one than one way, including reading it cover to cover or picking and choosing material from its chapters. In addition to reviewing the organization and chapters of this book, we will discuss its potential for sharing with local and global professional learning networks.

Book Organization and Chapters

This book is organized to first build on the foundations of co-teaching and then progress to topics that further amplify the strategies we discuss. In the same manner, we focus on partnerships, which encompass not only two credentialed teachers but also a wide array of educators whom co-teachers can partner with in a classroom, such as specialists and paraeducators. As the book progresses, it presents many opportunities for all teachers and educators to have a role in establishing and maintaining effective co-teaching cultures within their schools and districts. As a result, our goal is to zoom inward and then outward to help new and seasoned educators move forward with their co-teaching practice.

- **Chapter 1: Navigating Co-Teaching Partnerships**—With dynamic classrooms that move between physical and digital realms and also focus on equity, inclusion, social-emotional learning (SEL), and student academic growth, how do effective co-teaching partnerships manifest, and how do they look in practice? Additionally, this chapter focuses on finding the hidden potential of prospective co-teachers as well as one's own potential as a co-teacher.

- **Chapter 2: Introducing Co-Teaching Strategies**—In this chapter, we present eleven research-based co-teaching strategies, as well as examples of their implementation within primary and secondary classrooms. We weave these strategies throughout the book.

- **Chapter 3: Building and Maintaining Co-Teaching Relationships**—Relationships are critical elements for co-teachers as they navigate the school year and positively impact the students they serve. This chapter focuses on cultivating positive collegial relationships, implementing conflict management for teachers and students, building relationships with students, and developing strong classroom cultures within a co-teaching classroom. We share ideas for team building, including allowing time for critical discussion of educator pet peeves and individual systems to yield a strong co-teaching relationship. The knowledge and ideas in this chapter come through the experiential lens of over 150 co-teaching teams we've worked with.

- **Chapter 4: Synthesizing Efficacy, Attitude, and Essential Agreements**—Co-teaching partnerships are all about individual efficacy and attitude as well as how to make time to effectively plan, provide feedback, communicate with stakeholders and students, and navigate time in classrooms. These vital elements all come together when developing essential agreements on how co-teachers will provide instruction, grade student work, set up systems in the classroom, create equity and inclusion, and formulate responsibilities and put them into practice. Once co-teachers have created agreements, they should share them with parents and other stakeholders involved in the co-teaching process.

- **Chapter 5: Planning and Designing Lessons**—Planning and lesson design are critical components of a successful co-taught class. Co-teachers must engage in them strategically by learning systems to monitor and adjust their instruction. This chapter focuses on how to efficiently plan and design effective lessons co-teachers can use within any classroom setting. Furthermore, we provide ideas on finding time to plan, since effective lesson design is impossible without it.

- **Chapter 6: Integrating Instructional Strategies With Co-Teaching Strategies:** To impact student learning, co-teachers must be strategic in their practice and incorporate research-based instructional strategies along with their co-teaching strategies. This chapter features a wide variety of high-impact instructional strategies that you can use in all grade levels and areas of content, as well as examples of their integration with co-teaching strategies within primary and secondary classrooms.

- **Chapter 7: Co-Teaching in Classrooms Without Boundaries**—Co-teaching now takes place within classroom settings where instruction can occur within physical and digital spaces. This chapter focuses on how co-teachers can use a wide variety of instructional strategies along with integrating ed tech and AI tools to create effective and equitable instruction that can take place anywhere and at any time to meet students where they are in their learning.

- **Chapter 8: Integrating Specialists Into Co-Teaching**—This chapter explores the integration of various specialists, including special education teachers, bilingual educators, speech and language pathologists, and psychologists, within dynamic co-teaching environments. Emphasizing the need for all co-teachers to hold a solid understanding of special education, the chapter elaborates on the nuances of implementing accommodations and participating in IEP meetings. The narrative broadens to encompass bilingual education, recognizing all students as multilingual learners and underscoring the need for language development strategies in various contexts. A focus on the integration of speech and language pathologists and psychologists highlights their crucial role in this multidisciplinary approach. The chapter uniquely addresses the structure and components of integrated, collaborative, dual-immersion bilingual co-teaching and explores the complexities and richness of a co-teaching environment that embraces and integrates a variety of specialist roles for the benefit of all students.

- **Chapter 9: Co-Teaching in PreK and Early Childhood Settings**—More early childhood programs are co-teaching, collaborating, and building systems within their communities to support all learners. Sometimes the level of education differs in the preK classroom (such as one teacher with a master's degree in education and another with an associate of arts degree in child development); these educators can work together, sharing their gifts and knowledge. This chapter discusses creative systems of support for young learners and their co-teachers.

- **Chapter 10: Cultivating a Culture of Co-Teaching**—The final chapter of the book offers a guide for teacher and school leaders to establish a nurturing and successful co-teaching environment. It outlines pragmatic conflict-management strategies gleaned from situational case studies and proven educational leaders and highlights the importance of stakeholder buy-in, suggesting methods to make co-teaching systemic, sustainable, and widely accepted within the school community. This chapter delves into the logistical schoolwide challenges of co-teaching, detailing strategies for creating collaborative school structures—from planning with the master schedule to selecting co-teachers and conflict management between co-teachers and stakeholders. Last, it illustrates how school leaders can develop systems to support effective planning and lesson design, framing co-teaching as a vital strand that encapsulates the school's values and culture rather than just another program.

Local and Global Professional Learning Networks

Co-teaching is not an island, nor can it be accomplished in isolation. It is a collaborative effort that gains richness and effectiveness when integrated into your *professional learning network* (PLN), which encompasses educators you meet and connect with locally, globally, in person, and online to learn and grow together. Members of this network can reflect on, discuss, and fine-tune co-teaching strategies and methodologies. Your PLN serves as an invaluable repository of viewpoints that might be different from your own but no less enriching. This network offers a treasure trove of insights and strategies that co-teachers can adapt to fit their co-teaching context. A PLN is versatile, extending its reach from social media platforms like X (formerly known as Twitter), Threads, Instagram, TikTok, LinkedIn, and Facebook to more traditional settings within the school or district. When you discover an innovative co-teaching strategy, instructional strategy, ed tech integration, or lesson that engages all learners, share it with your PLN. For example, if you find an ed tech tool that streamlines collaboration between co-teachers, do not keep it to yourself in isolation; we encourage you to pass it along. In this book, we aim to become part of your PLN, sharing best practices and inspiring new approaches in co-teaching. Join the conversation with us using #CoTeachingEvolved on social media, and visit our website, https://coteachingevolved.com, for additional resources and updates. Together, co-teachers from around the world can transform the co-teaching landscape into a thriving community of shared knowledge and practice with the goal of supporting our students.

A Model That Can Work for Every Teacher

With co-teaching becoming increasingly more commonplace in schools, the need is greater for teachers to learn how to co-teach. We believe every teacher can become a co-teacher and that doing so means becoming a better teacher. Co-teaching provides opportunities for learning new instructional strategies that allow teachers to integrate a wide variety of techniques in tandem with their co-teaching partners. This unique experience incorporates the science of how we learn with the art of implementing these strategies together in the classroom.

Whether educators are beginning their careers or are experienced teachers, co-teaching opportunities may be spread throughout their time in the classroom. Sometimes they become career co-teachers. As we move toward full inclusion within our schools, we expect this trend to continue—especially for special education teachers as they move from teaching in more restricted classroom settings to co-teaching in general education classrooms.

This book embraces the ideas of continual improvement and instructional risk taking. Co-teaching requires teachers to try new practices or incorporate practices they may know well in a different context and setting with a co-teaching partner. It often creates unique scenarios, and there are challenges and rewards throughout the year. While co-teaching, however, you are never alone, enabling more discussion and reflection than many other teaching opportunities. Co-teaching is hard work, but it can be some of the most enjoyable and rewarding work you undertake in your teaching career.

As we enter a technology- and AI-driven era, it's becoming evident that traditional co-teaching strategies are in dire need of an overhaul. Gone are the days when one teacher leads while the other merely assists. A complex and interconnected world demands a more collaborative approach in our classrooms, which requires sophisticated integration of a multitude of co-teaching strategies, instructional strategies, and ed tech integrations to meet the needs of our students. Through the blend of research-based co-teaching strategies, cutting-edge instructional strategies based on cognitive science principles, and technology integration with the support of AI, co-teaching can transcend its historical limitations and transform itself to meet changing classroom challenges and to prepare our students to be lifelong learners in a dynamic world. By fostering strong partnerships among teachers, service providers, school leaders, families, and support staff such as paraprofessionals and classroom volunteers, these elements collectively create an instructional landscape where co-teaching not only thrives but also prepares our students to be agile and flexible thinkers, skilled communicators, and problem solvers. The simple yet profound reality is that, when executed effectively, modern co-teaching practices arm students with the indispensable skills and opportunities they need to navigate, contribute to, and flourish in a globalized and connected world.

Co-teaching is not possible without the willingness to change and the sharing of responsibility.

—E. Carrillo, co-teaching researcher and education specialist, personal communication, January 22, 2024

CHAPTER 1

Navigating Co-Teaching Partnerships

In a changing world, what do co-teaching partnerships look like in the classroom, and how do they work? How do they manifest, grow, and navigate in dynamic classrooms that move between physical and digital realms and focus on equity, inclusion, SEL, and student academic growth? All these questions are essential as two individuals come together to collaborate for the school year. A co-teaching partnership makes or breaks the school year, which is why it is important to cultivate them with care from the time they start to the time the partnership ends. As we begin this chapter about co-teaching partnerships and their cultivation, let's dive into an example from Matt's experience meeting potential co-teachers as his school began the process of creating new co-teaching partnerships for the upcoming school year:

> *In my large high school near the end of the school year, I found myself in an unusual but exciting meeting. As a mild to moderate special education teacher and an experienced co-teacher of several years who had taught with three co-teaching partners, I was in the principal's office with a dozen other educators, surrounded by donuts and snacks. A collaborative yet anxious spirit filled the room. This gathering was not just any meeting; it was a deliberate effort by school leadership to foster and create new co-teaching partnerships in our school of 3,500 students and 125 teachers. The event was designed to break the ice among general education teachers who had volunteered to co-teach and special education teachers like me, who were exploring which teachers might align best with their teaching practices and philosophies to develop a future co-teaching partnership for the upcoming school year. Before the meeting, I had completed a survey indicating my preferred content areas for the next academic year, choosing English and history while opting out of mathematics and science since I enjoyed teaching the former much more.*
>
> *After the initial meet-and-greet, the school organized no further events to facilitate interactions among potential co-teachers. Instead, it delegated the final pairing decisions to the department chairs and the principal. This process involved distributing, after the gathering, a final survey to the teachers, who listed their top choices for co-teaching partners*

once they had the opportunity to meet and talk. The objective was to form effective teaching pairs based on teacher preferences and subject expertise, but I found there weren't many opportunities to get to know teachers besides the normal pleasantries and introductory conversations. I felt I needed more information, such as a summarized narrative about each teacher—like a baseball card—and a digital portfolio of their work and craft. After some decent partnerships in the previous few years, I was nervous about selecting my top choices (or getting paired with someone I did not know) for the survey as well as whether my choices would be considered by the decision-making group of department chairs and the principal.

The school allotted two full days before the school year started to allow time for co-teacher partnerships, including mine, to review co-teaching strategies, discuss expectations, devise responsibilities, and begin backward planning. These days were crucial for planning and preparing, offering the newly formed co-teaching partnerships a dedicated window to align their teaching strategies, discuss curriculum, and set the groundwork for a collaborative and successful school year. I took advantage of these days with my co-teachers for the year, which helped set the groundwork for the school year.

When we analyze Matt's experience, many positives are evident as well as clear indications of why he was anxious about the process. What positives come to your mind regarding the process his school used? What areas would you change about the school's approach to creating co-teaching partnerships? How would you begin cultivating the relationship with your new co-teaching partners after being paired together? Note that you might have more than one co-teaching partner during a school year; Matt often had multiple because he was authorized to teach in many content areas. These are all important questions to consider, as facilitating and creating new co-teaching partnerships is critical to students' experience and success for the upcoming school year.

This chapter is about what co-teaching partnerships are, the types of co-teaching partnerships, and finding the hidden potential both of prospective co-teachers and oneself as a co-teacher. Our goal is to set the stage and explore basic foundational elements and examples of co-teaching partnerships. This foundation propels the conversation throughout this book, when we further outline building and maintaining co-teaching partnerships along with discussions relating to the attitude, time, and essential agreements it takes to navigate the ups and downs of the school year. We interweave elements of what it takes to create successful co-teaching partnerships with practical strategies of how to be an effective co-teacher and co-teaching partner, as we believe all of these elements depend on each other.

> **Key Themes and Ideas**
> ☐ A dynamic co-teaching classroom environment
> ☐ Co-teaching partnerships
> ☐ Types of co-teaching partnerships
> ☐ Hidden potential of prospective co-teachers
> ☐ Basic elements and examples of co-teaching partnerships

A Dynamic Co-Teaching Classroom Environment

Creating a dynamic co-teaching classroom is a multifaceted task requiring adaptability, communication, and a strong partnership between co-teachers. Co-teaching classrooms are ever-changing, catering to diverse student populations with a range of needs, along with the demands of the curriculum and standards that teachers are required to teach. The challenge for co-teachers lies in making numerous decisions that impact both the physical and digital learning environments that encompass classrooms. Within co-teaching classrooms, effective co-teaching requires establishing clear routines, norms, and feedback mechanisms, as well as deploying instructional strategies that resonate across both physical and digital spaces.

Modern classrooms blend physical interaction with digital tools, making it essential for co-teachers to be adept in both realms as they integrate effective co-teaching and instructional strategies. This synergy allows for a holistic and practical approach to student learning and engagement since the real world mirrors this dynamic. On top of this, communication with students, service providers, and students' families within both spaces is crucial.

Classroom management is another critical aspect to navigate in co-teaching classrooms, especially with the diversity of student needs. Co-teaching partnerships must develop and consistently apply norms and routines tailored to their class's unique dynamics as well as their own teaching and classroom management styles. Effective classroom management in co-teaching settings should incorporate culturally responsive teaching practices that acknowledge and respect students' diverse backgrounds. This approach can include establishing and maintaining norms and routines that reflect the values and expectations of different cultures. For example, a classroom might accommodate language diversity by incorporating visual aids and bilingual resources, which support non-native English speakers in understanding instructions and participating fully. As another example, morning carpet meetings or routines for the beginning of the period might include greetings in the multiple languages represented in the class. These adaptations of norms and routines can help ensure students are respected and engaged as well as cultivate a welcoming atmosphere, which not only supports individual student needs but also fosters a structured, inclusive learning environment. This is difficult to do without strategic coordination, communication, and trust between both co-teachers.

A significant part of co-teaching involves evaluating student progress, collecting data, writing goal progress, drafting IEPs, attending IEP meetings, and navigating communication and collaborative efforts with various stakeholders and service providers for students with disabilities. These responsibilities highlight the importance of having a dependable co-teaching partner. The ability within the partnership to delegate responsibilities and collaborate on tasks, including delivering instruction to students within physical and digital learning environments, is critical for success in ever-changing classroom environments.

A solid co-teaching partnership is the backbone of successful co-teaching, enabling co-teachers to share the workload, brainstorm solutions, and navigate the ups and downs and complexities of the classroom together. Most important, these partnerships can celebrate the big and small wins throughout the school year. This collaborative spirit not only eases the challenges of teaching but also enriches student learning and makes it a more sustainable and enjoyable experience for both co-teachers.

Co-Teaching Partnerships

We synthesize a wide range of components and several definitions to create our definition of co-teaching partnerships and what they embody. *Co-teaching partnerships* are collaborative classroom arrangements in which two or more professionals, often including a general and a special educator (or another service provider, paraprofessional, or adult or family volunteer), share instructional responsibility and authority in a diverse classroom setting (Atkinson, 2021; Scruggs, Mastropieri, & McDuffie, 2007). These partnerships are characterized by a set of key practices: negotiating differences and responsibilities, delivering instruction, differentiating instruction, sharing classroom authority, co-mentoring, planning, coaching in the moment, and immersing students in real-world teaching experiences that encompass various types of learning environments to general education and special education students (Stang & Capp, 2004; Thompson & Schademan, 2019).

Different elements may come into play, but this working definition encompasses various responsibilities and characteristics that should be present in these dynamic partnerships. Now, we will focus on the types of co-teachers, which will go beyond two credentialed teachers in the classroom.

Types of Co-Teaching Partnerships

There is a wide variety of co-teaching partnerships that we see in diverse co-teaching classrooms across the world. Co-teaching partnerships can embody credentialed teachers; credentialed service providers such as speech pathologists, occupational therapists, and psychologists; paraprofessionals; and classroom guest volunteers such as parents, family members, caregivers, and community members. Let's explore various examples of what each of these individuals can bring to a classroom environment through a co-teaching partnership.

- **Certified teachers:** Deliver instruction, co-plan and design lessons, assess student learning, differentiate instruction, collect data, monitor and adjust instruction, and provide feedback to students and student stakeholders (parents, families, or caregivers) and service providers.

- **Service providers (such as speech pathologists, occupational therapists, and psychologists):** Provide specialized support and implement specific services directed within an IEP; collaborate on IEP drafting, reporting, and collecting data; and may offer interventions and advise on establishing and maintaining student accommodations and modifications as directed by their IEP.

- **Paraeducators (classroom aides):** With supervision of a certified teacher, assist with classroom management, providing instructional assistance, leading small groups, providing individual and small-group support, and helping with supporting classroom activities, routines, and management.
- **Classroom guest volunteers (parents, family members, caregivers, and community members):** Assist small groups and individual students with guidance from teachers, provide learning experiences through discussing real-world opportunities (for example, sharing about their own careers), and help with classroom projects and school events.

All these educators can be part of a co-teaching partnership to a varying degree throughout a school year. Our focus will primarily be on the partnership between two certified teachers. However, much of what we discuss can apply to any educator in a co-teaching partnership.

Hidden Potential of Prospective Co-Teachers

Adam Grant (2023) proposes that to find the best candidates for a job, let them complete tasks directly associated with the future work to determine whether they have the potential to be great. Grant (2023) proposes mechanisms that we have modified to meet the needs of school systems. These include expanding on transcripts and developing personalized portfolios that describe co-teachers' professional journeys, providing models and examples of what high performance looks like for a job, and making interviews more personable by having candidates disclose more information about themselves before the interview takes place. As we move forward with this discussion, think of this first as a thought experiment followed by something that can be conducted at your school.

Teachers need to find the potential of others and of themselves as prospective co-teachers so they can determine if they can effectively accomplish the tasks associated with co-teaching. This is essential because the best candidates for a job demonstrate characteristics of success, evidence of knowledge, and experience with the tasks associated with the job (Grant, 2023). Teachers do not necessarily need to have experience co-teaching to meet this set of criteria. Rather, past education experiences, both in their own education and in teaching, can align to the tasks they would conduct in a co-teaching classroom, and these alignments work to find one's potential as a co-teacher. It's important to know a variety of key tasks in co-teaching classrooms before jumping into teaching in this environment. While teachers should have many of these experiences before going into teaching a co-taught class, not all are required by any means. The following list outlines the key tasks and skills potential co-teachers should have background in and knowledge about before entering a co-teaching partnership.

- Backward planning and daily planning
- Timely family and student communication

- Student and family feedback
- Ed tech integration into instruction
- Knowledge about implementing various instructional strategies:
  + Formative assessment
  + Guided practice
  + Modeling
  + Direct instruction
  + Retrieval practice
  + Pair share
  + Monitoring and adjusting instruction
- Knowledge of IEP and 504 documents
- Implementing accommodations for individuals and groups of students

Once teachers have reflected on their experiences and how those skills may align with the demands of a co-teaching classroom, potential co-teachers might consider how to demonstrate their potential as well as use matchmaking events to find hidden potential in others.

Your Potential as a Co-Teacher

As a prospective co-teacher, teachers should showcase their potential, including demonstration of mastery of skills in the previous list, as it may lead to a successful partnership in the future. Potential co-teachers can compile lessons, observation notes and provided feedback, and artifacts of the assignments, tasks, and assessments they have created. Showcasing this on a digital portfolio or folder to potential co-teaching partners and principals to review is a first step in having them see one's potential as a co-teacher. Alternatively or in addition to the digital portfolio, edit together several short recordings of lessons in a montage for this same group of educators to review. It can be short, two-to-five minute clips of various strategies that a teacher has implemented within their lessons. This can showcase their teaching style and offer a sneak peek at their mannerisms, classroom management, and routines. Sharing evidence will lead to better co-teaching partnerships.

Before moving forward, take a moment to fill out figure 1.1 as you begin to brainstorm your potential as a co-teacher. If you are a school or district leader, use a graphic organizer like this when curating candidates' potential for co-teaching in the future. Whether you are a seasoned co-teacher, new or potential co-teacher, or school leader looking for potential co-teacher pairings, this exercise will allow prospective co-teachers to list their strengths, skills, and evidence to demonstrate their potential as a prospective co-teacher.

Strengths as an Educator	Skills	Evidence

How Do You Best Communicate With Others?

FIGURE 1.1: Finding your potential as a co-teacher.

*Visit **go.SolutionTree.com/instruction** for a free reproducible version of this figure.*

Matchmaking Event to Find Hidden Potential

Another opportunity to find hidden potential of co-teaching partnerships is for school and teacher leaders to create a matchmaking event at the school site where all possible co-teachers get to meet and discuss teaching and learning. During the gathering, they complete a survey about their experience related to teaching and co-teaching that asks them specific questions related to their teaching philosophy, experience, and skills they believe they have in their repertoire. Following that experience, school and special education teacher leaders ask various teachers to team up together for an hour and backward plan a couple of lessons and then teach the lesson within a current co-teaching class. The principal, assistant principal, instructional coach, or a seasoned co-teaching pair observes each partnership. Following the observations, the observer compiles notes, and each co-teacher completes a survey documenting the planning process and the lesson itself: how the lesson went, what strategies they employed, and honest feedback about the experience with their co-teaching partner. Then, school and teacher leaders who are assigned to pick co-teaching partners synthesize the survey responses and notes from the observation. Finally, this committee selects co-teaching partners for the upcoming school year.

Basic Elements and Examples of Co-Teaching Partnerships

The success of co-teaching partnerships hinges on a blend of interpersonal and professional components that we have derived from research and from seeing these components in action in real classrooms. First, we focus on the research. Then, we provide two partnership examples that illustrate what the components from the research look like in practice from how both co-teachers begin their classroom experience together through various points throughout the year and how to manifest these partnerships at the individual teacher level.

The Research: Effective Co-Teaching Partnerships

It's vital to consider key research for effective co-teaching partnerships. John-Michael L. Nix (2021) highlights the critical role of positive interdependence and interpersonal sensitivity, which surpass even the importance of formal teaching qualifications as characteristics necessary for a successful co-teacher partnership. This means co-teachers can be independent after roles are clarified and are also able to openly discuss their feelings related to their work with their co-teaching partner. These elements foster a shared vision for student and classroom success tailored to the unique needs of each class they teach together. Because co-teachers are open to discussing their roles and feelings with each other, they develop and maintain a shared vision for their collective classrooms and what success may look like for individual students. V. Sue Atkinson (2021) further contributes to this perspective by emphasizing the need for shared instructional responsibility, effective role negotiation, and attentiveness to the requirements of special education students. Again, being open to feedback and communicating how one may feel about a situation and their role is essential for being effective.

Research by Nix (2021) and Atkinson (2021) builds on the work of Friend (2008) and Kristin K. Stang and Gordon Capp (2004) on the previously discussed components as well as several structural components. Stang and Capp (2004) underscore the significance of consistent communication and collaboration coupled with regular planning sessions. This ensures alignment in classroom and learning objectives as well as the strategies that co-teachers deploy within their classroom instruction and the establishment and maintenance of their classroom culture. Friend (2008) adds to these findings by focusing on the practical and relational dimensions of co-teaching. This includes establishing co-planning routines, nurturing positive interpersonal dynamics, clarifying roles and responsibilities as co-teachers, and securing administrative backing and support.

Collectively, these components from the research body form the basic framework for an effective and dynamic co-teaching partnership, enabling teachers to collaborate and communicate effectively as they navigate changing classroom environments. We continue to expand on these components as we progress through the book in our discussions of planning, establishing and maintaining relationships with co-teachers, co-teacher attitude, time, and essential agreements.

What does this framework look like in real co-teaching classrooms? First, we provide an example of the components in action within Mrs. Thompson and Mr. Lee's third-grade classroom. Then, we showcase them within Mr. Patel and Ms. Garcia's seventh-grade science classroom. In each example, we break down individual actions by each co-teacher that helped positively impact their co-teaching partnership.

Classroom Example 1: Third-Grade Co-Teacher Partnership

At the start of the school year in a third-grade classroom, Mrs. Thompson and Mr. Lee are setting the stage for a successful partnership. They prioritize building a relationship based on mutual respect and understanding, recognizing that their interpersonal dynamics are as crucial as their teaching skills. They spend time before the year starts discussing their teaching philosophies, strengths, and areas for growth, ensuring positive interdependence. A week before class begins and backward planning commences, they agree on shared instructional responsibilities, with Mrs. Thompson taking the lead in literacy, given her expertise, and Mr. Lee focusing on mathematics. They also plan strategies to address the diverse needs of their special education students, ensuring an inclusive environment from the outset. To do this, they build out a backward plan that includes modifications, accommodations, and differentiations of the lessons they will provide to their students for each unit in each content area. Additionally, they want to ensure equity in everything they provide their students. As a result, they analyze student languages and cultural backgrounds and plan individualized notes on each student to get to know them better. As the year progresses, Mrs. Thompson and Mr. Lee fill out each student mini portfolio on a Google Sheet, which includes not only demographic information but also students' interests, hobbies, and favorite subjects.

Halfway through the year, Mrs. Thompson and Mr. Lee's co-teaching relationship has been moving along well as they continue to navigate the ups and downs of the school year. Their initial planning and role clarification at the beginning of the year have paid off. They have established a rhythm for co-planning time asynchronously and during their designated planning sessions, using these sessions to reflect on their teaching strategies and student progress. They have been able to use their reflections and student data as barometers for how they monitor and adjust their teaching and how they are presenting the curriculum's content to their students. This consistent and ongoing communication has allowed them to adapt their co-teaching strategies and key instructional strategies to the evolving needs of their students. Together, they celebrate small victories, like the improvement of their struggling students' reading levels, and tackle challenges, like finding effective ways to engage their more advanced learners as they work on opportunities to extend learning.

How did individual actions by each co-teacher help support them in creating a successful partnership? These actions are essential to note, as small actions by each individual co-teacher can make a decisive, positive difference in the trajectory of the co-teaching partnership. Mrs. Thompson spearheads literacy activities by taking the lead in the planning session, but she also actively listens to Mr. Lee. Both co-teachers focused on leading but also listening, which contributes to Mr. Lee having the confidence to integrate his mathematical expertise and take the lead in that content area. They regularly review and adapt their instructional strategies, with Mrs. Thompson offering insights from her literacy background and Mr. Lee contributing his numeracy skills. They take time to do this at the beginning of each planning session by reviewing the various trends and themes they see from an instructional perspective and analyzing student performance via the latest formative assessment data. This collaboration ensures both teachers are actively involved in the entire learning process as well as active participants in their co-teaching partnership.

As the school year nears its end, the successful partnership between Mrs. Thompson and Mr. Lee is evident. The positive relationship they built at the beginning of the year has grown stronger, and their shared instructional responsibilities have led to significant student progress. When observing their classroom instruction and collaboration, both co-teachers are in sync, and there is a visible synergy between them. Their regular co-planning sessions have evolved into creative brainstorming sessions, where they share innovative ideas and reflect on their teaching practices from the day and the week through their review of student data and personal anecdotes.

Classroom Example 2: Seventh-Grade Co-Teacher Partnership

In their seventh-grade science classroom, Mr. Patel and Ms. Garcia are embarking on their co-teaching journey as experienced co-teachers, but this is their first year co-teaching together. They start the year by establishing a foundation of positive interdependence and interpersonal sensitivity. To do this, both recognize the importance of their professional relationship, share their expectations and teaching styles, and agree to support each other's strengths with dialogue and a planning document with essential agreements. They divide the curriculum based on their expertise, with Mr. Patel focusing on ed tech integration, assessment, and differentiating instruction and Ms. Garcia on providing instruction related to the science curriculum, designing inclusive lab experiences, and providing feedback on student assignments and tasks. After reviewing their roster and the students who have 504 plans and IEPs in their co-taught sections, they identify strategies to support their diverse learners by developing a set of accommodations and supports embedded in all assignments, tasks, and assessments for the school year. Each student in this class receives these supports—not just those with special needs. In this way, students with special needs receive necessary support, and the learning environment is equitable for all students.

By midyear, Mr. Patel and Ms. Garcia have developed a strong, collaborative partnership. Their commitment to consistent communication through texts, email, and common planning time has been key to their success. They regularly discuss student progress, adapt lesson plans, and share feedback on co-teaching strategies and instructional strategies they have integrated into their lessons. This ongoing dialogue has helped them refine their co-teaching approach; they have both evolved over the course of the year as they've adjusted as new co-teaching partners. Their science lessons are more engaging and effective because they have had to innovate and design new lessons and classroom routines to meet their students' needs.

This co-teaching partnership also manifests success with their individual actions. Mr. Patel and Ms. Garcia divide responsibilities based on their strengths but maintain that, at times, various responsibilities may ebb and flow from one teacher to another depending on the circumstances. Mr. Patel's focus on ed tech and assessment complements Ms. Garcia's expertise in science instruction because they can take the lead on planning each component of the lesson during both their collaborative and individual planning time. They hold frequent planning sessions and communicate daily via text messages, in which Mr. Patel shares digital tools and strategies and Ms. Garcia provides input on scientific content and lab activities before finalizing their lessons. This co-teaching partnership is characterized by continual dialogue and communication, allowing them to refine their co-teaching strategies and instructional approaches to their lessons while using their strengths to complement each other.

As the year concludes, the impact of Mr. Patel and Ms. Garcia's co-teaching is clear. Their initial efforts in establishing a solid partnership have led to a classroom where students are excited about science and feel supported. This was not without its ups and downs, since it took time to develop a classroom routine and culture. Their co-planning sessions have become a space for innovative planning and the integration of new co-teaching strategies, such as parallel and station teaching, with which they saw major dividends during science labs. Reflecting on the year, both teachers feel a sense of accomplishment and look forward to continuing their successful partnership next year in teaching sections of seventh- and eighth-grade science together.

These scenarios illustrate how to effectively implement the components we highlight in co-teaching partnerships at different grade levels, demonstrating the positive impact on both teachers and students throughout the school year. Additionally, the individual actions of each co-teacher helped establish and maintain their partnership. Co-teaching is hard work. But consistent elements and small individual actions can make a world of difference for both co-teachers and, most important, for their students.

Conclusion

In this chapter, we introduced co-teaching partnerships and how to find the hidden potential in oneself and others as co-teachers. We also addressed how many different educators and volunteers can also take on the role as a co-teacher in a wide variety of ways. Finally, we delved into the basic components that can help support successful co-teaching partnerships. We provided examples of research-based collective and individual actions of co-teachers and broke down each scenario to help make clear how they positively impact their co-teaching partnerships throughout the course of a school year.

Remember, what we discuss in this chapter is only the beginning of our focus on co-teaching partnerships. In the next chapter, we introduce eleven co-teaching strategies. And then, throughout this book and most notably in chapters 3 and 4, we outline how to positively impact co-teaching partnerships further.

> **ADDITIONAL RESOURCE TO CONSIDER AFTER READING THIS CHAPTER**
>
> **Hidden Potential: The Science of Achieving Greater Things—Talks at Google** (www.youtube.com/watch?v=EZBz5c5IWTU) is an eighteen-minute video in which an organizational psychologist expands on his thinking. This can help co-teachers find their strengths and opportunities to achieve a complementary and successful partnership.

Reflection and Action: Next Steps

Directions: After reading about co-teaching partnerships in chapter 1, what do you think were the main ideas and key details from this chapter? Write at least three main ideas and key details. Then, discuss how you can apply what you have read to your co-teaching partnerships.

Main Ideas

Key Details

Next Steps

Co-Teaching Evolved © 2025 Solution Tree Press • SolutionTree.com
Visit **go.SolutionTree.com/instruction** to download this free reproducible.

The success of co-teaching is similar to a marriage commitment; it relies on mutual trust, acceptance of responsibility, and respect from the professionals working in the class with the common belief that all parties are working with the common and united goal—doing what's best for students.
—K. Santos, education specialist, personal communication, January 28, 2024

CHAPTER 2

Introducing Co-Teaching Strategies

In 2018, Belinda attended a Center for Education Diplomacy event in Washington, DC. On the stage was a panel of top researchers from the countries in the world with the top-ranking Program for International Student Assessment (PISA) exam scores: Finland, China, Singapore, and Japan. In the audience of over four thousand educators from the United States, a U.S. citizen went to the microphone and asked, "You have all been in the United States for several weeks talking and visiting our schools; why would you say we are behind other nations in education?" The Finnish researcher said they had discussed this very concept the night before as a group and had an answer. You could hear a pin drop as everyone leaned in to hear his response. He said U.S. teachers are running around paying other teachers (he was referencing the internet site Teachers Pay Teachers), recreating lessons, and working individually. Meanwhile, Finnish teachers are using research-based strategies and implementing them daily in classrooms in co-teaching situations. Most of the research they implement is from the United States. He explained that in other countries, teachers team together to analyze data and evaluate lessons and student behavior to create purposeful goals to make a difference each time they facilitate any group of students. This shared teaching carries a mutual respect; the educators work as a team. They plan, teach, assess, and reflect together. There is much to learn from the international community about co-teaching. Désirée von Ahlefeld Nisser (2017) purports that co-teaching in Sweden is a way to promote justifiable, research-based inclusive practices. He writes that participatory democracy, collaboration, and team building all have a place when teachers work together to promote equity. In some places around the world, co-teaching is seen as a systematic strategy for student improvement (Walsh, 2012).

Our takeaway here is that co-teaching doesn't just happen. There are established, research-based strategies that can provide guidance and take co-teaching from a nebulous idea to a realized practice. We have made brief mention of some co-teaching strategies already; in this chapter, we provide detailed explanations and examples of each one. Before diving into the eleven co-teaching strategies, Belinda shares an experience from an international school in Tbilisi, Georgia, in eastern Europe:

> I spent three years consulting and watching schoolwide inclusion growth at this school. It is a sixteen-hour flight from my home, so when I went, I was there for a week or two. I will never forget my last visit; I witnessed so many teachers using a variety of co-teaching strategies. I entered a fifth-grade classroom at around 9:00 a.m., and they were just breaking into parallel teaching. The general education teacher and the learning services (special education) teacher

> *split the class in half for about twenty minutes of direct instruction on an upcoming literacy assignment (parallel teaching). At around 9:20, students returned to their seats and worked independently. The co-teachers circulated around the classroom, using formative assessment to check on students (shared teaching). At approximately 9:35, the general education teacher called four students over to a small table on one side of the room to preteach an upcoming lesson. The learning services teacher continued to monitor students working independently for about ten minutes and then conducted a review of the literacy lesson with the students still in their seats (alternative teaching). At 10:00, the co-teachers jointly introduced four stations to the class (graze and tag). One shared about station 1, the other about station 2, and so on. The students then cycled through fifteen-minute stations for the next hour. Both teachers taught a station, and the other two stations were independent (station teaching). At about 11:15, the co-teachers brought the students together for a quick teacher role-play as an anticipatory set for the book they were going to begin reading as a class (role-play). In one morning, I witnessed this fabulous co-teaching team use six of the eleven co-teaching strategies! The entire time I watched, students were engaged and seemed to be enjoying the learning, and the teachers were successfully working together.*

Co-teaching strategies were originally introduced in education literature in the 1960s. Education research in this area became well known when Cook and Friend (1995) introduced the terminology in their descriptions of several scenarios in which general education and special education teachers worked together. As indicated in the introduction (page 1), *co-teaching* describes a situation where two educators collectively plan, organize, deliver, assess, and reflect on instruction (Friend & Barron, 2016).

Cook and Friend (1995) also describe co-teaching as when "two or more professionals deliver substantive instruction to a diverse or blended group of students in a single physical space" (p. 2). Both educators become active participants in the instructional components. The level of activity is different depending on the stage of co-teaching and the strategy the team chooses to implement. This chapter defines eleven strategies and provides a few examples of how teachers from preK to the college level have used these strategies.

> **Key Themes and Ideas**
> ☐ A three-stage co-teaching strategy sequence
> ☐ The eleven co-teaching strategies
> ☐ The role of collaboration

A Three-Stage Co-Teaching Strategy Sequence

Expanding on some of the common terms used in the original co-teaching research introduced by Cook and Friend in 1995, and written about by Wendy W. Murawski (2009) and others, Belinda introduces a co-teaching sequence in three stages: (1) supportive co-teaching, (2) team co-teaching, and (3) advanced co-teaching (Karge, 2015, 2023b).

Some authors use the term *co-teaching model*. However, we prefer to use *co-teaching strategy*. Education models comprise the philosophical foundation or beliefs about learning—for example, progressive or traditional education models. Various writings break these down by philosophy to include postmodernism, progressivism, essentialism, and perennialism. Models typically provide a description. On the other hand, a strategy is a plan. We provide each of the eleven co-teaching strategies as a plan for instruction that involves both teachers working together to implement it. Both co-teachers are actively involved in every aspect of the instruction (Karge, 2023b). Table 2.1 provides names and definitions of the strategies in each stage.

TABLE 2.1: Co-Teaching Strategy Quick-Reference Guide

Strategy	Definition
Supportive Co-Teaching	
One teach, one assist	One educator is teaching, and another is assisting. The educator who is teaching is typically sharing the instructional information to the students.
One teach, one observe	One educator takes the lead and imparts the knowledge or leads a discussion. The second educator observes the teaching and the students, often taking data as they observe.
One teach, one support	An educator provides the instruction, and the other "does something to enhance and support the instruction" (Karge, 2015, p. 6). The supportive educator might create a visual, paraphrase the instructional content, or take notes on a whiteboard or computer.
Team Co-Teaching	
Graze-and-tag teaching	One educator teaches while the other educator "grazes" (that is, strolls the room viewing what students are working on and how they are understanding the concepts). The educators shift roles when the other educator adds to or teaches another concept.
Parallel teaching	Each teacher teaches the same lesson simultaneously to half the class (that is, to different groups of students). Typically, the teachers are in the same room at the same time. If there is an open area outside or a neighboring classroom, sometimes one group will move to another location.
Station teaching	Prior to station teaching, the educators plan the goals and objectives for the lesson. Sometimes they develop a generic plan, and then the educator working at a specific station spends more time developing their individual station. The students are divided into heterogeneous groups. Teacher 1 is assigned to teach one group, and teacher 2 is assigned to work with an additional group. Sometimes there are additional independent groups. The students rotate from one station to another. Every student participates at every station.
Alternative teaching	As educators plan, they consider how they will divide students into groups. Teacher 1 works with the enrichment group while teacher 2 reteaches a concept.
Advanced Co-Teaching	
Conversation teaching	Both teachers act as the stars of their own reality show. The co-teachers preplan the content and then have an educational conversation in front of the students.
Role-play teaching	The co-teaching team plans and shares a think-aloud, characterization, or debate in skit format with the entire class.
Interactive teaching	Richard A. Villa, Jacqueline S. Thousand, and Ann I. Nevin (2013) refer to it as complementary co-teaching and describe it as each co-teacher doing something to enhance the instruction provided by the other teacher. For example, co-teachers might engage in an interactive dialogue during a modeled lesson.
Shared teaching	Collaborative teaching teams of educators fully share all responsibilities for the classroom, doing what one teacher traditionally does (plan, teach, assess, and reflect), taking full responsibility for every aspect of the classroom.

Source: Karge, 2015.

*Visit **go.SolutionTree.com/instruction** for a free reproducible version of this table.*

The following section discusses each of these strategies in much more detail.

The Eleven Co-Teaching Strategies

We describe each of the strategies in detail in this chapter and provide examples throughout the book. Most teams will move through the three stages in the following order, with some juggling of strategies within each stage.

Supportive Co-Teaching

The three supporting co-teaching strategies are very similar. In each case, one of the educators carries the primary instruction, and the other either assists, observes, or provides minimal support. Villa and colleagues (2013) note that supportive co-teaching is frequently a favored approach by novice teachers. While it's important that teachers who are new to co-teaching start with these strategies and build up a foundation of experience with them before moving on to the more advanced strategies, we suggest educators move through these strategies quickly so the team can work together to use team co-teaching and advanced co-teaching.

1. ONE TEACH, ONE ASSIST

In this co-teaching strategy, one educator teaches, and another assists. The educator who is teaching typically delivers the instructional information to the students while in front of the class. The educator who is assisting circulates the instructional area and provides support as needed. For example, if students need one-on-one tutorial assistance or a tap on the shoulder to remind them to focus, the assisting teacher steps in while the co-teacher continues to lead the lesson. In fact, there is virtually no actual co-teaching going on. Sadly, as Thomas E. Scruggs, Margo A. Mastropieri, and Kimberly A. McDuffie (2007) indicate in their research, this is the dominant form of co-teaching that teachers use most often. Like Scruggs and his colleagues (2007), we have observed that educators across North America and the world who practice co-teaching have not received professional learning detailing the other strategies, and they rely on one teacher teaching and the other merely serving as an assistant.

Figure 2.1 provides a visual of one teach, one assist.

- One teacher leads the lesson for the whole class, and the other teacher serves as an assistant.
- The lead teacher has primary responsibility for all aspects of the lesson.
- The danger with this strategy is that one teacher does all the work, which can challenge collaboration.
- This method is wonderful for teachers in training during field practicum, residency, or student teaching.

FIGURE 2.1: Co-teaching strategy 1—One teach, one assist.

2. ONE TEACH, ONE OBSERVE

During one teach, one observe, one educator takes the lead and imparts the knowledge or leads a discussion. The second educator observes. This strategy can be used for student teaching. However, it is also an excellent strategy for systematically collecting data. For example, an English language specialist might observe a predetermined small group of students and collect language samples. Or a speech and language therapist might observe a first-grade teacher during a phonics lesson. After the observation, the speech and language therapist might work with the first-grade teacher to use one of the remaining strategies during the next lesson. Or an intervention specialist might observe a particular student to collect data to determine whether the student is a candidate for Tier 2 of the school's multitiered system of supports (MTSS).

Figure 2.2 provides a visual of one teach, one observe.

- One teacher leads the lesson for the whole class, and the other teacher observes.
- This method is an excellent approach to deepen shared understanding of students and about each other's teaching practice.
- If co-teachers use one teach, one observe exclusively, it may appear that the observing teacher has been relegated to the role of assistant (Friend, Cook, Hurley-Chamberlain, & Shamberger, 2010).

FIGURE 2.2: Co-teaching strategy 2—One teach, one observe.

3. ONE TEACH, ONE SUPPORT

During one teach, one support, one educator provides the instruction, and the other "does something to enhance and support the instruction" (Karge, 2015, p. 6). The supportive educator might create a visual, paraphrase the instructional content, or take notes on a whiteboard or computer. Support means different things to different educators, and clear communication is necessary to determine the best approach for working together.

Access a video example of this strategy:

https://bit.ly/3T4jTb1

Figure 2.3 (page 34) is a planning template for educators new to co-teaching. The lead co-teacher, the one who will provide the instruction, should have the overall instructional objective (purpose)

One Teach Instructional Objectives	One Assist	One Observe	One Support	Why
The student will read aloud from grade-level text with increasing fluency and accuracy. Ms. D. will call on students to read.		Mr. R. will have a list of students and make notes on those who have difficulty reading aloud or with fluency		This aligns with standard 8.6.

FIGURE 2.3: Supportive co-teaching planning template.

*Visit **go.SolutionTree.com/instruction** for a free reproducible version of this figure.*

in the first column. Then the role of the person doing the assisting, observing, or supporting should be noted, with the rationale (why) in the final column. The why becomes important in terms of justifying why two teachers need to be in the classroom.

Figure 2.4 provides a visual of one teach, one support.

- One teacher leads planning and presenting of lesson content to the whole class.
- The other teacher provides support. They may rephrase statements, ask questions, listen, and suggest next steps.
- Alternatively, the other teacher may write key ideas on a whiteboard for students to use in their notes.

FIGURE 2.4: Co-teaching strategy 3—One teach, one support.

Team Co-Teaching

As teachers implement team co-teaching, they should continually check to make certain that what they are doing "needs" two of them. That is, if one teacher can do it alone, then maybe it isn't necessary to have two teachers. The ultimate goal is to impact student learning. What are two educators doing together that is stronger than what one can do alone? This should be a key question continually on your mind as you implement co-teaching. In team co-teaching, students experience smaller groupings and opportunities to participate in instruction that differ from traditional rows or whole-class learning, a definite benefit.

4. GRAZE-AND-TAG TEACHING

Graze and tag is a term originally introduced by wrestlers in the Midwest (Cornal, 2021). One wrestler takes the advantage or lead, and then the other wrestler overcomes this position and moves to another. The different positions and forms engage the viewer. During graze and tag, one educator teaches while the other educator "grazes" (that is, strolls the room viewing what students are working on and how they are understanding concepts), and the role shift occurs when the other educator adds or teaches another concept. For example, if third-grade co-teachers are reviewing a story with their students, one educator might introduce the activity and ask how the story began, the other educator would jump in and ask questions about the plot, and then the first educator would ask about the end of the story. This sharing of instruction involves minimal planning; however, the teamwork demonstrated within the instruction time is highly valued by the students as they listen and participate. Educators who use this strategy report their colleague often asks inspiring questions or makes comments that they themselves had not thought of, thus adding value to the lesson (Carrillo, 2023).

Figure 2.5 provides a visual of graze-and-tag teaching.

- The lead teacher role shifts between co-teachers during instruction.
- While one teacher leads instruction, the other "grazes" or assists students, monitors task behavior, and insists on rigorous learning: correct grammar, spelling, format. The grazing teacher plays a scholarly role.
- The shifting roles allow teachers to share their expertise or approach the material in new ways.

FIGURE 2.5: Co-teaching strategy 4—Graze-and-tag teaching.

5. PARALLEL TEACHING

Sometimes student learning improves with more opportunities to ask questions or more time to respond. During parallel teaching, each teacher simultaneously teaches the same lesson to half the class (that is, each teaches to different groups of students). Typically, the teachers are in the same room at the same time. If there is an open area outside or a neighboring classroom available, sometimes one group will move to another location. Collaborative planning yields the content of the lesson, and the class is divided into two separate, heterogeneous student groups. Each educator instructs only their group. Teachers appreciate the smaller group size, as often they can provide more one-on-one support (Karge, 2015). The materials are presented in different ways, depending on the individual teaching preferences, but the content is identical. Figure 2.6 provides an example. Each of these teachers taught the exact same lesson to half of the class, using the same approach, individualized for the particular learners in the specific parallel group.

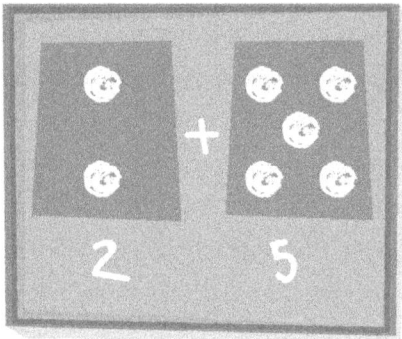

FIGURE 2.6: Parallel teaching example.

Access an example of this strategy:

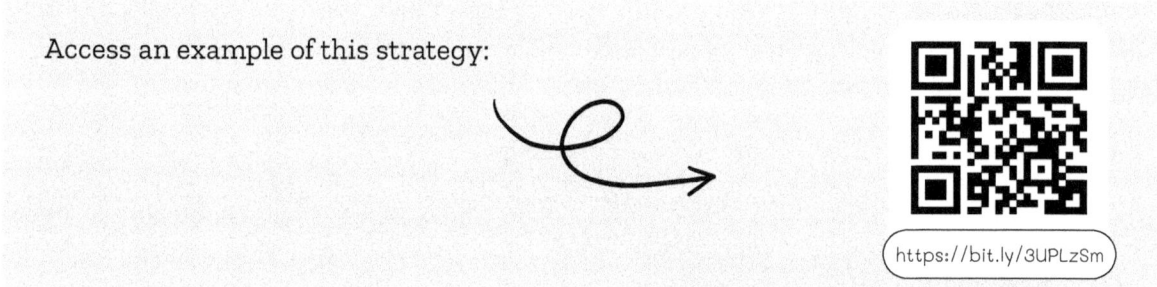

https://bit.ly/3UPLzSm

Figure 2.7 provides a visual of parallel teaching.

- Co-teachers jointly plan instruction.
- Teachers independently deliver content to separate, diverse groups of students. They both teach the same information simultaneously to the divided class.
- Students have more opportunities for participation and individual support.

FIGURE 2.7: Co-teaching strategy 5—Parallel teaching.

6. STATION TEACHING

In station teaching, the students are divided into heterogeneous groups. One teacher is assigned to teach one group, and the other is assigned to work with another group. Sometimes there are additional independent groups. The students rotate from one station to another. Every student participates in every station. The benefit of station teaching is the opportunity for students to move (brain break), and the teaching is typically in smaller segments (learning chunks), supporting long-term memory (Murawski & Spencer, 2011). Prior to station teaching, the educators plan the goals and objectives for the lesson. Sometimes they develop a generic plan, and then educators working at specific stations spend more time developing their individual station.

Figure 2.8 provides a visual of station teaching.

- One teacher works with part of the class on unit of study A.
- The other teacher works with part of the class on unit of study B.
- The rest of the class works at an independent station, individually at their desks or computer.

FIGURE 2.8: Co-teaching strategy 6—Station teaching.

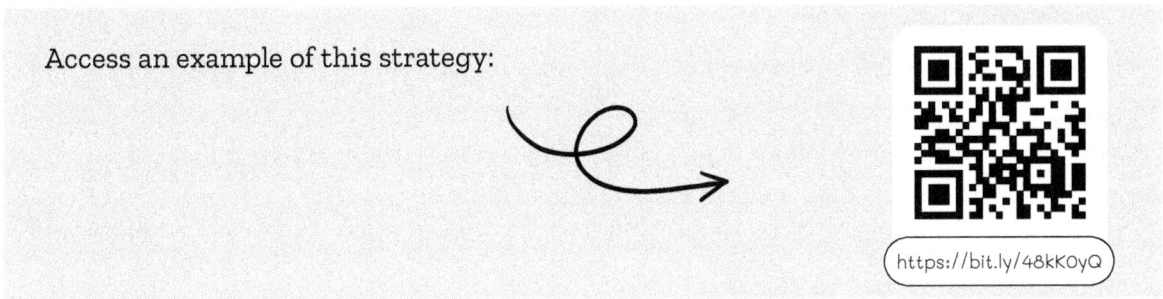

Access an example of this strategy:

https://bit.ly/48kK0yQ

7. ALTERNATIVE TEACHING

Alternative teaching is a co-teaching strategy in which one teacher provides instruction to a main group of students while the other co-teacher works directly with a smaller group of selected students. Within the smaller group of students, the goal is to provide more intensive direct instruction, modeling, and review. Additionally, goals could include remediation, preteaching vocabulary, or formative assessment. This co-teaching strategy provides an opportunity to address specific student needs without interrupting the instructional flow of the entire classroom (Friend et al., 2010). As educators plan, they consider how to divide students into groups. One teacher works with the enrichment group, while the other reteaches a concept. A very creative secondary mathematics co-teaching team Belinda worked with in Southern California used this strategy once a week. They gave a three-problem assessment every Thursday. The students who were able to correctly respond to all three joined the enrichment group. The students who missed one were able to decide whether they wanted to join enrichment or go to the reteach group. Students who missed two or three were asked to attend the reteach group. The groups changed weekly depending on student skill ability. The teachers took turns working with the enrichment and reteach groups.

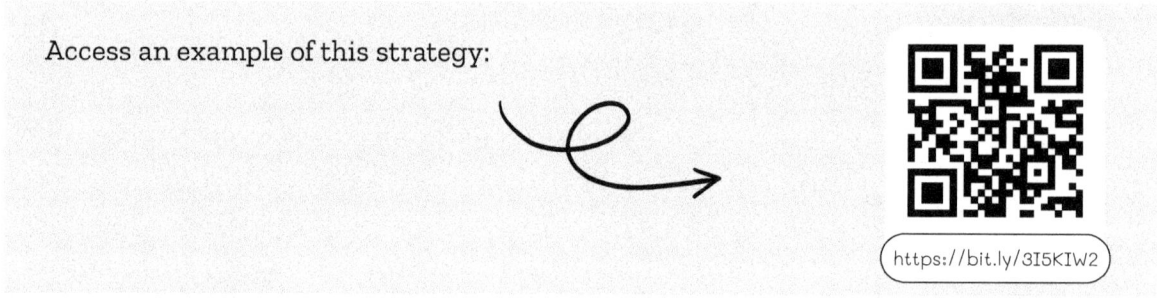

Access an example of this strategy:

https://bit.ly/3I5KIW2

Figure 2.9 provides a visual of alternative teaching.

- Students are divided into two groups that are based on immediate need rather than ability or tracking.
- The first teacher focuses on enrichment.
- The other teacher focuses on reteaching.

FIGURE 2.9: Co-teaching strategy 7—Alternative teaching.

Advanced Co-Teaching

Advanced co-teaching strategies include conversation teaching, role-play teaching, interactive teaching, and shared teaching. These strategies tend to require more planning and experience to execute. As a result, before trying these strategies, we recommend practicing the prior co-teaching strategies to the point where your team can plan and switch between them with ease. Then, once you are comfortable implementing the first seven co-teaching strategies with a degree of success, your co-teaching team can begin experimenting with the final four co-teaching strategies. They have a higher degree of variability and require a level of synchronization within a co-teaching partnership to make them work well. Thus, as you read about these next four strategies, evaluate your co-teaching partnership and what degree of experience you have together, as these factors are key to which co-teaching strategies you will want to use in your practice.

8. CONVERSATION TEACHING

Talk shows and reality television can offer compelling viewing. During conversation teaching, both teachers are the "stars" of their own reality show. The co-teachers preplan the content and then have an educational conversation in front of the students. The students are the audience. They listen, watch, and absorb content. The co-teachers dig deep and demonstrate inquiry in front of students (Karge, 2018).

For example, a very creative middle school mathematics team from Southern California introduced writing large numbers by having the general education co-teacher (Mr. J.) tell the special education co-teacher (Mrs. T.) what to write in front of the students. Mr. J. asked Mrs. T. to write one million using zeros. Mrs. T. wrote the answer incorrectly, and, using a story, Mr. J. guided her on how to rewrite the correct response. The dialogue continued, and Mrs. T. made errors she predicted students on her special education caseload who were in the class might make. She then asked clarification questions of Mr. J. to highlight and reinforce the concept learning. The students enjoyed "eavesdropping" on the teacher conversation and learned while doing so.

Co-teaching research in secondary schools validates the practice of conversation teaching when implemented with fidelity (Hamdan, Anuar, & Khan, 2016; King-Sears, Stefanidis, Berkeley, & Strogilos, 2021). It's especially useful at the secondary level because curriculum and standards are more rigorous and students often need more ample instruction.

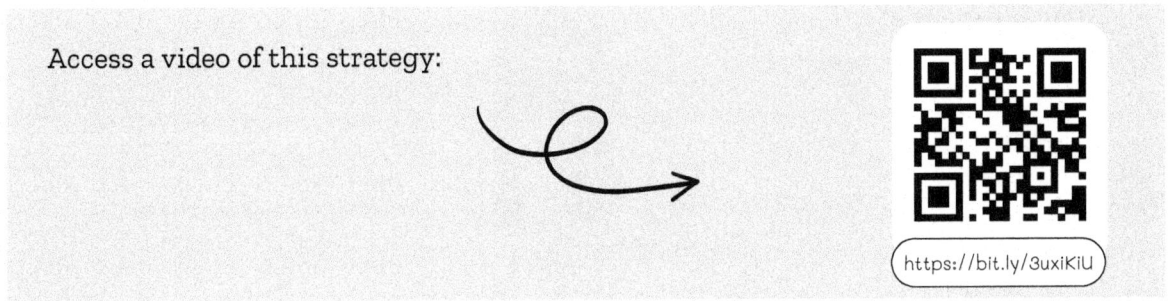

Access a video of this strategy:

https://bit.ly/3uxiKiU

Figure 2.10 (page 40) provides a visual of conversation teaching.

FIGURE 2.10: Co-teaching strategy 8—Conversation teaching.

9. ROLE-PLAY TEACHING

Role-play teaching allows the co-teaching team to plan and share a think-aloud, characterization, or debate in skit format with the entire class. Sometimes, the teachers wear costumes or a funny hat. Other times, they might mime. The performance is captivating, and students enjoy the show. Students recall this unusual "performance and generalize the knowledge obtained from viewing" (Karge, 2015, p. 19).

When Belinda was co-teaching, during about the middle of a sixth-grade class co-teaching assignment, arguing among classmates became a problem. Belinda and her partner incorporated a role-play designed to illustrate appropriate social skills for solving problems with peers in the lesson. They recreated the argument from the prior day and then went through social skill steps to demonstrate how to solve the problem. The students were extremely engaged during the co-teaching role-play. They followed up by posting a weekly social skill and praising students with verbal rewards when they exhibited the skill. Belinda noticed a significant decline in arguing among classmates the remainder of the year.

Figure 2.11 provides a visual of role-play teaching.

FIGURE 2.11: Co-teaching strategy 9—Role-play teaching.

10. INTERACTIVE TEACHING

Interactive teaching describes teachers who collaboratively plan and use a variety of co-teaching approaches, with the common thread being an interactive element. The teachers both take the instructional lead and work side by side to implement the teaching responsibilities during one period or hour a day. Calling it complementary co-teaching, Villa and colleagues (2013) refer to interactive teaching as each co-teacher doing something to enhance the instruction provided by the other teacher. In a fifth-grade class, during a lesson on plant life cycles, one co-teacher leads a discussion by modeling how to plant seeds in the community garden while the other co-teacher circulates to assist students with the hands-on activity of planting the seeds, followed by ensuring students are writing down their observations in their science journals. Another example of interactive teaching takes place in a co-taught tenth-grade English class. In this lesson, one co-teacher leads a Socratic seminar on the themes of a novel, while the other co-teacher provides a small group real-time formative assessment with mini whiteboards related to the themes of the story. In both examples, interactive teaching provides opportunities for an interactive element of a lesson, such as the act of planting a seed or debating, as well as an opportunity for students to receive one-on-one or small-group support simultaneously.

Figure 2.12 provides a visual of interactive teaching.

- Interactive teaching leads to doubled brain power as well as multiple exposures to text and topics, since both teachers are sharing their subject matter expertise (Scruggs et al., 2007).
- Interactive instruction means planning the lesson, carrying out the instruction, and assessing student outcomes collectively.

FIGURE 2.12: Co-teaching strategy 10—Interactive teaching.

11. SHARED TEACHING

Shared teaching describes collaborative teaching teams of educators who fully share all responsibilities for the classroom, doing what one teacher traditionally does (that is, plan, teach, assess, and reflect) and taking full responsibility for every aspect of the classroom. They demonstrate to their students that they respect each other and are comfortable sharing the teaching stage (Murawski & Spencer, 2011). During shared teaching, teachers work together all day in the same classroom or teaching simultaneously for multiple periods to deliver exemplary lessons. Co-teachers share the teaching, and students experience each educator's strengths and expertise (Villa et al., 2013).

Many preschool and kindergarten classrooms are now co-taught all day using the shared teaching strategy. In practice, having two educators sharing the teaching provides more opportunity for individualized attention, differentiation, and modeling, which ultimately caters to students' learning needs. Additionally, younger students may require closer supervision, more emotional support, and more frequent interventions. Furthermore, having two educators in the room means they have more eyes, ears, and hands geared toward managing the dynamics of the classroom with the goal of ensuring safety and fostering a nurturing and predictable environment. As a result, shared teaching in preschool and kindergarten enhances the quality of instruction and creates a more supportive and responsive learning space for students.

Figure 2.13 provides a visual of shared teaching.

FIGURE 2.13: Co-teaching strategy 11—Shared teaching.

The Role of Collaboration

Collaboration is vital in co-teaching, which involves more than simply having two teachers in the same classroom; it requires a strategic partnership in which both educators actively and strategically collaborate to deliver instruction to a diverse group of learners. Murawski (2009) has used the term *collaborative teaching*. Friend (2000) initially wrote about collaborative teaching, cautioning that just because two teachers interact, one cannot assume it's collaborative. Collaboration is a very specific relationship that includes dialogue, planning, and joint decision making (Hughes & Murawski, 2001; Murawski, 2009). The eleven co-teaching strategies described in this chapter give a variety of options for collaboration. However, our hope is that teams expand this definition of collaboration and take the opportunity to meet and discuss the eleven co-teaching strategies. Co-teachers can explicitly discuss how to use each strategy within their specific co-teaching environment, share insights with others at the school, and explore further context. Building a community of practice where teams of co-teachers share and engage in collaborative inquiry cycles can strengthen the entire process (Feller, Myers, & Smith, 2022). *Collaborative inquiry cycles* are a component of professional learning communities (PLCs), which require ongoing job-embedded learning by educators to enhance student outcomes (DuFour, DuFour, Eaker, Mattos, & Muhammad, 2021).

In practice, this requires co-teachers at the partner and department level to dive into reflective exercises, conduct research, and evaluate feedback from coaches or other instructional leaders. As they go through the collaborative inquiry cycle, they can uncover trends and devise action plans. The observations and experiences from this exercise build a collaborative culture of continuous co-teaching improvement.

Twenty-four co-teachers (twelve co-teaching pairs) at an elementary school in rural Texas that Belinda worked with show how this process looked. They were trained as part of the school's implementation of the PLC process (DuFour et al., 2021). They divided into grade-level groups; grades 1 and 2 had three co-teaching teams each, and grades 3, 4, and 5 consisted of two co-teaching teams. They met faithfully twice a month to use the decision-making cycle for data collection (see figure 2.14) to guide their discussions. They looked at pre- and post-curriculum data for each instructional unit (gathered from a pretest and a post-test implemented for each unit), made data-based decisions for interventions, and brainstormed strategies in their grade-level teams for instruction and progress monitoring. As they talked through the interventions, they discussed which of the eleven co-teaching strategies they would use and how to implement them. At the next team meeting, they again came together to review, revisit, and refine as needed. These meetings were intentional and conducted at the same time every other week to form an effective community of practice (Trust & Horrocks, 2018). All teams met in the same room. The principal and school instructional coach moved from group to group: listening in, adding to the discussion, and asking questions to dig deeper into the student learning data as well as the implementation of co-teaching strategies as instructional tools to enhance student learning.

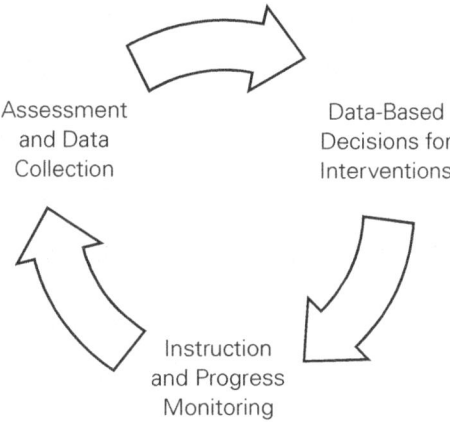

Source: Karge, 2023b, p. 167.

FIGURE 2.14: Decision-making cycle for data collection.

Conclusion

In this chapter, we described three stages, eleven co-teaching strategies, and the concept of using collaborative inquiry cycles. We suggest that teachers move quickly past strategies 1–3—but do not skip them—and spend quality time using strategies 4–11. When each co-teacher actively engages in the instructional process, true co-teaching takes place (Bacharach, Heck, & Dahlberg, 2010). Which co-teaching strategy would you like to try?

Regardless of the approach, both educators should proactively communicate and actively participate in the task of teaching during the allocated co-teaching time. In our experience, veteran co-teachers continually share that the variety the eleven strategies offer builds motivation and enjoyment. These co-teaching strategies go beyond the five strategies originally introduced by Cook and Friend (1995) and allow for more depth and greater investment in the instruction both teachers offer (Karge, 2023b).

As we move further in this book, these eleven co-teaching strategies are key to integrating instructional strategies and ed tech within lessons. You will see how you can use them in physical and digital classroom spaces, as there are infinite possibilities for how you can integrate and sequence them within instruction. With practice, many of these co-teaching strategies will become second nature, and you will notice how often you are switching between them throughout your lessons.

> **ADDITIONAL RESOURCES TO CONSIDER AFTER READING THIS CHAPTER**
> - **2Teach Global (https://2teachllc.com)** is an education consulting company that provides numerous resources related to co-teaching and inclusive teaching on its website. 2Teach Global's CEO is Wendy Murawski, who is widely cited in this book and is one of the foremost experts on co-teaching.
> - From the nonprofit research and development organization CAST, **"What Is Co-Teaching? An Introduction to Co-Teaching and Inclusion" (https://bit.ly/3yPmMos)** is an informational article that provides a general overview of co-teaching practice and a look at the most popular strategies and their implementation.

Reflection and Action: I Noticed, I Wondered

Directions: After reading chapter 2 on co-teaching strategies, write down several key themes you noticed about each of the co-teaching strategies presented in this chapter. Then, write down at least three to five questions or statements that relate to your next steps of taking what you learned in this chapter and applying the strategies to your co-teaching classroom.

I Noticed	I Wondered

Co-Teaching Evolved © 2025 Solution Tree Press • SolutionTree.com
Visit **go.SolutionTree.com/instruction** to download this free reproducible.

Student outcomes in co-taught classes are strongly impacted by the amount that the teaching partners invest and believe in co-teaching. Relationship building between the teachers and with their students is essential for positive outcomes. No matter the structure of the co-taught class, all students should be viewed as "our students." Co-teachers need to trust each other, treat each other as equals, be willing to compromise, and have strong communication skills.

—T. Marquez, special education co-teacher, personal communication, January 19, 2024

CHAPTER 3

Building and Maintaining Co-Teaching Relationships

In 1996, several teachers from Brea Unified School District in Southern California were invited to a professional development learning session sponsored by California in collaboration with the Schwab Foundation. The session focused on multiage classes and teacher partnerships. It also included several sessions on general education–special education co-teaching. Two of the general education teachers, Ms. C. and Ms. M., listened intently, went back to their school, and began collaborating. The next year, they asked the principal and superintendent if they could take down the wall between their classrooms and teach in one large open room. At the time, Ms. C. was teaching fifth grade, and Ms. M. was teaching fourth. Each had thirty students. They co-taught with sixty students in one large room, sometimes team teaching together in the front of the room or role-playing for all sixty, and other times using a variety of co-teaching strategies to divide the group. When the special education teacher, Ms. S., came into their room, she was able to stay for two time blocks, since there were two teachers. This allowed for station co-teaching and alternative co-teaching with twenty students each. Ms. C. and Ms. M. co-taught until they retired. Over the years, they had built and maintained a successful partnership and saw the value and enhanced benefits of co-teaching in their student outcomes on both formative and summative assessments. They attribute their retention in the teaching field to co-teaching. And due to the relationship they had built during their long-standing co-teaching partnership, they remain in contact even in retirement.

Building a successful co-teaching *partnership* and fostering a co-teaching *relationship*, though of course they are related, involve distinct elements. A co-teaching partnership is defined by a collaboration between two educators rooted in mutual respect and understanding of the work, where each partner contributes to providing equitable and inclusive instruction to all students (Atkinson, 2021; Scruggs et al., 2007). In chapter 1 (page 15), we discuss co-teaching partnerships as a set of key practices: negotiating differences and responsibilities, delivering instruction, differentiating instruction, sharing classroom authority, co-mentoring, planning, and coaching students. In contrast, a co-teaching relationship relates to the interpersonal dynamics between co-teachers, encompassing the ability to navigate the challenges and successes of teaching together in a classroom. While partnerships focus on the functional work aspects of teaching roles and responsibilities, relationships delve into the social-emotional and communication skills needed to maintain a productive, professional, and harmonious teaching environment (Scruggs et al., 2007). That's the focus of this chapter: the dynamics of the relationship between co-teachers that they build and maintain. As we discuss co-teaching relationships, elements of co-teaching partnerships will intertwine, such as the dynamics of the work itself and the perceptions of both teachers of their relationship as colleagues working together.

The lack of a good co-teaching relationship can have serious consequences for the success of the partnership, the culture of the classroom and even the whole school, and, of course, the resulting levels of student learning. To illustrate, we recall an administrator we worked with who shared that the school was having a union issue related to co-teaching:

> *When we asked her to expand on the issue, she reported that teachers thought it was unfair that they had to plan together and did not want to put in the perceived extra time to co-teach. As we asked the administrator to reflect more deeply, she shared that the district had moved to a co-teaching format a few years before as part of an inclusion initiative. There was no preplanning time, no professional learning to introduce various co-teaching strategies, and no negotiation or even information session about the initiative with the teachers' union. The teachers were just told this was the new approach. As you can imagine, the education culture in that school was not positive, and teachers were not successfully building healthy relationships. In hindsight, no one thought it was important to provide time to build and support co-teaching relationships. Ultimately, the district sought the advice of a private consultant, who spent time with the union representatives, hosted several meetings to learn their issues, and then conducted systemic professional development on co-teaching over a two-year period. This district has seen an increase in teacher requests to co-teach, along with a significant rise in test scores. A very different outcome than where they started!*

There are many complex tasks involved in developing a healthy co-teaching partnership. While engaged in writing this book, we asked co-teaching teams from around the world to share with us their suggestions. The consensus themes from over 150 co-teaching teams, grades preK to college, appear in the first section of this chapter. As numerous co-teaching partners shared, it takes time to build the relationship and equal time to maintain it. This is why we recommend, after the initial professional learning, allowing co-teaching teams to continue to work together for a few consecutive years. It is also recommended that teachers have a say in selecting their co-teaching partner, instead of haphazard assignment of teams by administration. The second part of this chapter focuses on how these relationships lead to strong partnerships that in turn lead to better student outcomes.

> **Key Themes and Ideas**
> ☐ Fourteen suggestions for building and maintaining co-teaching relationships
> ☐ Strong partnerships for better student outcomes

Fourteen Suggestions for Building and Maintaining Co-Teaching Relationships

These fourteen factors underpin the development of supportive, enjoyable, and healthy co-teaching partnerships, and in turn, student progress is evident in these classrooms, often over the single-taught instructional classes.

1. Build a professional relationship.
2. Start small.
3. Use collaborative team planning time wisely.
4. Find a middle ground.
5. Set norms for each other and the class.
6. Use each other's strengths.
7. Let go of control.
8. Be gracious.
9. Be open minded.
10. Take time to debrief.
11. Share any and all student feedback.
12. Have open communication.
13. Share space and time.
14. Know it is worth your time and energy.

The following sections discuss each in more detail.

Build a Professional Relationship

The health of a professional relationship contributes significantly to the implementation of co-teaching. We have heard many stories of co-teaching teams that did not work well together for a variety of reasons. Both teaching and learning contexts suffer if strong partnerships are not established (Jenkins & Murawski, 2024). It is hardly surprising, then, that we would want to carve out quality time to build professional relationships. Professional connectedness is often developed when co-teachers find similarities on a personal level as well. For example, a co-teaching team with teachers who each had young children of their own agreed to arrive and depart school each day at teacher report time; however, each Thursday evening at 9:00 p.m., when their children are in bed, they get on Zoom and co-plan. At first, they just planned; however, as the professional relationship grew during those Thursday night sessions, they learned more about each other, their families, and why they went into teaching. These jewels of knowledge made their co-teaching time stronger. In their words, their professional and personal worlds *clicked*, and this enhanced their time in the classroom with students. One of the co-teaching partners learned her colleague enjoyed coffee in the early morning and often brought her a specialty coffee as a thank-you gift for their successful partnership. This small display of gratitude acknowledged the professional relationship they built.

Start Small

Every team we talked with agreed co-teaching teams must begin small. As mentioned in chapter 2 (page 29), we recommend building on professional knowledge and expertise by beginning with supportive co-teaching (one teach, one assist; one teach, one observe; and one teach, one support). In most cases, this means one of the teachers will take the teaching lead by teaching the content, and the co-teacher will assist (for example, taking notes on the board for students to observe), observe (for example, recording behavior counts to keep track of on-task behavior), or support (for example, walking around the classroom and keeping students focused with proximity). Once partnerships have established a comfort zone in this area, then the co-teaching pairs move to team co-teaching (graze-and-tag teaching, parallel teaching, station teaching, and alternative teaching). Finally, once the partnership is further developed and they have reached the appropriate level of comfort, the pairs can move on to using the advanced co-teaching strategies (conversation teaching, role-play teaching, interactive teaching, and shared teaching). We recommend caution: take it slow but build on the process. Too many teachers new to co-teaching get stuck on the first level, supportive co-teaching, and never move away from using these three strategies. When this occurs, resentment often forms as there is not a divided workload.

Use Collaborative Team Planning Time Wisely

Many of the teams we surveyed and spoke with work in schools that have implemented the PLC process and report that the collaborative team planning time that takes place in a PLC is a great place to dig in and plan as well as learn from each other to improve student learning opportunities. Whether you use team time, your planning period, or your own time, the time must be spent wisely. One of the values of working as a team is sharing each other's expertise (DuFour et al., 2024). During planning time, make sure to establish timelines and assign preparation tasks. Co-planning skills will improve as the co-teaching team spends more and more time together. Be sure to document your planning for future reference (so that next year you can add on to it, not recreate it!). When you struggle to find planning time, the use of a travel journal (a shared, live Google Doc or Word document) in which each of you electronically write comments can provide impromptu learning between the co-teaching partners. We discuss planning time in more detail in chapter 5 (page 81).

Find a Middle Ground

Negotiate ahead of time. Identify what each member of the partnership believes in. Have the critical discussion of what individual systems both teachers have been using and how they can be integrated into co-teaching. Discuss respective educator pet peeves to clear the air. How can co-teachers build on these to move from *mine* to *ours*? Successfully doing so allows them to implement co-teaching with informed perspectives. Again, *ours*, not *yours and mine*, should be your mantra. Along with this thought process is a give and take in lesson planning, classroom organization and management, and direct (or nondirect) teaching approaches. Finding middle ground will allow both co-teachers to feel successful.

Set Norms for Each Other and the Class

For many co-teachers, setting norms means making sure they agree on their vision for behavior and classroom setup and posting so they are visible to their students. These are similar to the essential agreements that co-teachers should come to for greater efficacy, as we discuss in chapter 4 (page 59); norms, in essence, act as sub-agreements. These measures are certainly important, and all co-teachers should consider them. Several of the co-teaching teams we have worked with indicate they had used three of the four concepts suggested by Jade Wexler, Devin M. Kearns, Erin K. Hogan, Erin Clancy, and Alexandra Shelton (2021) to improve implementation of their practices: (1) monitor fidelity of implementation, (2) integrate evidence-based practices, and (3) determine roles to set their co-teaching instructional norms. (The fourth concept is more about the paper's specific topic, so we have omitted it as it's not generally applicable.) Wexler and colleagues (2021) write about implementing evidence-based literacy practices in co-taught classrooms. The teams we have worked with see the importance of evidence-based strategies as a norm for their co-teaching.

Use Each Other's Strengths

It is important to use each other's strengths to become better co-teachers and support *all* students. As co-teachers, we want to have a strengths-based approach through an equity lens. What this means is that there should be no sense of hierarchy, but there should be opportunities for both teachers and students alike: "Each individual should feel like an integral part of the collaborative relationship, despite having significantly different contributions to the work" (Jenkins & Murawski, 2024, p. 54). In a well-run co-taught classroom, the lead teacher role should shift between co-teachers during instruction. When one co-teacher is stronger at behavior management and the other at data monitoring, both co-teachers complement and learn from each other, and their personal skill sets are enhanced by the experience. This takes planning, experience, and a true understanding of each other's strengths as teachers.

Let Go of Control

Although some teacher preparation programs do use the co-teacher training method, most teachers learn to teach solo. Many teachers are used to being alone in every aspect of teaching. The co-teaching teams we have worked with emphasize the importance of letting go of control. Think of the co-taught classroom as any other relationship; it is a give and take. Neither co-teacher needs to be in control for every planning session, teaching event, assessment, or reflection of the lesson. When co-teachers can let go of that control and share it with a colleague, they find their work is stronger and student learning levels are higher. Relinquish control and trust your colleagues (Jeong & Eggelston, 2021).

Many of the teams we spoke with say that as they learned to trust their colleagues, it was easier to let go of classroom and overall teaching control, and they found that it improves all aspects of teaching and learning.

Be Gracious

Greet each other with a smile and talk informally. Grace goes a long way. When one of the co-teaching partners makes an error, see it as a learning opportunity. As in any relationship, kindness goes a long way. When one of the pair has a bad day (personally or professionally), the other can step up and take the lead.

Be Open Minded

A crucial aspect of co-teaching relationships is being open minded. Many of the teams we have worked with tell us that they learned so much from their co-teaching partners. Watching someone else introduce a concept or reteach using an accommodation can provide professional growth. As planning takes place, listen with an open mind; the suggestion just might grant students access to the content a co-teacher has taught for many years in a very different yet informative way.

Take Time to Debrief

Much of the teaching literature focuses on the teach-learn-assess-reflect cycle (Hall & Simeral, 2015). Co-teaching is no different. It is vitally important to take time to debrief. Co-teachers can debrief not only lessons but also their working relationship, job sharing, individual connections to students, classroom culture, and relationships with parents. Are both co-teachers engaging in shared decision making and problem solving? Are they merely playing nicely while physically in the room at the same time, or are they sharing the space in a truly collaborative way? Talk about this and debrief to learn, grow, and extend your co-teaching practices (Jenkins & Murawski, 2024).

Share Any and All Student Feedback

It should be a given that joint evaluation of student progress is important, yet the co-teachers we spoke with voiced the concern that sometimes, one person does not have access to the gradebook or cannot enter grades, and thus the grading falls on the one with access. Co-teachers can talk to administrators or coordinators and figure out the back end of the LMS so two teachers can be added to one class or period.

Share other types of feedback as well. Several of the co-teaching teams we worked with say they make it a point to tell each other if a student expressed difficulty with a lesson or enjoyed a component of the lesson. These shared feedback statements allow both members to feel a part of the whole.

Have Open Communication

A primary question for co-teachers should always be, How will we ensure regular open communication with one another? Sharing information should be open and confidential between co-teachers.

Teachers should decide before they begin co-teaching when and how to discuss issues with each other. Who will communicate with administration? Is this communication they want to do together, or does it make sense for just one of them to take on the role of consistent communicator with administration to give them a window into the classroom and keep them updated on how the co-teaching is going? Are both co-teachers engaging in shared decision making and problem solving? Are they truly collaborating, or are they merely physically in the room at the same time, sharing the space? These are good questions to ask each other and openly discuss the responses.

Share Space and Time

Interpretation of the roles each co-teacher is to perform in the classroom helped so many of the teams we have worked with. This sounds a bit ambiguous; however, when we think of any human relationship that involves shared space and time, eventually each person falls in their lane, so to speak, and refines how they work together to sustain the relationship. For instance, in an elementary school co-teaching team, one teacher might specialize in leading mathematics and science lessons, while the other focuses on language arts and social studies, but both collaborate on lesson planning and share classroom management responsibilities to maintain a balanced and supportive classroom environment. Students will take note of the positive collegial relationship co-teachers display.

Know It Is Worth Your Time and Energy

A common relational view shared by veteran co-teachers and first-year teams alike is that co-teaching is worth it. This is something that will be evident to outside observers: "When co-teaching is taking place, leaders should see something beyond what they would see if only one teacher is in the classroom" (Karge, 2023b, p. 54).

Strong Partnerships for Better Student Outcomes

Talking about relationships might feel a little ambiguous or touchy-feely, but when co-teachers take the time to intentionally foster their relationship, the partnership is strong, and so are the results. Fostering relationships can equate to a stronger partnership as the relationship evolves and each teacher gets to know the other.

An example of the student progress co-teachers can experience took place in an international elementary school Belinda worked with in El Salvador. Teaching is in English even though the primary language of most of the students is Spanish. In both first and fifth grades, the co-teaching teams realized their weakest area of student growth was oral fluency while reading. The data showed a complete flatline—meaning that neither grade level had made any progress in the three years prior. Three different groups at grade 1 and three different groups at grade 5 had made no progress. Belinda provided a professional learning session detailing how to dig into every aspect of data. It was during a co-teaching data dig that this deficit was revealed.

The intervention specialist co-taught with each of the general education teachers. It was decided during the data session that the interventional specialist (a trained special education teacher) would come into the first-grade classroom for an hour each day and the fifth-grade classroom for forty-five minutes each day. During that time, the teachers would use one of the advanced co-teaching strategies (conversation, role-play, interactive, or shared co-teaching) to introduce the reading lesson (twenty minutes). They would then break into alternative teaching groups for small-group fluency for the remainder of the time. During these groups, the co-teachers would read aloud with the students, including various read-aloud activities (popcorn reading, choral reading, and so on). Then the intervention specialist would pull three students a day to read aloud to her outside of the classroom while the general education first- or fifth-grade teacher did a whole-group lesson with the students who were left. In one trimester of consistent implementation, the first-grade average fluency jumped twenty points (see figure 3.1)! These first-grade students moved from the 25th to the 75th percentile on the standardized oral reading fluency data comparison, created by University of Oregon researchers Jan Hasbrouck and Gerald Tindal (2017). Remember, they had been flatlined for three years prior. This is very impressive student growth. The teachers shared that the difference was the intentional co-teaching of fluency. Their already established healthy partnership led to ease of implementation and successful co-teaching for both teachers and students.

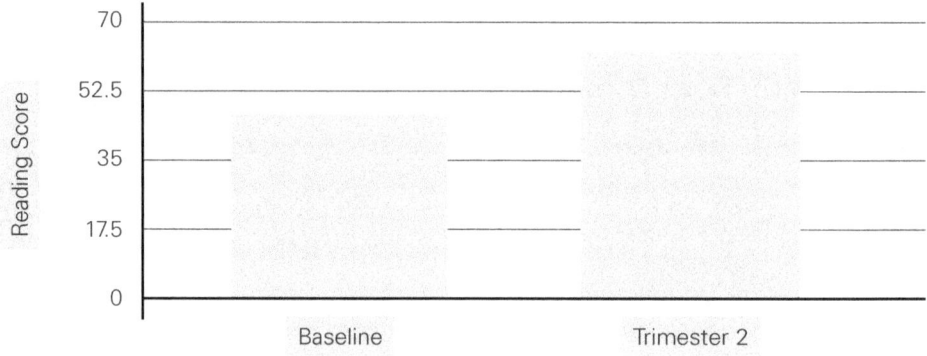

FIGURE 3.1: Oral reading fluency in first grade.

Similarly, at the same time, a huge increase was seen by the fifth graders as well. They moved from the 50th percentile to the 90th percentile. See figure 3.2 for a comparison of their reading scores that translate to these percentiles.

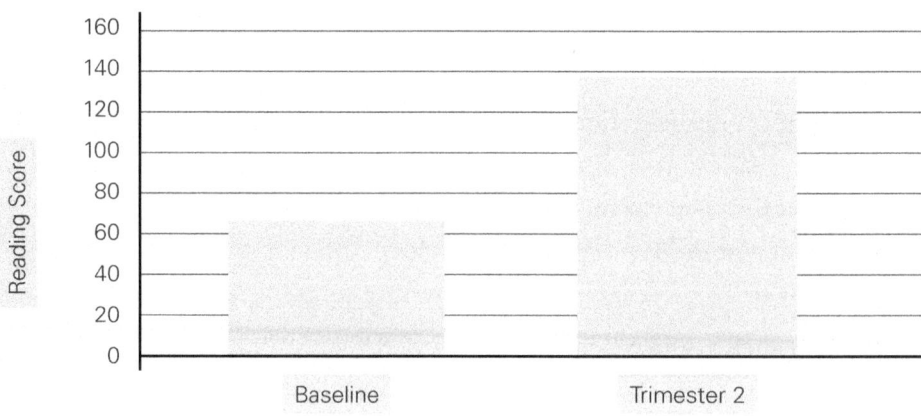

FIGURE 3.2: Oral reading fluency in fifth grade.

These three teachers realized they had taken a risk by spending so much teaching time on oral fluency, yet it was something their students needed and something the school was encouraging. When they debriefed with Belinda, they commented that, had they not taken the time during the data dig to really look for an area of need, they may have missed the opportunity to collaborate as co-teaching teams and in turn for their students to show such substantial growth.

When Belinda asked the principal what had been done initially to bring together the co-teaching teams, he shared that after the preliminary co-teaching assignments, the teachers took the Myers-Briggs Type Indicator and shared profiles with their partners. They then received time to discuss teaching and their instructional philosophies. He asked each team to come up with a goal and vision for their co-teaching and, once they had a collaborative vision, to make an action plan. This administrator gave the co-teaching teams time to develop the steps they would take to move their co-teaching forward and then asked them to create lesson plans and define their roles and responsibilities for the first month of school. This intentionality built the partnerships. The total time allocated for this planning was twelve hours. Ultimately, with the structure in place as well as the allocated time, both co-teachers not only got time to establish their co-teaching partnerships, but they also had time to begin fostering their relationship as co-teachers by getting to know each other more as professionals and as people. In summary, the steps the school took to cultivate strong co-teaching partnerships were as follows.

1. Take Myers-Briggs Type Indicator.
2. Share profiles with co-teaching partner.
3. Discuss teaching and learning preferences.
4. Create a goal and vision for your unique co-teaching team.
5. Form an action plan with next steps.
6. Plan lessons and define roles and responsibilities for the first month.

Conclusion

In addition to the fourteen factors and the initial steps for cultivating a partnership, we would like to add the importance of always making certain students come first. Every co-teaching relationship should focus on being student minded. While we have emphasized the importance of spending time on adult relationships in this chapter, we don't mean that it should minimize the importance of student relationships. Keeping students front and center means thinking through how co-teachers will build connections with students and help them understand their teachers. From the simple things, such as both teachers greeting students as they enter the classroom, to more complex notions, such as conflict management, the team should be consistent. Be transparent with students and establish norms and expectations together. Co-teaching can be a lot of fun when implemented as a team.

A healthy co-teaching relationship also serves as a model for students; in fact, for some students, the co-teaching relationship may be the only positive adult relationship they see. Cultivating positive collegial relationships among all involved builds community. This chapter shared the thoughts of many co-teaching teams in the fourteen factors used to build and maintain co-teaching relationships. Highlighting one leader's intentional initial steps for cultivating a strong co-teaching partnership and then seeing the results of a data dig remind all of us that the time invested on the front end can help schools reap many rewards as the co-teaching teams develop and work together.

RESOURCES TO CONSIDER AFTER READING THIS CHAPTER

- Take a free personality test based on the **Myers-Briggs Type Indicator (www.truity.com/test/type-finder-personality-test-new)** to shed light on your strengths and your co-teacher's strengths and to begin building a collaborative co-teaching partnership and relationship. Review each other's strengths and begin determining next steps on setting up the necessary structures and essential agreements to get your co-teaching classroom up and running.
- **NERIS Type Explorer (www.16personalities.com/free-personality-test)** is another personality test you and your co-teacher can use to learn more about each other and how to work best with each other.
- **"Co-Teaching 101: Working With Your Co-Teacher" (https://diverselearnerscoop.com/blog/co-teaching-101-working-with-your-co-teacher)** is a post on the Diverse Learners Cooperative blog that provides tips on how to build a relationship with your co-teacher.
- The Cult of Pedagogy blog post **"Co-Teaching: How to Make It Work" (www.cultofpedagogy.com/co-teaching-push-in)** outlines not only co-teaching strategies but, more important, how to navigate and build co-teaching relationships with your co-teacher.
- The MiddleWeb blog post **"Turning Around a Co-Teaching Relationship" (www.middleweb.com/44819/how-we-turned-around-a-co-teaching-relationship)** by Tan Huynh focuses on how to rebuild a co-teaching relationship that has not gone as planned.
- The Edutopia video **"Building Relationships With Empathy Maps" (www.edutopia.org/video/building-relationships-empathy-maps)** by Jorge Valenzuela focuses on how we can use empathy maps to learn more about each other so we can work better together.

Reflection and Action: *I Used to Think* Versus *Now I Think*

Directions: After reading chapter 3 about building and maintaining co-teaching relationships, fill out the following graphic organizer. Describe what you used to think about this chapter's topics of discussion. Then, after you have spent time reflecting on the chapter's content, outline what you now think about these topics.

I Used to Think	Now I Think

Co-Teaching Evolved © 2025 Solution Tree Press • SolutionTree.com
Visit **go.SolutionTree.com/instruction** to download this free reproducible.

Some of the most important collaborations that need to be in place for successful co-teaching include co-establishing lesson objectives, deciding on clear roles for each teacher, thinking through proper spaces where instruction happens, and working with and learning from different specialists to ensure individual student needs are addressed.

—C. Weatherill, third-grade teacher, personal communication, January 30, 2024

CHAPTER 4

Synthesizing Efficacy, Attitude, and Essential Agreements

Teachers' attitudes and belief in themselves and others are critical to their success and sustainability as teachers (Wray, Sharma, & Subban, 2022). As we emphasize in this chapter, daily consideration of these factors in the ways co-teachers work together is key to a successful partnership.

Early in Matt's career, he had two different co-teachers and two self-contained special education sections he taught by himself. This scenario gives a window into that experience:

> *I had three preps but also two distinct co-teachers to collaborate with throughout the year. Each period I had with each co-teacher occurred each day, consisting of one-hour and two-hour block periods, along with a caseload of over twenty-five students. I often wondered at the beginning, How do I have enough time? Often, we did not have time to adequately plan or work together to use effective co-teaching and instructional strategies. My two co-teaching partnerships that year offer contrasting narratives.*
>
> *One co-teaching partnership was with an English and language arts teacher. We had a one-hour planning block that overlapped throughout the week. At the beginning of the year, we came together and developed a variety of essential agreements and a planning schedule, which helped us immensely. We had great cooperation and planning, but we did not have enough time to thoroughly plan because of the other responsibilities I had. Still, our class had a number of co-teaching strategies in place, such as team teaching, one teach, one observe, and parallel teaching.*
>
> *For my other co-teaching partnership, I worked with a government and economics teacher. We had only one period together and did not have an active planning block. Additionally, both of us had very different philosophies on how a class functions and different abilities to use strategies and technologies. At the beginning of the year, we did not spend much time coming together to build essential agreements. I am sure you can see where this is going. Our class looked unorganized at times. We mostly followed the general education teacher's lesson plan with implemented adaptations and accommodations. As a result, we mainly*

> *used the one teach, one assist and one teach, one support co-teaching strategies. Ultimately, without planning time, our instruction was not dynamic, which resulted in a lack of student engagement at times.*
>
> *These two scenarios affected my attitude and belief in myself as an educator. I thought one co-teaching class went well, while we really struggled in the other one. Additionally, I had a hard time juggling everything I had to do. The year's scattered workload overwhelmed me; I did not know where to focus, as all my co-teaching classrooms and partnerships had to compete for my time and energy. Ultimately, this is a prime example of the importance of planning time and schedules.*

Do co-teachers believe in themselves and others and their practices as educators? How does this impact their ability to work with others and provide positive and honest feedback and collaboration? This chapter delves into these questions. Additionally, it covers how co-teachers must come together and determine how they will interact, communicate, and function within the classroom setting by learning more about each other as well as creating essential agreements, which make up the pillars of any co-teaching partnership.

> **Key Themes and Ideas**
> ☐ Efficacy and mindset
> ☐ Elements of co-teaching that maximize co-teacher efficacy
> ☐ Essential agreements for greater co-teacher efficacy

Efficacy and Mindset

Have you ever felt that your attitude and your perceived belief in your abilities affect you as a teacher? There is no doubt that going into the day confident and positive is better than doubt and negativity. Attitude ties directly into how teachers feel about their practice and their efficacy. *Self-efficacy* refers to our perceived belief in our capabilities to complete a given task (Bandura, Freeman, & Lightsey, 1999). *Collective efficacy* relates to a group's shared belief and perceived abilities to execute a given set of individual and collective actions (Hattie, 2023; Krammer, Gastager, Lisa, Gasteiger-Klicpera, & Rossmann, 2018). High degrees of self-efficacy and collective efficacy correlate with higher degrees of student achievement (Hattie, 2023).

Susanne Garvis and Donna Pendergast (2016) share Albert Bandura's foundational work on the concept of self-efficacy as an indicator of motivation, a good compass for achievement. Robert Klassen and Virginia M. C. Tze (2014) conducted a meta-analysis that includes 9,216 teachers, and their findings reveal a significant correlation between teacher self-efficacy and teaching performance. Self-efficacy is critical for co-teachers and teachers in general to succeed and enjoy what they do daily. Additionally, it helps them resiliently navigate the ebbs and flows of teaching throughout the school year. Last, teacher self-efficacy impacts student motivation and achievement, which is a huge factor alongside all its teacher job satisfaction benefits (Mojavezi & Tamiz, 2012; Viel-Ruma, Houchins, Jolivette, & Benson, 2010).

We emphasize the importance of self-efficacy for both co-teachers within their partnership as well as that of school leaders and co-teachers in leadership roles; an effective co-teaching program and effective partnerships rely on the confidence and capabilities of each individual involved in both teaching and managing as well as leading the program.

Concurrently, self-efficacy and collective efficacy are required for the systems that make it possible to implement co-teaching in classrooms and schools. These systems include how co-teaching is planned in the school's schedule, teacher planning time, the tools co-teachers receive, and the perceptions of how co-teaching should look in that particular school's context. Additionally, elements of school system design (discussed in chapter 6, page 101) help propagate higher levels of self- and collective efficacy. For example, schools that have a focused direction in terms of their vision and goals promote instructional risk taking, provide collaborative planning time and structures, and advocate for deeper learning; these factors contribute to efficacy, and these schools tend to exhibit higher levels of achievement (Fullan & Quinn, 2016). These elements impact teacher efficacy as individuals and as co-teachers.

Collective efficacy also matters greatly at the classroom level; when collective efficacy is strong in co-teaching teams, there are significant positive results in student outcomes (Krammer et al., 2018). Have you ever walked into a classroom and seen a high or low degree of efficacy among teachers? Observing and evaluating efficacy of teachers and the collective efficacy of a group of teachers and staff is a good exercise. Let's focus on how self-efficacy and collective efficacy may affect teachers' ability to collaborate with their co-teachers as well as help them provide impactful instruction. Teachers with a high degree of self- and collective efficacy typically are supported with resources, have positive and supportive relationships with colleagues and school leaders, and share goals and values (Skaalvik & Skaalvik, 2019).

There are several classroom and school system variables that impact co-teachers' self-efficacy and collective efficacy as teams. Many scenarios in each of these two categories can positively and negatively affect self- and collective teacher efficacy, which ultimately may impact the attitude of teachers. Let's explore some of these elements, which we've divided according to their positive and negative impact on self- and collective efficacy.

Positive Elements That Impact Efficacy

There are numerous ways to boost self- and collective efficacy. These include shared planning time (Friend, 2008; Simon, 2017; Wilson, 2016), a collaborative community of practice (Jenkins & Murawski, 2024; Trust & Horrocks, 2018), mentoring (Anderson & Karge, 2020), celebrations (Karge, 2023b), administrative support (Esposito, 2023), and an instructional risk-taking culture (Henriksen et al., 2021). These elements must work in tandem with each other throughout the school year to give teachers the opportunities to truly believe in themselves and their abilities to make a positive impact in the classrooms they serve.

Negative Elements That Impact Efficacy

Have you ever struggled to find time to plan? Have you ever had to work with a colleague whose disposition did not complement yours? Have you worked with a partner or team without setting boundaries and essential agreements? Have you worked with grade-level and department teams with no shared planning time and without a collaborative culture? Have you lacked adequate administrative support and professional learning opportunities? All these situations relate to the inverse of the positive variables discussed in the previous section. Ultimately, the goal for co-teachers is to boost their efficacy by focusing on how they can ensure the positive variables and eliminate as many of the negative variables as possible. Each positive variable builds on the others to establish and maintain positive and effective co-teacher efficacy. Let's jump into these variables that can maximize teacher efficacy between co-teachers.

Elements of Co-Teaching That Maximize Co-Teacher Efficacy

The positive variables that impact self- and collective efficacy among co-teachers ultimately improve each teacher's attitude toward their daily work as they navigate the challenges they face together. The following sections dig deeper into these variables, including shared planning time, a collaborative community of practice, mentoring, celebrations, administrative support, and an instructional risk-taking culture.

Shared Planning Time

Shared planning time is critical for collaborating on lessons throughout the week as well as reviewing student data to drive instruction (Simon, 2017; Wilson, 2016). Teachers get the opportunity to coordinate, connect, and manage various challenges and tasks such as anticipating behavior challenges, differentiating instruction, assessing student work, reflecting on practice, and communicating with families and stakeholders. Sometimes they simply reconnect and calibrate after a lesson or series of lessons. Shared planning time creates the potential to significantly improve student outcomes (Friend, 2008). Successful co-teaching requires time investment in every element of the relationship to enhance the experience for both teachers and ultimately the students they support (Rytivaara, Pulkkinen, & de Bruin, 2019).

In teaching and education, time is always of the essence (Syrek, Kühnel, Vahle-Hinz, & De Bloom, 2022). This is especially true in shared planning time, as it may not regularly occur each day. Instead, it may take place strategically throughout the week. Researchers Kenneth W. Thompson and Mirah J. Dow (2017) discuss how intensity and effort in shared planning and organization are key to the overall effectiveness of the co-teaching partnership. Therefore, shared planning time must be strategic. But how do co-teachers optimize this time?

First, having a system of organization is key to success. A shared digital and physical space is optimal to organize digital files and physical papers. The digital folder should contain all content that you will place on an LMS, long- and short-term working planning documents, IEPs, IEPs at a glance, student data, and key stakeholder communication. A shared Google Drive folder is a good vehicle because you can organize your files into folders and subfolders. Physical organization can look similar: use a filing cabinet with tabs and folders to sort important documents. Additionally, within the classroom, designate a space where students receive and turn in work products.

Second, the workflow of short-term and long-term lesson planning is another key organizational piece all co-teaching partners must develop. By *workflow*, we mean the planning process, generating and creating the content, interconnecting it with selected ed tech tools, and finally integrating the content into instruction. Access to a pacing guide broken down into long-term and weekly lesson planners is the first step. You can then divide the pacing guide based on units for content and skill areas and align each unit with formative and summative assessments. The short-term plan is the weekly lesson plans where you have developed each area of content, hyperlinked them, and uploaded them to the LMS for students to access. Generally, more strategic planning takes place at the end of a unit as co-teachers review summative data before building the next unit. During this time, both co-teachers discuss which instructional and co-teaching strategies they will use for each lesson. With this in place, planning can become asynchronous. As they sketch out the unit on the long-term plan, each co-teacher takes a role in asynchronously planning various components of the lesson (that is, formative assessment, content and visuals, differentiations, and so on). Co-teachers can also asynchronously divide the tasks of communication between students and families as well as providing feedback and grading student work.

The third element to maximize planning time is to ensure administrative tasks do not take over. For example, at the school level, ensure that no IEP meetings will be conducted over the course of the planning period. Shared planning time is also not an opportunity to cover classes. Devote this time exclusively to tasks that you and your co-teacher must do synchronously, saving the rest for your individual planning time. Creating these systematic boundaries helps alleviate burnout. Additionally, it makes co-teaching sustainable and more effective (Jomuad et al., 2021).

To support teachers in their planning workflow, it is worth noting the availability of a wide variety of AI tools, such as Google Gemini, ChatGPT, Claude, and Microsoft Copilot, along with a multitude of other AI-integrated tools. A set of shared prompts and planning data to input to help build teaching content and materials may make this time more effective and efficient, giving co-teachers more time to focus on thinking and discussing what the teaching will look like. Be sure to use the prompt structure of providing a role for the AI, stating a task, and providing specific details about the task and various constraints (such as a model text, rubric, tone, grade level, and so on; Fitzpatrick, Fox, & Weinstein, 2023). Ask AI to differentiate text or content for your students. Such a prompt may look like the following:

> *You are two co-teachers teaching middle school social science. I have copied and pasted a text excerpt into the chat as a model. [Insert text excerpt here.] You will use this as your model to differentiate the text to various reading levels in your classroom. We would like the reading levels of this text to be at the third-, sixth-, and eighth-grade levels.*

> *Additionally, include a list of key vocabulary words and their definitions generated within a table before each passage so students can be front-loaded with critical vocabulary before diving into the text.*

Include prompts like this within a shared document and folder that both co-teachers can access. Throughout the year, as the co-teachers use more prompts, they can add them to this document to employ in the future. Co-teachers using AI to help with planning, differentiation, and content creation will notice that prompts to complete each of these tasks are usually very similar. What may change in the prompts is the specified model text, standards, objectives, and the content being delivered to students. As a result, co-teachers will have a repository of prompts they can use at any time throughout the year, which they can copy and paste into their AI tool of choice to help them complete a wide variety of tasks.

Collaborative Community of Practice

A collaborative community of practice is key to improving not only the efficacy of teachers but also the effectiveness of co-teaching while lessening the workload for teachers. A *collaborative community of practice* is a culture with system in place to ensure teachers work together to solve problems that align to the school's mission, vision, and student needs. A collaborative community of practice includes six key elements (Trust & Horrocks, 2018). The first element is leadership roles. Each member of the co-teaching partnership is a teacher leader who drives their own learning by collaborating and working with their co-teaching partner. A tenth-grade co-teacher shares:

> Instead of waiting on the professional learning workshop that was scheduled four months into the school year, we were able to share co-teaching articles and learn from each other. Then, when we arrived at the training, our community of practice already knew this was something we wanted to implement with fidelity, and we were ready to learn! (B. Witmore, personal communication, October 21, 2023)

Once the teachers take the lead and are responsible for their own learning and practice, the other elements (personalized learning, guiding principles, organizational support, social learning, and purpose) fall into place to enhance teacher efficacy (Trust & Horrocks, 2018).

The second element, personalized learning, may include attending trainings online or in person, with or without the co-teaching partner. One teacher may attend a summer institute and the other a series of online modules. The key is the time to meet, review, and learn from each other as they grow their craft and build their community of practice. As co-teaching teams share their learnings with each other, their guiding principles, the third element, come into play. In this case, *guiding principles* refer to the etiquette with which the co-teachers interact and engage in a community of practice. For example, if there are only thirty minutes to meet, a guiding principle may be to stay focused by not responding to text or phone messages and to come to the community of practice ready to share previous learnings by bringing a summary or bulleted list. This allows each member to quickly inform their co-teacher of the learning and then for the two of them to jointly explore ways to include the learning in their teaching practices.

The fourth element is organizational support. Administrative support is necessary (we discuss this in depth in chapter 10, page 165, and later in this section); however, this element goes deeper than just administrative support. The school as an organization needs to see the value of co-teaching. When school colleagues who are not currently co-teaching see the benefits, co-teaching teams gain a sense of purpose and a feeling of support for their work. Seeing co-teaching as a strategy that contributes to the school's mission and vision allows for serious conversations with school staff and leaders who oversee the master schedule to make sure the co-teaching partners have joint planning time and that their teaching schedules align. Another component of organizational support is parent knowledge of co-teaching. When each of these parties is informed and sees the connection to the mission and vision of the school, the practice of co-teaching can move forward.

Torrey Trust and Brian Horrocks (2018) call the fifth element *social learning*, as all communities of practice are a social process. Learning from the knowledge of others and sharing one's own expertise provide each co-teacher with a feeling of job satisfaction. This type of reciprocal learning culture is prevalent in strong communities of practice. Murawski (2010) likens this close-knit co-teaching connection to a marriage. The purpose of each partner in the co-teaching relationship is pivotal.

The final element, purpose, is instrumental: the primary purpose of any co-teaching strategy is to improve student learning and achievement. When two teachers work in tandem with shared goals and purpose, they demonstrate a community of practice that supports a positive culture and collective efficacy.

Mentoring

Think about your mentors. What did they do to encourage you to do your best work? Why is it that you remember them? Did the mentor support your professional growth? Maybe the mentor helped you build your teaching toolbox with evidence-based instructional practices. Our guess is the mentor supported your self-efficacy, and ultimately, the students you worked with benefited academically, behaviorally, socially, and emotionally.

As Belinda puts it, "To *mentor* means to walk alongside" (Karge, 2023b, p. 72). The concept involves an experienced educator guiding a less experienced co-teacher. As co-teachers develop self- and collective efficacy, they may need an experienced mentor or mentors to walk alongside them. Consider both a content-specific mentor as well as someone who knows the ins and outs of co-teaching to work with teams to build collective efficacy. This type of ongoing mentorship is important to all teachers, regardless of how long they have been teaching (Anderson & Karge, 2020). Mentors can share pedagogical knowledge and strategies to enhance lesson planning, instruction, classroom management, and other elements of co-teaching (Cordie, Brecke, Lin, & Wooten, 2020). The mentor helps navigate the complexities of co-teaching dynamics. Mentors can guide co-teachers in assessments and reflections of teaching practices as well as analyzing outcomes and adjusting based on classroom observations and co-teaching discussions.

If conflict arises, mentors can play a vital role in helping co-teachers find solutions and build a positive working relationship. A productive mentor relationship can help to build substantial self-efficacy among co-teachers.

Celebrations

Recognition plays a significant role in boosting co-teacher confidence and efficacy. When others acknowledge teachers' efforts and successes, we have seen in our experience that it positively impacts co-teachers' beliefs in their own teaching abilities. During conversations with the students, leaders at a high school in Washington that Belinda worked with learned that student test scores had improved in part due to the co-teaching situation in an English class. Figure 4.1 shows the data. The individually taught class was first period; the same teacher who taught the first period co-taught the second as well. The material was identical. The second-period co-taught class included five students with disabilities. The teacher administered identical pre- and post-tests on the same days in both classes. After the leaders saw these substantial gains, they celebrated by having pizza delivered to the class. During the celebration, the administration shared the test scores and talked to the students about their learning experiences. The students candidly shared their belief that having two teachers made it easier to learn and remember the material. Not only did the students benefit from the celebration—they talked about it for weeks and were undoubtedly motivated to continue studying, learning, and achieving—but the teachers received a significant boost in self-efficacy as well. Celebrating the improved test scores elevated the teachers' belief in what they were doing in the co-taught class. It encouraged them to advocate for additional periods of co-taught collaborations.

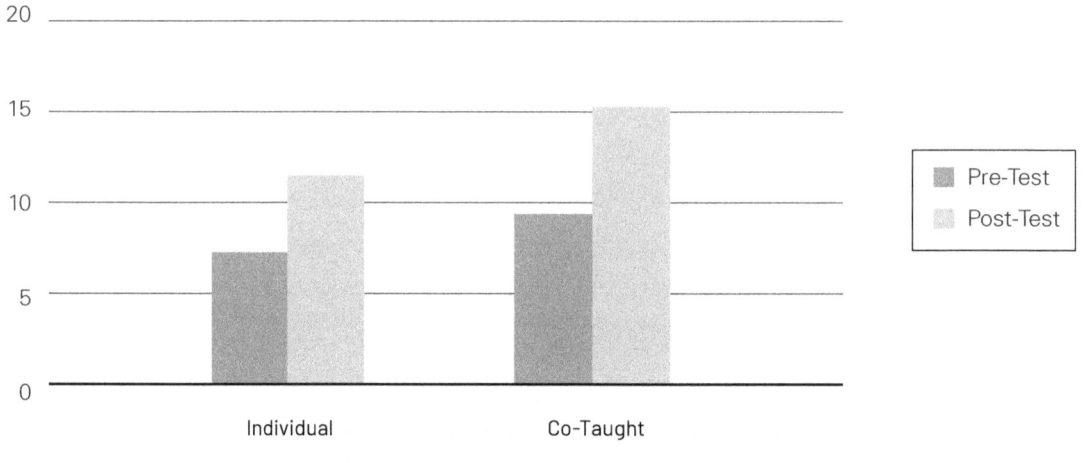

Source: Karge, 2023b, p. 175.

FIGURE 4.1: Pre- and post-test scores in individual and co-taught high school English classes.

Celebrations build positive social learning, boosting the whole class and giving co-teachers a boost as well. When a student comes early to class or helps another student, take the time to celebrate the unique talents and strengths of the student (Dieker, 2007). Keep a running list and make sure you share a positive comment about each student as the year progresses. Celebrating each student publicly helps them feel special and allows their peers to hear and see the value of their classmates.

Administrative Support

Administrative support (as discussed further in chapter 10, page 165) fosters teacher efficacy, leading to a more positive school culture (Esposito, 2023). Administrative support includes resource allocation, which includes management of shared resources and technology as well as coordinating schedules for co-teacher planning periods and classroom teaching. It also encompasses checking in and establishing effective communication channels, giving the administrator knowledge of effective practices and opening the door to recognize the co-teaching team for its successes and encourage continued progress. Additionally, ensuring co-teachers have access to data-monitoring tools and establishing systems for progress monitoring build efficacy among all involved.

Instructional Risk-Taking Culture

Co-teachers grow their self-efficacy when they're part of a culture that values continual improvement by experimentation where they feel safe to try new strategies, techniques, and teaching challenges even with a risk of failure. This instructional risk-taking culture impacts the quality of education and the overall learning experience for teachers and students (Henriksen et al., 2021). Discuss successes and failures, even when the experiment does not yield the expected outcome. This sort of culture promotes a growth mindset and demystifies risk taking, which can lead to enhanced learning experiences for both educators and students.

During a training in El Salvador in 2022, a co-teaching team talked about trying engagement strategies for the first time. The teachers tried the team-pair-solo strategy, but it was not successful. When they reflected on the lesson, they realized they needed to back up and teach the students how to work in teams and pairs before they used the engagement strategies. The co-teaching team had taken a huge risk, as typically one of them merely lectured and the other assisted. Once they taught the students to work in groups, they realized the risk had produced growth. They spent the 2022–2023 school year trying other engagement strategies and built their lessons around the eleven co-teaching strategies. They reported significant growth in their own teaching abilities as well as student outcomes. Taking a risk led to positive self-efficacy.

Essential Agreements for Greater Co-Teacher Efficacy

Productive and constructive co-teaching relationships that have positive outcomes for teachers and students come from establishing and maintaining essential agreements throughout the co-teaching partnership. *Essential agreements* in this context are philosophical and systematic agreements on what teaching and learning will look like in a co-teaching partnership. Each co-teaching partnership's agreements differ, but the process of creating and maintaining them can be similar: identifying who co-teachers are as teachers, developing the agreements, and using AI to maximize time and embody them.

Who Co-Teachers Are as Teachers

Co-teachers should establish essential agreements before the school year starts. The earlier they discuss, agree on, and put into practice their essential agreements, the stronger their partnership will be. The process of developing the essential agreements involves first identifying who each co-teacher is as a teacher: their teaching philosophy, what that looks like daily, and their thoughts on how they interact with students and build relationships with them. Co-teaching partners should dive deeply into aspects of their teaching philosophy, such as the nature of instruction, grading, how to implement inclusive classrooms, and how their previous experiences with teaching, co-teaching, or both have shaped them. Each co-teacher identifies their strengths and areas of improvement as a teacher and discusses this openly with the other. To see this in action, review figures 4.2 and 4.3 (page 70), as they provide a guided pathway for these critical conversations before you develop your own essential agreements.

Teaching and Learning Philosophy	How Do I Teach? What Do My Lessons Look Like on a Daily Basis?	Thoughts on Interacting With and Building Relationships With Students
My teaching and learning philosophy relates to being primarily teacher led followed by gradual release to provide student-centered opportunities to demonstrate their learning. I like to model and provide instruction integrated with ongoing formative assessment during guided practice. I also like to provide students multiple opportunities during independent practice to demonstrate their skills and proficiency in the content and skills we are covering in class.	My lessons follow this format: interactive formative assessment, review, and guided practice that's engaging along with student collaboration strategies such as cooperative learning strategies. This is then followed up by independent practice that may take place in stations that are either physical or digital stations where students practice the skills and content they are learning. Last, I prefer to have a formative assessment at the end of each lesson to review student data.	Generally, I believe it takes time to develop relationships with students. I try to gauge shared interests, activate students' prior knowledge with pop culture references, and use humor. Over time, I believe this will help me develop relationships with my students. However, I acknowledge that I need to ensure that I am professional with students, while showing empathy and understanding to my students. In the same light, I need to ensure my routines and norms in my classroom have firm boundaries on student behavior and expectations.

Communicating With Students' Families	Thoughts on Grading and Providing Feedback	Thoughts on Inclusion and Equity and How They Manifest in the Classroom Setting
I try to remain in contact with families and students through our class's learning management system. I send out family and student announcements throughout the week to keep them updated on all things that are going on in class. With this strategy, I attempt to limit email as much as I can. I have a twenty-four-hour reply rule for email over the course of the school week. My goal is to problem solve and be an advocate for my students as well as be transparent with families regarding student behavior and performance in my class.	For grading, I use a standards-based grading approach. Each student is graded by their performance on assessments they can retake as much as they would like related to the concepts and skills we cover in class. Each unit is divided up into four major assessments that students take. Besides assessments, students are given practice opportunities and summative projects for each semester that they will be completing. Regarding providing feedback, I first and foremost try to provide whole-class feedback during instruction. Then, during independent practice time, I focus on giving my students more personalized feedback that then gives them another task to complete to put that feedback into action.	I want to provide as many opportunities as possible for students. This is exemplified in retaking assessments as much as possible and receiving many opportunities for practice and one-on-one support. Additionally, I want to ensure all students can see the content and instruction whenever they can through our LMS. I upload videos and additional resources to help reteach and practice the content and skills of our class.

Co-Teaching Experience	Understanding of IEPs and Special Education Law	Implementing IEP Services and Accommodations or Modifications in Instruction
I have co-taught once before, but only for one period years ago. I did not plan with the co-teacher often. Maybe only once a month. However, I did enjoy the opportunity to have another teacher in the class working with me to teach and support student learning.	I have reviewed all students with IEPs and 504 plans that I've had in my classes over the years. I generally evaluate the first page of the IEP as it outlines the disability of the student as well as their services and goal pages. These help me get a picture of the students' needs and services to holistically support them.	If I have several students in my class who have accommodations, I first try to embed as many as I can within my instruction. This looks like providing extra time for assessments, retakes, visuals, notes available on request, and more (depending on the year). Then, I try to look at each student to see if I can implement their accommodations with the help of their IEP team. This same strategy is something I do with modifications as well.

FIGURE 4.2: Essential agreements—Individual co-teacher brainstorming template.

*Visit **go.SolutionTree.com/instruction** for a free reproducible version of this figure.*

Strengths	Shared Strengths and Areas of Growth	Areas of Growth
Co-Teacher 1: » Planning, ed tech integration, developing routines, direct instruction and modeling, guided practice, and assessment » Communicating with families and students through the LMS » Collaborating with department members on pacing and aligning curriculum to district benchmarks and state standards Co-Teacher 2: » Planning instruction and incorporating cooperative learning strategies to support student collaboration » Working with students who have accommodations, modifications, and services that need to be embedded into classroom instruction » Building relationships with students and families	Strengths: » Planning instruction » Using a wide range of instructional strategies in their instruction Areas of Growth: » Using various forms of assessment to support student learning (that is, verbal, demonstration, writing, and projects)	Co-Teacher 1: » Assessing students using a wide variety of assessment strategies (that is, verbal, demonstration, writing, and projects) » Modifying classroom routines as the year progresses » Working with students who have an IEP or 504 plan Co-Teacher 2: » Integrating ed tech into their instruction to support student learning and assessment » Collaborating with teachers on planning and delivering instruction » Using various forms of assessment to support student learning (that is, verbal, demonstration, writing, and projects)

FIGURE 4.3: Essential agreements to identify shared strengths and areas of growth.

Visit go.SolutionTree.com/instruction for a free reproducible version of this figure.

Essential Agreement Development

After learning more about each other as educators, it is time to discuss where the co-teaching partners can agree about how their classroom will function. The goal is to take areas both co-teachers have strengths and expertise in as well as a general agreement on. This will look different for each partnership. Additionally, fundamental essential agreements may evolve over time when philosophical differences are nuanced because of the context of the classroom, such as with ed tech integration or behavioral supports. We recommend agreeing on the following when developing and finalizing the essential agreements to start the year.

- Combined teaching and learning philosophy
- Designing and deploying lessons
- Creating an equitable and inclusionary classroom and implementing IEP services and accommodations
- Assessing, grading, and providing students with feedback
- Planning lessons
- Communicating with students and families

These are all fundamental areas where agreement between co-teachers is essential. The dialogue will require patience and the ability to avoid taking differences personally. Development and implementation of these essential agreements better the students and school community both co-teachers serve. Going into the conversation with this in mind may help deescalate the natural need to be right because it focuses more on shared understanding to make everyone's experience the best it can be in the classroom.

Essential agreements can start as an overarching theme followed by bullet points. For example, let's look at designing and deploying lessons. The overarching theme could look like this: "We will design and implement lessons with UDL principles and using effective co-teaching strategies along with instructional strategies that engage students and provide opportunities for all to learn." Then the bullet points can illustrate further what this means.

- We will design our lessons to have listening, speaking, writing, and problem-solving components.
- Our lessons will provide content that our students can consume and process in a variety of ways, such as visuals, audio, diverse instructional strategies, and differentiated content.
- We will deploy all our lessons from our Canvas LMS.
- We plan to use ReadTheory, Google Workspace, and Edpuzzle as our main ed tech tools.
- We will focus on the co-teaching strategies of team teaching, one teach, one observe, and parallel teaching.
- Our instructional strategies will include cooperative learning and thinking routine strategies.

Sentence frames and guiding questions can help facilitate focused dialogue. The goal of these conversation starters is to help propel the conversation toward the development and implementation of your essential agreements. Use the following to help develop your partnership's essential agreements.

- One essential agreement we could consider is . . .
- In order to promote _____, we should agree to implement _____ .
- What are some general expectations we should set for ourselves to ensure a successful partnership?
- What are a number of themes from our own philosophies that we can combine and implement in the following areas?
- How can we hold each other accountable for upholding our essential agreements?
- What resources or support will we need to implement these essential agreements effectively in our co-teaching classroom?

The following dialogues provide examples of a secondary English teacher and special education teacher coming together to develop several essential agreements. Use them as a model for your own conversation on essential agreements.

In the first dialogue, we see how a pair of co-teachers decide on an essential agreement for how their co-taught class will function. The pair agrees on several essential agreements in this dialogue, such as setting clear expectations, inclusivity, culturally responsive teaching, and a couple of their classroom routines. Mr. Patel is a secondary English teacher, while Ms. Hernandez is a special education teacher. They have been selected to teach two sections of ninth-grade English together. Neither co-teacher has co-taught together or with others in the past. Throughout this dialogue, they will begin to formulate essential agreements for their class before they begin the school year, which they will likely expand further in future dialogues as they round out how these essential agreements will play out in their co-teaching classroom.

> **Ms. Hernandez:** So, Mr. Patel, I believe it's important that we establish some essential agreements for our co-taught English class as we begin the school year. It's our first time co-teaching. Once we agree on these things, we can really think about building out what our class will look like and function. What do you think?
>
> **Mr. Patel:** I completely agree. I think it's important for us to be on the same page and set clear expectations for ourselves and our students. I want to be on the same page as much as possible.
>
> **Ms. Hernandez:** Great. Well, one essential agreement I believe we should consider is respecting and incorporating elements of each other's philosophies on teaching and learning. What do you think?
>
> **Mr. Patel:** I believe that's a good one to start with. I know we have a few philosophical differences, but I think we can learn a lot from each other if we're open minded.
>
> **Ms. Hernandez:** Definitely. Another agreement that I think is important is making sure that all our students feel included and valued in our classroom. What do you think? How should we create an equitable and inclusive space?
>
> **Mr. Patel:** I agree. I believe it's important for our students to feel like they belong and that their voices are heard in our lessons and for them to have opportunities to share their voices in our class and beyond. I think we could start by being intentional about our language and making sure we're using inclusive pronouns and examples that reflect the diversity of our students. Additionally, I believe in everything we do, we should focus on UDL as the baseline for all the instruction we provide.
>
> **Ms. Hernandez:** That's a good point. And we could also make sure that we're incorporating multiple perspectives and voices in our lesson plans and discussions to be culturally responsive.

Mr. Patel: Yes, definitely. Another essential agreement we should consider is being consistent with our classroom management as well as how we plan to communicate with students, service providers, and families. What do you think, and how do you think we should implement this?

Ms. Hernandez: I completely agree. Our students need consistency to feel safe and supported in our classroom. We should set a series of classroom routines and expectations for our students. We also need procedures for who speaks to whom about what's going on with a particular student. We always cc each other in emails. We can also do all our communication with our students and the vast majority of their families through our LMS.

Mr. Patel: This is a good start! What are some ways we can develop routines to help ensure consistency in our classroom management?

Ms. Hernandez: Let's start by creating a clear set of expectations and consequences and making sure that we're both enforcing them consistently with our students. For example, no phones. We can also be sure to have restorative conversations. On top of this, we can have a multiple-warning system before a restorative conversation will be required and further escalation with service providers and administration thereafter if the issue is not resolved.

Mr. Patel: Agreed! We could also make sure that we're communicating with each other regularly and checking in on our students' progress and behavior. During planning time, we can review student data, divide progress monitoring, and present level updates for our students who have upcoming IEP meetings. We can send communications out to service providers and families if we believe it necessary based on student progress.

Ms. Hernandez: That's a good idea! So, let's recap. Our essential agreements so far are respecting each other's philosophies about teaching and learning and incorporating elements, making students feel included and valued, consistency in classroom management and communication, and guidance from UDL for lesson design. Do you have any other suggestions, Mr. Patel?

Mr. Patel: I believe those are great so far. I'm excited to start implementing them in our classroom. We will write them down and then focus on what they will ultimately look like when we begin implementing them in our classroom.

Ms. Hernandez: Me, too. I am ready to go. This is a solid foundation that I think our students are going to benefit a lot from as we start the year together.

In the next dialogue, we see a crucial discussion between the same two co-teachers as they disagree and then come to consensus regarding an essential agreement for their co-teaching classroom at the beginning of the school year. Their conversation centers on the pivotal decision of choosing an appropriate grading system for their ninth-grade English class. While Mr. Patel leans toward the traditional grading methods he's familiar with, Ms. Hernandez advocates for a standards-based approach, highlighting its benefits for a diverse range of learners, including their students who have IEPs and 504 plans. This dialogue showcases the process of negotiation and collaboration, reflecting the challenges and opportunities inherent in co-teaching partnerships.

> **Ms. Hernandez:** Mr. Patel, I've been thinking about our grading system for this school year. I really believe we should consider a standards-based grading approach. It focuses on mastery of content and skills, which I think would be beneficial for all our students, especially our students with a 504 plan or IEP.
>
> **Mr. Patel:** Standards-based grading? I usually use traditional grading methods. I'm not sure how that would work with our ninth-grade English curriculum. It seems like a big shift, as my curriculum in the past has been based on the number of points certain assignments and assessments are worth.
>
> **Ms. Hernandez:** I understand your concerns. This is a huge change! But think about it—standards-based grading allows us to clearly define learning objectives and assess students on their progress toward these objectives. It's more transparent and equitable, as it requires continuous assessment and opportunities for students to earn mastery throughout the school year, and everyone learns at different paces.
>
> **Mr. Patel:** That sounds great in theory. But how do we align this with the current curriculum and ensure it's fair to all students? The traditional system has worked well for me in the past.
>
> **Ms. Hernandez:** By using standards-based grading, we can tailor our instruction to meet students where they are in their learning journey. It's about providing multiple opportunities for students to demonstrate their understanding. This way, we're not just grading tasks but grading actual learning and progress. It also provides our students with numerous opportunities to showcase their learning.
>
> **Mr. Patel:** That does sound beneficial, especially for differentiating instruction with the wide variety of learners we will have in our classrooms. But I worry about how students and families will react to this, as many students may have not experienced this type of grading system in their school career.
>
> **Ms. Hernandez:** We can educate all stakeholders on its benefits. This system gives students a clearer understanding of their strengths and areas for growth. It's about learning, not just earning a grade. We can hold a parent-teacher forum early in the year to explain this approach. We can provide slides, record it, and place it onto our LMS so it stands as the foundation for what we are doing this year in our class.
>
> **Mr. Patel:** I see your point. It could foster a more growth-oriented mindset among students and their families. And you're right; it does seem more equitable, particularly for students who need more time to grasp certain concepts as well as offering students an opportunity to go back and master previous concepts and skills, if needed, throughout the school year.

> **Ms. Hernandez:** Exactly! And we'll be there to support each other in this transition. We can start with a couple of units. Additionally, I can share with you how I've done this in the past. What do you say?
>
> **Mr. Patel:** All right, let's give it a try. Standards-based grading it is. We'll work together to implement it effectively and see how it supports our students' learning.
>
> **Ms. Hernandez:** Great! I believe this will make a significant difference in our co-taught classroom. I'm excited to see how it will positively impact our students' learning experiences, as I believe it will be easier for our diverse learners to navigate the class once they get used to it.

Figure 4.4 offers a template to develop these agreements and shows how a co-teaching pair might use it.

Combined Teaching and Learning Philosophy	How Will We Design Our Lessons?	How Will We Create an Equitable and Inclusive Classroom and Implement IEP Services and Accommodations?
We will practice mutual respect and integrate the following elements into our combined teaching philosophy: cultural responsiveness; consistency in instruction, classroom management, and communication with students and families; and open-mindedness toward different teaching styles and strategies.	Underpinning each lesson will be the notion of inclusivity and UDL principles. Our lesson design goal is to cater to students' diverse learning needs in an inclusive and culturally responsive manner. Additionally, collaboration will be key to lesson planning.	We will create a classroom environment where all students feel valued and included. This involves using inclusive language and considering the diverse backgrounds of students in our teaching.
How Will We Assess, Grade, and Provide Students With Feedback?	**How Will We Plan Lessons?**	**How Will We Communicate With Students and Families?**
We will develop equitable and fair systems to support student feedback and grading such as standards-based grading and flexibility to meet individual student needs.	We will plan lessons collaboratively with backward planning. Then each of us will individually create certain assignments, assessments, and slideshows.	We will maintain consistent communication with students, service providers, and families, using strategies like joint emails and leveraging our LMS for broader communication.

FIGURE 4.4: Essential agreement template part 1.

*Visit **go.SolutionTree.com/instruction** for a free reproducible version of this figure.*

Through these conversations, we hope the essential agreements you and your partner come up with can help you navigate your co-teaching classroom and the challenges and triumphs it may encompass throughout the school year. Starting with a solid foundation is critical for maintaining your self-efficacy as well as the collective efficacy of your partnership. As the year progresses, come back to these essential agreements to revise them. We recommend doing this quarterly or semesterly, as it gives enough time to progress monitor to see what's working and what needs improvement.

AI for Maximizing Time and Embodying Essential Agreements

AI can support co-teachers in brainstorming and building essential agreements as well as grading rubrics, standards-based assessments, assignments, syllabi, and planning documents that embody these essential agreements. For example, co-teachers may come up with essential agreements related to grading, classroom routines, and assessment. They can prompt a generative AI tool to create drafts based on the details they discuss and work out for each essential agreement they develop. Over time, co-teachers can prompt the AI with feedback and revisions to refine their agreements as they progress to a finalized set.

The same method can help them create classroom content that incorporates the essential agreements. For example, let's focus on a grading rubric and how both co-teachers incorporate an essential agreement on standards-based grading into their prompting to generate drafts of the rubric. Co-teachers can provide the AI tool with the following prompt to begin developing the rubric for various skills in the class:

> *You are two co-teachers teaching middle school mathematics. Our standards relate to the following state standards, Common Core standards, and district standards: [insert standards]. Now, we would like you to develop a rubric on how we can assess student learning. We want assessments to be standards based with a four-point rubric on four areas: (1) problem solving, (2) methodology, (3) explanation of their methodology, and (4) correctness. Incorporate our essential agreement related to standards-based grading into this rubric language: each student will have an opportunity to redo each assessment throughout the term to work toward achieving the highest standard possible found in our assessments and rubrics. This rubric will be the basis of other rubrics we will develop based on the content and skills we are teaching in each unit. For each of the following rubrics after the first generation of the rubric, we will input the content and skills it will cover. Be sure to make the language on the rubrics friendly to students at the sixth-grade level.*

Co-teachers can replicate prompts like this for course syllabi, classroom routines, and assessments. They can easily construct a syllabus if each partner agrees to various themes for their classroom, such as the grading system, how to turn in work, assessment, routines, communication, and more. They can address each of these specific areas directly within the prompt to generate drafts of the syllabus, which they can refine through further prompting and editing.

Along with rubrics and syllabi, co-teachers can harness generative AI to help them build content for their class, such as graphic organizers, worksheets, assessments, and assignments. If co-teachers agree on what they would like for a specific task, they can prompt the AI to generate drafts of this content. An example of a prompt for a graphic organizer preceded by a word problem for a practice assignment on adding and subtracting fractions might look like this:

> *You are two co-teachers teaching middle school mathematics. Develop a word problem that adds and subtracts fractions at the sixth-grade reading level. Besides the word problem, develop a graphic organizer as a table that helps students capture key ideas related to the word problem, such as the values of the fractions being added and subtracted as well as their final methodology to solve the problem. Generate two additional differentiated word problems that use these same concepts and are easier and harder to solve for our sixth graders, for a total of three word problems. Be sure to incorporate a four-point rubric in a table on four areas: (1) problem solving, (2) methodology, (3) explanation of their methodology, and (4) correctness. Last, incorporate our essential agreement of standards-based grading into the language of the rubric and in the directions of the problem set: each student will have an opportunity to redo each assessment throughout the term to work toward achieving the highest standard possible found in our assessments and rubrics.*

The AI can generate this type of word problem with three different variations, as well as graphic organizers that students can use. The output will also include a rubric using the standards-based essential agreement embodied within it for students and co-teachers to employ for this problem set. The co-teachers can also place the prompt and the initial drafts of content that the AI tool generates into documents that they store in the shared virtual storage for their co-taught class. As a result, co-teaching partners can develop and tweak this content as much as they like throughout the school year. This can help cut down on time they spend developing content to use with their students.

Co-teachers can also employ generative AI to help them brainstorm and review data in line with their agreements. For example, a co-teaching partnership of elementary school co-teachers wants to focus on an upcoming phonics lesson that aims to build vocabulary and help students decode high-frequency words. Co-teachers can use the AI prompt to make sure it relates to their lesson goals, what their data say (ensure all names and identifying information are removed), and other variables, such as outside-the-box ways to make the lesson engaging, related to students' prior knowledge, and culturally responsive. With these variables, co-teachers can construct prompts that can help them plan this upcoming lesson. Employ simple one- or two-sentence prompts at first, followed by more in-depth prompts as you get more used to the technology. The goal of this collaboration with the AI tool is to generate useful ideas, begin constructing a lesson, and then, ultimately, use its content with students.

Generative AI offers a transformative approach to developing and executing essential agreements and streamlining the ideation and development of diverse content co-teachers can use in their classrooms. From constructing grading rubrics to crafting accessible syllabi, AI's capacity to assist in the creative process is invaluable as co-teachers transform essential agreements into tangible action. This technology not only accelerates the development of teaching resources like graphic organizers and customized assignments but also enhances the brainstorming process, bringing fresh perspectives and innovative ideas to the forefront for co-teachers to curate, revise, and transform. The integration of AI into co-teaching practices promises more efficient, collaborative, and dynamic classrooms, allowing co-teachers to dedicate more time to their students.

Conclusion

Throughout this chapter, we illustrated the importance of self- and collective teacher efficacy. Efficacy in your teaching practice throughout the year can impact how you teach your students and how effective you can be within your co-teaching partnership. The relationship in co-teaching partnerships heavily depends on efficacy. We also discussed variables that can affect efficacy positively and negatively and the essential elements that contribute to efficacy.

We also focused on the need to formulate essential agreements on how a co-teaching classroom will look and function. We outlined how this happens in practice and why it is important in maintaining a strong and effective co-teaching partnership, as the year will deliver many challenges and opportunities to celebrate the progression of students and teachers' practice. Last, through the prioritization of co-teaching partnerships through developing, revising, and maintaining essential agreements, co-teachers can foster positive and collaborative classroom environments that benefit students, service providers, families, and each other.

> **RESOURCES TO CONSIDER AFTER READING THIS CHAPTER**
> - Teachers', leaders', and collective self-efficacy by Megan Tschannen-Moran (https://mxtsch.pages.wm.edu/research-tools): These are survey scales you can utilize with teachers, leaders, and collective school sites to determine degrees of efficacy during a given time.
> - The Edutopia blog post "Shared Agreements for Working Together Benefit Teachers and Administrators" (https://bit.ly/3KuCCaA) by Jorge Valenzuela outlines how setting clear expectations can help improve the school working environment.

Reflection and Action: Agree, Argue, and Inspired

Directions: After reading chapter 4 on efficacy, attitude, and essential agreements, what do you agree with and argue with, and what inspired you?

Agree

Argue—What do you question or oppose?

Inspired—How will you take action?

To be most successful in co-teaching, partners need to be flexible and communicate ... but to make the most positive impact on students, co-teachers absolutely need to co-plan for diversity! This is where UDL, differentiation, and specially designed instruction come in.

—W. Murawski, researcher and expert in co-teaching, personal communication, January 20, 2024

CHAPTER 5

Planning and Designing Lessons

Planning and lesson design are critical to co-teaching success (Chitiyo & Brinda, 2018; Cook & Friend, 1995; Guise, Habib, Thiessen, & Robbins, 2017; Karge, 2023b; Murawski, 2009). Both educators come together not only to map out the unit, the week, or daily lesson but also to incorporate strategies to support all learners within the class. Planning and lesson design vary from one co-teaching partnership to another, but as with any aspect of teaching, there is only so much time you can devote to it. The quality of strategic planning, established workflow, and open and thorough discussion of teaching strategies and philosophies throughout the year can make or break the instruction and culture of a co-taught classroom.

Before jumping into the context of this chapter, Matt shares his experience with how planning and workflow evolved throughout his partnerships and career as a co-teacher:

> *During my first few co-teaching partnerships, the approach to planning varied. At the beginning of my career, I taught with two different co-teachers in only one period, each in two different subject areas: English 12 and government. The government co-teacher gave me the unit plan but did not plan daily lessons. The English teacher collaborated on a backward plan and daily lesson plan synchronously once or twice throughout the week to address the backward plan and then asynchronously to build out daily lessons. Additionally, while each class had a similar routine and structure, in the government class, the planning was inconsistent and the textbook drove the curriculum and lessons, creating a monotonous experience for students. The English class, in which the planning was strategic, used the textbook as a supplemental source for the curriculum.*
>
> *As a result, the English class was very dynamic, using various co-teaching strategies, while the government class only used two—team teaching and one teach, one assist. Differentiation and the nature of instruction and routines differed greatly across the two classes because of the planning or lack of planning that took place. Additionally, roles and responsibilities as well as understanding of shared teaching philosophies and practices were very clear in the English class. In the government class, this did not happen on a consistent basis.*
>
> *Both co-teachers that year had their strengths. The buy-in for co-teaching was a huge indicator. The English co-teacher worked hard to collaborate on establishing planning and workflow routines as well as creating a shared understanding of how instruction and the*

> *classroom would function. The government co-teacher participated in minimal collaboration. As a result, I am sure you know which class was taught more effectively.*
>
> *That year, I was trying to keep my head above water as a special education teacher. My mistake as a co-teacher was not transferring the same successful planning from one class to another. This shift took place during my third and fourth year of teaching. I learned my lesson. There was a huge difference between each class. This experience demonstrated early in my career the importance of strategic long- and short-term planning as well as coming to a consensus early on how we would like our instruction and classroom routines to look within our co-taught classroom.*

Planning and lesson design require many elements to succeed, such as establishing roles and workflow and breaking down teaching philosophies and strategies to support student learning. Therefore, this chapter breaks down how to plan both synchronously and asynchronously in an efficient and collaborative manner, both long and short term. Additionally, we discuss how co-teachers can incorporate instructional strategies and routines in their classroom to provide effective instruction. This interrelates with how teaching roles and responsibilities, along with openly discussing teaching and learning philosophies, form a foundation of effective instruction from the beginning through the end of the school year.

> **Key Themes and Ideas**
> ☐ Long- and short-term planning with workflow in mind
> ☐ Shared teaching philosophies and integration into classroom instruction
> ☐ Roles and responsibilities in planning and workflow
> ☐ Instructional and co-teaching strategy and routine incorporation into lessons

Long- and Short-Term Planning With Workflow in Mind

When we plan, we must keep instructional design in mind. *Instructional design* consists of a progression of recognizing, explaining, and putting together a sequence to apply an intensive learning system to support student outcomes (Beebe, Mottet, & Roach, 2013). How teachers achieve this—the workflow—is key to effectiveness and sustainability. Instructional design with workflow in mind means co-teachers strategically plan how they deliver instruction as well as the instructional planning process throughout their partnership, from backward lesson design to everyday lesson planning (Mills, Wiley, & Williams, 2019). They focus on integrating strategies and content that can help all students learn. We believe in modern classrooms that transcend both physical and digital realms (Rhoads, McLaughlin, & Moore, 2022). Thus, this section outlines how to long- and short-term plan by establishing a shared organizational structure for the planning itself. Then, we focus on the roles of both co-teachers in lesson-planning structure. Last, we zoom in on how this workflow occurs by looking at how we can leverage technology to boost our efficiency and organization while ensuring planning can take place synchronously and asynchronously.

Establishment of a Long-Term Plan

Long-term planning refers to desired learning outcomes aligned with standards, which are then used as a benchmark to plan backward (Wiggins & McTighe, 2011). Content and skill-based standards provide an opportunity to see what students need to learn. Teachers then break up the learning into segments that not only teach students the standards but also provide opportunities to measure progress along the way to monitor and adjust instruction. Therefore, long-term planning creates a flexible framework within a given time period to teach and measure learning. Then, short-term planning takes those goals and breaks them down on a weekly and daily basis. This is where instructional design comes into play, as well as integrating strategies for helping students best learn skills and content. What does this look like in practice? First, we must see how two co-teachers ideate and then put into action how they will organize the class and the structure of the lesson; then, they establish roles and how they will plan and put it all together in practice.

When two teachers come together, both bring to the table how they have planned in the past. In some scenarios, polar opposites can come together. Convening before the school year begins is critical to starting a successful co-teaching relationship and partnership. One of the first things they discuss is how they will plan their lessons and organize their lesson structure. Both facets go hand in hand; with the structure of the lesson in mind, co-teachers can break down the workflow of how they plan.

To begin, co-teachers must have a conversation about the structure of their lessons and how they design them. One example is to share a simple breakdown of a lesson sequence. Regardless of the grade level or content, you can break your lesson down into segments, such as formative assessment, guided practice, independent and collaborative practice, and formative assessment, while integrating instructional strategies such as station rotation as a key element that takes place in the lesson. If both co-teachers bring this to their first meeting, it will greatly improve their ability to organize how to structure and plan for lessons.

The next step involves planning lessons. Co-teaching involves many forms of strategies (Karge, 2023b). Therefore, it's important to first adopt a less-is-more mindset, which will allow the team to start simple for the first month or so and then slowly integrate more instructional strategies and co-teaching strategies over time. We recommend trying out no more than three co-teaching strategies and five instructional strategies to start. When planning, first start with the unit breakdown in each content and skill area that you are teaching. Then, as you both think backward to go forward, develop a weekly planner that will eventually work toward the final unit assessments and tasks that help teachers assess and measure student learning and growth. We recommend a shared Google or Word document with each day of the week listed in the top row. Within each daily column, co-teachers break down the daily lesson or lessons, outline the role of each co-teacher, and include hyperlinks connecting content that students and teachers will work with. The last row is a place to list the standards co-teachers are using. Figure 5.1 (page 84) provides a simple template with an example of how it might look after co-teachers have filled out the first day of the week.

Monday	Tuesday	Wednesday	Thursday	Friday
Writing Introduce narrative writing using the book *Charlotte's Web*. Co-teacher A models how to begin a story using an exciting hook while co-teacher B annotates on a shared document. **Reading** Students brainstorm their story settings after reading excerpts of chapters 1 and 2 of *Charlotte's Web* in reading groups. Differentiated: After guided reading, three groups of students receive three distinct tasks in a jigsaw. Group A writes descriptions of the setting, group B draws settings, and group C uses story cubes for inspiration to illustrate and write descriptions of the setting. **Mathematics** Begin unit on fractions. Introduce simple fractions using fraction tiles. Team teach to model simple fractions as well as worked examples. Then, work on simple fraction worksheets in three groups where two groups are teacher led (groups B and C). Differentiated: group A—basic, group B—intermediate, group C—advanced.				

Monday	Tuesday	Wednesday	Thursday	Friday
Standards **Writing:** Write narratives to develop real or imagined experiences or events using effective technique, descriptive details, and clear event sequences (CCSS.ELA-Literacy.W.4.3). **Reading:** RL.4.1—Refer to details and examples in a text when explaining what the text says explicitly and when drawing inferences from the text (CCSS.ELA-Literacy.RL.4.1). **Mathematics:** 4.NF.A.1—Explain why a fraction a/b is equivalent to a fraction (n × a)/(n × b) by using visual fraction models, with attention to how the number and size of the parts differ even though the two fractions themselves are the same size. Use this principle to recognize and generate equivalent fractions (CCSS.Math-Content.4.NF.A.1).				

Source for standards: National Governors Association Center for Best Practices & Council of Chief State School Officers, 2010a, 2010b.

FIGURE 5.1: Weekly backward planner.

*Visit **go.SolutionTree.com/instruction** for a free reproducible version of this figure.*

Planning Roles of Co-Teachers

In the weekly backward planner that aligns with the unit's major learning goals and standards, co-teachers have created a sequence of tasks and opportunities to build skill and content knowledge. Now, to fill out the backward planner, co-teachers must assign themselves roles. This is so each co-teacher will know which of them will devote their time and effort to planning throughout the year. One teacher may be willing to develop the daily slide deck, while another may want to create the documents and ed tech tool integrations students will interact with in the class LMS. Besides dividing up the planning roles, co-teachers must determine how planning will take place over the course of the year. For example, in one to two in-person or online synchronous meetings before each week of teaching commences, the pair can work out a sketch or outline of the planning and who will write each section—we call this the skeleton of the backward planner.

Once they have created the skeleton of the lessons for the week, each co-teacher will have various roles in developing the content they will deploy for the lessons, differentiating tasks, creating assessments, and uploading materials onto the class's LMS. Figure 5.2 demonstrates the breakdown of planning roles by both teachers. Initially, these should remain the same week to week. Over time, the co-teachers can adjust their roles depending on how planning and instruction is going throughout the semester.

Co-Teacher 1	Co-Teacher 2
» Complete skeleton outline and co-teaching strategies for the week » Create all English and mathematics tasks for the week » Develop mathematics formative and summative assessments » Create weekly lesson slideshow » Upload and place the weekly lessons and materials in LMS	» Complete skeleton outline and co-teaching strategies for the week » Create differentiated material for English and mathematics tasks » Upload and place all content from the weekly backward planner onto the LMS

FIGURE 5.2: Planning role breakdown for elementary school co-teachers.

*Visit **go.SolutionTree.com/instruction** for a free reproducible version of this figure.*

Digital and Physical Organization

Another important facet that goes along with planning and establishing roles related to planning is the digital and physical organization of instructional content and classroom materials (Brown & Green, 2018). It is essential during your initial conversations with your co-teacher to determine how to organize your classroom content and materials (Karten & Murawski, 2020). Let's dive into how this can be done for digital content, how to support organizational planning with AI, and considerations for the physical classroom.

DIGITAL CONTENT

Since planning should take place using a shared digital Google or Word document, co-teachers should create digital folders within Google Drive or OneDrive that relate to the unit of study, the week, and then the content in relation to assignments and tasks as well as assessments. They can't place it between different digital folders. Thus, creating a shared folder system where both teachers can create and access content is essential. This organization can then support the unit and weekly backward planning when co-teachers place hyperlinks within the backward plan document to the content created and organized within the digital folders. Figure 5.3 shows how you might organize digital folders for either an entire class or a subject area you are teaching.

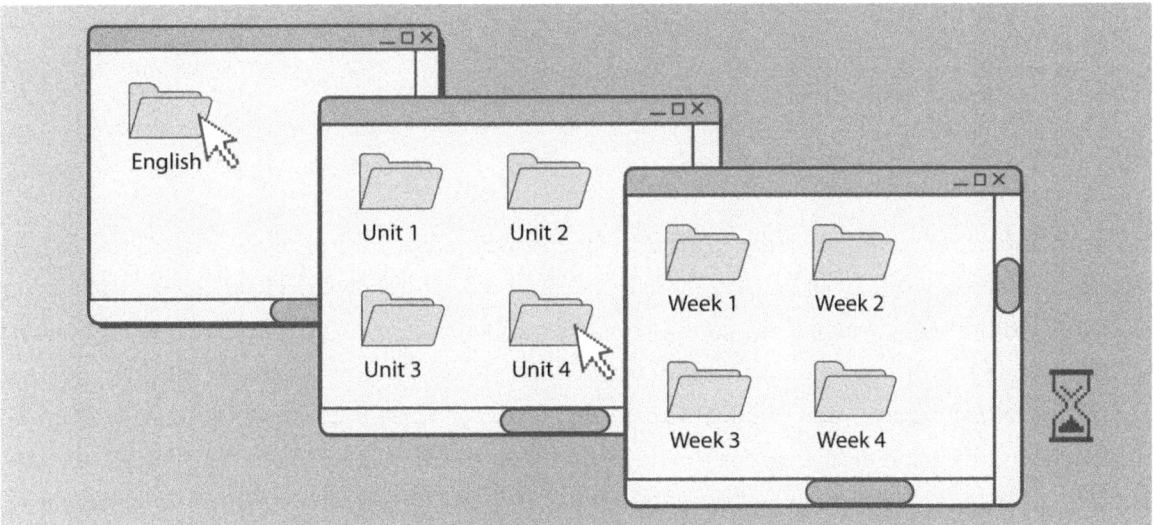

FIGURE 5.3: Digital folder organization structure example.

Another important aspect of digital organization is shared access to calendars. Each planning period, IEP meeting, learning services team meeting, or 504 meeting can appear on the calendar. Having a shared digital calendar allows both co-teachers to see the week in advance and determine how to plan for possible meetings and events. This is very important, as co-teachers must be on the same page regarding their calendars. It creates transparency and a sense of organization. Be sure to share your work calendars before the school year begins.

GENERATIVE AI FOR PLANNING SUPPORT

Co-teachers are increasingly using assistants to support them in their planning: AI copilots. AI copilots—mainstream generative tools such as ChatGPT, Microsoft Copilot, Google Gemini, and Claude—help teachers plan lesson plans, develop content for teacher and student use, and differentiate tasks, assignments, and assessments to meet student needs. While planning, it is important to have these tools open and available to support brainstorming, developing lessons and content, and differentiating content.

As a team, you are working on drafts you will continue to revise until you are ready to finalize and place them where you can store and deploy to students (such as Docs, Slideshow, Sheets, Drawing, and so on). Prompting requires continual practice and skills developed over time with use of the AI tools. Additionally, it is important to discuss that you must evaluate and analyze all content you do develop before moving forward. Generative AI tools are not accurate at times and can make errors. Thus, be judicious and aware of these risks. However, these tools can save hours of time planning and differentiating content for your lessons and students. You can use that time instead with students without having to plan outside of normal working hours.

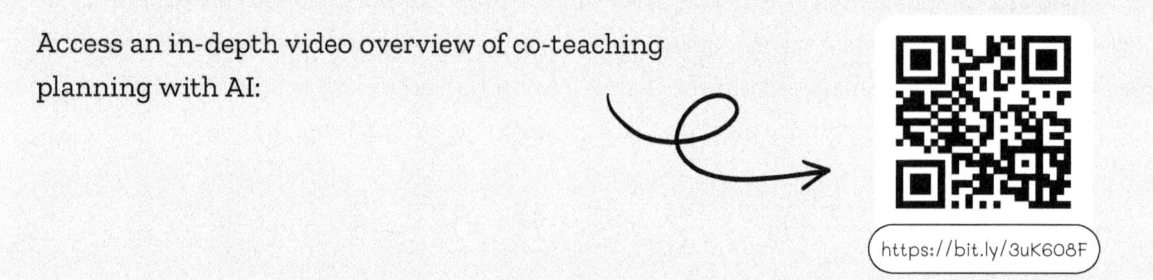

Access an in-depth video overview of co-teaching planning with AI:

https://bit.ly/3uK608F

PHYSICAL CLASSROOM

Just as important as digital organization is the physical organization of the classroom. Where will both teachers' work areas be? Are there front and back whiteboards? How do you want desks arranged? Additionally, where is the computer cart, and how will students retrieve their computers? All of these are important organizational decisions that also segue into classroom routines. Aharon Kellerman (2014) suggests that physical and virtual spaces can be important ways to satisfy human needs. The gratification of having one's own space, either in person or online, is essential for confidence in co-teaching. One strategy to get your physical classroom organized with your co-teacher is to diagram the design before moving any furniture. Before finalizing the drawing, think of how you will be instructing students, such as the types of co-teaching strategies and instructional strategies you will implement. Additionally, what will your classroom routines be? For example, how will the beginning and the end of class time look? What will transitions from one task to another look like? Take each of these into consideration before moving anything around.

Shared Teaching Philosophies and Integration Into Classroom Instruction

As the year begins, have an in-depth conversation about each co-teacher's strengths, areas of improvement, and philosophies regarding teaching and learning (Friend, 2019; Karten & Murawski, 2020). This should include a thorough breakdown of thoughts related to equity, content and curricular knowledge, classroom routines, instructional strategies, feedback and grading, differentiating instruction, and cultural responsiveness to the students you serve. Much of this conversation relates to dispositions, values, and expertise. There will be agreement and disagreement. However, consensus must come on a wide variety of areas for any new partnership or continuing partnership to succeed. One strategy, illustrated in figure 5.4, is to break down each co-teacher's thoughts and beliefs in these areas and then note shared teaching philosophies to integrate into your classroom.

Co-Teacher 1	Co-Teacher 2
Teaching Philosophies	**Teaching Philosophies**
» Engaging students » Use of formative assessment » Individualization » Extensive written lesson plans » Real-world connection	» Students learn from each other » Use of formative and summative assessments » Use of differentiation » Multiple sources of technology
Shared Teaching Philosophies for Our Class	
Our co-taught class will be an engaging place for students to learn from each other as they experience real-world connections to their learning using individualization, differentiation, and multiple sources of technology. Written lesson plans will include formative and summative assessments.	

FIGURE 5.4: Breaking down teaching philosophies to create a shared philosophy.

*Visit **go.SolutionTree.com/instruction** for a free reproducible version of this figure.*

Remember, these conversations go hand in hand with developing essential agreements as discussed in chapter 4 (page 59). With instruction such a pivotal aspect of a classroom and co-teaching partnership, we reemphasize these conversations because they are critical not just at the beginning of the year but throughout. Understanding what instruction looks like, as well as ensuring both co-teachers are on the same page within your partnership, both help facilitate instructional transparency and keep both partners aligned throughout the planning and implementation of instruction.

Having difficult conversations before the school year begins is critical for each new co-teaching partnership. Co-teachers often face the challenge of reconciling differing beliefs, philosophies, and practices. Douglas Stone and Sheila Heen (2014) emphasize the importance of understanding each other's perspectives when difficult conversations arise. They suggest that mutual respect and active listening are key to maintaining a strong relationship and navigating difficult conversations.

To reach consensus on a challenging issue, co-teachers can employ several strategies, such as collaborative brainstorming (with and without the use of AI to assist in generating ideas), role-playing scenarios, and seeking external mediation and counsel from another co-teaching colleague or school leader (Knight, 2011). For example, one co-teacher might prioritize strict routines related to classroom management to maintain order, while the other may be more flexible with routines and managing student behavior. To come to a consensus about classroom routines and management, they could develop and implement a system where structured routines and activities that are teacher led alternate with more flexible student-driven activities. For behavior, both co-teachers can write down their non-negotiables, and together, they can determine how they will react to those behaviors and remain consistent. By engaging in open dialogue, co-teachers can compromise on a wide variety of important facets for a successful co-teaching classroom where their shared teaching philosophy encapsulates the strengths of both co-teachers, ultimately benefiting their students.

This can be a reoccurring conversation for co-teaching partners who have worked together for one or more years; it's important to consistently reflect on and discuss thoughts related to teaching and learning and how to improve. Over time, you can establish, reinforce, and modify classroom routines, instructional models, and strategies you will implement within your classroom.

Co-teachers need to talk about their differences and come up with a proactive plan. For example, the noise level of the classroom can be an issue if one teacher prefers a quiet atmosphere and the co-teacher is more comfortable with an environment where students are constantly talking. Co-teaching relationships must be developed: "It cannot be assumed that co-teaching or team teaching relationships occur naturally or evolve in a healthy manner" (Clancy, Rosenau, Ferreira, Lock, & Rainsbury, 2015, p. 73). A discussion of roles and responsibilities can prove critical, as many special education co-teachers feel like glorified assistants instead of co-teachers (Friend et al., 2010). Taking the time before working together to discuss not only philosophies but also how each of the co-teaching strategies will be implemented can serve the team well.

Roles and Responsibilities in Planning and Workflow

Planning and managing the work for co-teachers can be the Achilles's heel of a successful partnership. If they do not divide roles and responsibilities equitably, resentment and guilt for not doing enough or for doing too much may percolate to the surface, causing a strain in the relationship. Just as important as discussing teaching philosophies is fairly dividing the tasks required for the class they are teaching. Co-teaching contexts are incredibly diverse, so cast a wide net when considering roles related to planning, content creation, student feedback, communication, and integrating instructional strategies into your classroom. Elementary and secondary co-teaching classrooms have different contextual features, such as student population, the content and skills being taught, the amount of instructional and language differentiation required, and technological knowledge of the co-teachers.

After analyzing these variables, think about how best to devise who takes the responsibility of lesson planning, content creation, communication, and implementation of various strategies into the classroom. Figure 5.5 provides a breakdown of these roles along with specifics about how those divisions will look. Co-teachers should discuss workflow in tandem with the role breakdown. For every outlined role and responsibility outlined, there must be a workflow procedure and sequence of how that will occur to keep it consistent and transparent for both co-teachers. Hashing this out is key to the planning process. It will be evident when it is not; a student, parent or caregiver, or school leader is sure to point it out.

Role	Responsibility: Co-Teacher's Name	How Will It Happen?
Lesson planning	Mr. Jones	On Google Doc Mr. Jones will draft the initial lesson plans on the shared weekly Google Doc, which will then be refined by Mr. Mann during their synchronous planning time the week prior to when the lessons will take place in class.
Content creation (assessments, assignments, and so on)	Mr. Mann	After the rubric is determined, add formative assessments to help achieve the rubric components. Mr. Mann will design the primary content students will interact with (that is, documents, activities, integrations) throughout the week's lessons while Mr. Jones will differentiate the content with the help of AI.
Student feedback and grading	Mr. Jones	Will add rubric when writing lesson plan Depending on the task, either Mr. Jones and Mr. Mann will use automated grading for assessments and will provide the trends to the entire class during whole-class feedback opportunities throughout the week. Each will also designate time to meet with students throughout the week. Mr. Mann will input all major assessments into the gradebook.
Selecting strategies to be implemented in class	Mr. Mann	Will define ahead of time on Google Form During their synchronous planning time, they will determine, based on the objective, standards, and student needs, which co-teaching strategies and instructional strategies they will integrate into their lessons before selecting and building out the content for those lessons.
Student and parent or caregiver communication	Mr. Jones and Mr. Mann	Joint letter to families Mr. Jones will handle the majority of communications with families, but both will attend IEP meetings, parent-teacher conferences, and important meetings together.

FIGURE 5.5: Division of labor and responsibilities.

*Visit **go.SolutionTree.com/instruction** for a free reproducible version of this figure.*

Instructional and Co-Teaching Strategy and Routine Incorporation Into Lessons

After deliberating and agreeing on a shared teaching philosophy, planning workflow, and division of labor, one remaining element is necessary to finalize effective lessons for your students. Let's focus on selecting critical instructional strategies and classroom routines to integrate into your lessons. First, we cover establishing and maintaining structures for classroom routines. Then, we outline how to select instructional strategies and establish an instructional repertoire you can integrate into your lessons throughout the school year; we discuss synthesizing these with co-teaching strategies in chapter 6 (page 101). An additional consideration is making time for the planning to take place.

Strategies for Classroom Routines

Establishing and maintaining structures for classroom routines culminates in instructional design (Wiggins & McTighe, 2011). All lessons should contain elements of formative assessment, guided practice, independent and collaborative practice, and metacognition. With these important elements in place, teachers can use strategies centered on retrieval practice, interweaving, scaffolding, worked examples, and whole-class and individualized feedback. Going further, they can break down strategies with thinking routines that scaffold instruction, student thinking, and task completion within a sequence (Rhoads & Lim, 2022). In figure 5.6, we define each of these important instructional design categories and then define and illustrate instructional strategies that you can deploy in your classroom.

	Engagement	**Collaboration**	**Assessment**	**Feedback and Reflection**
Definition	*Engagement* is opportunities for thinking that teachers create (Ritchhart, Church, & Morrison, 2011). Lessons need clear objectives and goals and give learners ownership of their work as well as autonomy over time to develop cognitive engagement (Pedler, Yeigh, & Hudson, 2020).	*Collaboration* involves two or more students working together on a task. Successful collaboration means keeping in mind *cognitive load*, which is information our memory can process at a given time, affecting how students learn. Consider several factors for the collaborative activity (Leahy & Sweller, 2008; Sweller, 1988). • Task complexity • Expertise of student • Team roles • Team size: three to four students • Students' prior knowledge • Homogeneous teams	*Assessment* is the collection of and review of information generated by students to support their learning (Banta & Polomba, 2014).	*Feedback* is information about students' performance intended to improve their learning (Wisniewski, Zierer, & Hattie, 2020). When students "employ metacognition, they become consciously aware of themselves as problem solvers, which enables them to actively seek solutions to any problems they encounter, rather than relying on others to tell them what to do or to answer their questions" (McGuire, 2015, p. 35).

	Engagement	**Collaboration**	**Assessment**	**Feedback and Reflection**
Example	Students engage in think, write, pair, share; they first think about a response to a problem. Then, they write their response. Following that, they discuss what they have written and their thinking with a partner. Finally, teachers select pairs to discuss their answers, thinking, and distinctions in how they got to that solution or answer.	Students collaborate in small groups for project-based learning. Teachers front-load content and provide scaffolded tasks over time to help students research, think, and come up with conclusions. Each group is differentiated based on students' skill sets, which also dictates the task complexity for the groups. Last, teachers give roles to students throughout the project.	Students complete a formative assessment using interactive slides, such as Google Slides, Pear Deck, or Nearpod, in which they problem solve and answer questions. Teachers collect data on student performance to monitor and adjust their instruction to further differentiate and reteach.	One co-teacher presents three major bullet points on which students did well in addition to two bullet points summarizing areas the entire class needs to improve in. Then, both co-teachers give students individualized verbal and written feedback as well as additional actions for students to complete to follow up on the feedback.
Instructional Strategies	**Notice and wonder:** Students receive an image, video, 3-D representation, or written statement to view and to think about. After time to process, students write out three to four observations of what they notice. Then, teachers prompt students to write down one to two questions on what they wonder about that particular phenomenon and what they may want to learn more about. According to preference, teachers weave student-to-student conversations and whole-class discussions into this strategy (Rumack & Huinker, 2019).	**Think, write, pair, share:** Teachers present students with a prompt or problem and ask them to think. After providing wait time, teachers allow them to write an answer or solve the problem at hand. Once the time has elapsed, they pair with a partner. During the group discussion, teachers prompt them to outline the steps they used to solve the problem and to discuss their answer. Last, pairs share with the class each partner's methodology and answer (Kagan & Kagan, 1994; Karge, 2023b).	**Retrieval practice as a formative assessment:** Students receive physical or digital flash cards or slides that ask them to problem solve or recall information from a previous class session. This methodology can help boost long-term memory and retention (Roediger & Butler, 2011). This can occur anytime within the scope of the lesson but often takes place at the beginning and end of the lesson to gauge student performance and understanding.	**Whole-class and small-group feedback:** Teachers provide positive and reinforcing feedback to the entire class with major trends in two to three bullet points. Then, they give specific and actionable feedback, including steps to help students see where they are going and how to get there during small-group instruction.

FIGURE 5.6: Elements of instructional design definitions and examples.

After you have a set of instructional strategies that you can interweave into each element of instructional design, you can use them again and again. Using the less-is-more mindset, you can create routines around strategies that work for each element of instructional design and plan around them on a daily and weekly basis. With an instructional tool kit of up to five strategies for each element of instructional design to choose from, your planning time efficiency and instructional effectiveness as co-teachers will only improve.

Co-teachers can select and implement instructional strategies and co-teaching strategies from their tool kit into their weekly backward plan by having an organizer like the one in figure 5.6 (page 93). Strategy selection is based on student need, how co-teachers want to teach the skills and content, and how comfortable they are with the instructional strategies within their tool kit. Both co-teachers must consider each of these areas before thinking of implementing the instructional strategy. Additionally, if technology is involved, the co-teachers should further consider how they can use the tool to further access and equity and amplify student learning (Rhoads & Lim, 2022).

For novice teachers or teachers who are just learning instructional and co-teaching strategies, it might be beneficial to consistently develop into the planning routine the three phases of contemplative practice, which include (1) predict, (2) plan for, and (3) respond (Chandler & Budge, 2023). Using the predict, plan, respond format provides a thought process for powerful student care and classroom organization. As a co-teaching team, try to predict student interactions and engagement within the classroom routine, plan for any challenges, necessary differentiation, or UDL strategies, and be ready to respond with additional tools for the instructional and co-teaching strategies.

Strategies for Instructional Use

As co-teaching partners, it's important to select instructional strategies based on a list of criteria to best meet student needs. Additionally, co-teachers can focus on the design of their lesson and integrate instructional sequences of strategies throughout. Here is a set of criteria that co-teachers can use to evaluate instructional strategies they would like to consider for an upcoming lesson.

- Student needs
- How co-teachers want to teach content or a specific skill
- Efficacy of co-teachers to implement instructional strategy or co-teaching strategy
- Technology integration consideration (varies)

Given these criteria, co-teachers can select from a list of potential strategies shared in figure 5.7 what to incorporate into their lessons throughout the week; space is provided at the top of the figure for that purpose. For example, if a key need is student engagement, strategies like a notice-and-wonder thinking routine or four corners might be appropriate. For collaboration, consider think, write, pair, share or project-based learning with embedded scaffolds. Select assessment strategies like retrieval practice using flash cards or formative assessment using interactive slides based on the assessment needs of the lesson.

Monday	Tuesday	Wednesday	Thursday	Friday

Standards
Instructional Tool Kit
Engagement   • Notice-and-wonder thinking routine   • Take one, get one   • Four corners
Collaboration   • Think, write, pair, share   • Project-based learning with embedded scaffolds
Assessment   • Retrieval practice using flash cards   • Formative assessment using interactive slides   • Project-based learning work product   • Summative multiple-choice and short-answer assessment
Feedback   • Whole-class feedback   • Small-group feedback   • One-on-one conference   • Written or audio-recorded feedback on a work product
Metacognition   • Lesson reflection of performance   • Summary of major learning points
Other Strategies to Consider   • Social-emotional learning: Beginning- and end-of-class check-in   • Guided instruction: Direct instruction with modeling and scaffolds
Co-Teaching Strategies (Karge, 2015, 2023b)
Supportive Co-Teaching   • Co-teach strategy 1: One teach, one assist   • Co-teach strategy 2: One teach, one observe   • Co-teach strategy 3: One teach, one support
Team Co-Teaching   • Co-teach strategy 4: Graze-and-tag teaching   • Co-teach strategy 5: Parallel teaching   • Co-teach strategy 6: Station teaching   • Co-teach strategy 7: Alternative teaching
Advanced Co-Teaching   • Co-teach strategy 8: Conversation teaching   • Co-teach strategy 9: Role-play teaching   • Co-teach strategy 10: Interactive teaching   • Co-teach strategy 11: Shared teaching

FIGURE 5.7: Backward planner and strategy tool kit.

*Visit **go.SolutionTree.com/instruction** for a free reproducible version of this figure.*

Incorporating these strategies into the weekly planner involves aligning them with the specific objectives and standards for each day. Co-teachers should discuss and agree on which strategies best meet the criteria for each lesson segment, ensuring that they complement each other's teaching style and knowledge repertoire. The process of collaborative planning with selection criteria as the guide for co-teachers helps ensure that each lesson integrates high-impact, research-based instructional strategies.

Figure 5.7 (page 95) puts together everything we discuss in this chapter in a graphic representation that you can use to plan with your co-teacher. It not only provides strategies to consider but also allows you and your co-teacher to place them within your long- and short-term planning. Before we conclude this chapter, think about how you can use the template and methodology provided to help create planning routines that are efficient, effective, and equitable for both co-teachers.

Time to Plan

Co-teachers can use all the strategies in this chapter when they establish and maintain consistent planning time. In preparation for writing this book, we reflected on the many ways teachers find time to plan. Belinda shares systems that co-teaching teams she has worked with have used, including once-a-month release, morning coffee, PLCs, planning period, and personal time.

ONCE-A-MONTH RELEASE

At an elementary school in Southern California, Christa and Michelle, both fourth-grade teachers, have the opportunity to plan for half a day once a month. The site administrator provides two substitute teachers for the morning. These same substitutes then cover another co-teaching team in the afternoon. With a substitute covering both classes, the teachers can strategically plan for all content areas and incorporate strong instructional strategies they want to implement. The time also allows for the review of past planning and general discussion of how the co-teaching process is going.

MORNING COFFEE

At a high school in Colorado, Jim and Kent arrive early every Friday morning and meet for coffee and planning time. They both coach athletic teams on campus and find the early Friday morning time slot effective, as their respective teams typically have afternoon games or practices on Fridays and both teachers are regularly available in the morning. They use the time to evaluate the previous week and plan for the week ahead. In their co-teaching situation, they use Friday's classes for makeup work and study hall, allowing them a bit of a break as well.

PROFESSIONAL LEARNING COMMUNITIES

At an international school in Africa, co-teachers Magaly and Kesha are members of a schoolwide PLC along with six other co-teaching teams, all middle school teachers. The PLC process in the school calls for fifty minutes of collaborative meeting time for co-teachers every week. Once a month, the co-teaching teams meet as a group during the designated collaborative grade-level meeting time, during which they share co-teaching strategies and techniques. Then, during the other three meeting time slots, Magaly and Kesha meet as a pair to plan, assess, and reflect on their practice.

PLANNING PERIOD

Many schools have planning periods. It is common practice at secondary schools and many elementary schools to build in the planning period while students are at "specials" (that is, music, physical education, and so on). At these sites, co-teaching teams have the benefit of scheduled planning time.

Mark and Jen co-teach ninety minutes each day. Mark is a fourth-grade teacher, and Jen is the special education teacher. Jen meets with Mark during his planning period twice a month. The pair finds this time allows them to review student work and plan for upcoming lessons that include appropriate accommodations and supports for all students.

PERSONAL TIME

New York educators Marian and Marcella are new to co-teaching. They requested and received the approval to experiment as the first co-teaching team at their school. They did not realize the importance or value of co-planning time and did not negotiate for such time. However, they value their time together. Both teachers are young moms. It works for them to put their children to bed, and then, every Thursday at 9:00 p.m., they meet on Zoom and plan. When asked about giving up personal time, Marcella explains, "I used to plan alone at night; it is a lot more productive to plan with a colleague" (M. Leamons, personal communication, May 27, 2023).

Conclusion

In this chapter, we covered how to plan and design lessons with your co-teacher. Devising how planning will take place, developing a shared teaching philosophy, dividing up the labor of planning and instructional integration, and establishing and maintaining classroom routines and instructional integrations are important elements all co-teachers must discuss at the beginning of their co-teaching experience and throughout their partnership. Workflow was a critical theme, as co-teachers need efficiency to plan and devise effective lessons without taking more time than necessary. The chapter also described how to plan synchronously and asynchronously and divide the labor required to not only create the lesson structure and content but also select the instructional strategies from a revolving tool kit. This, in turn, makes planning even more efficient and lessons more effective. Last, based on suggestions from veteran co-teachers, we addressed various key conversations and dynamics to determine at the beginning of the year to ensure successful planning and lesson design. Creating a shared teaching philosophy is necessary before planning commences. Division of labor helps create shared responsibility for how planning and its implementation will take place in your classroom.

ADDITIONAL RESOURCES TO CONSIDER AFTER READING THIS CHAPTER

- The nonprofit organization Digital Promise provides a free tool called the **Learner Variability Navigator (https://lvp.digitalpromiseglobal.org)** that can help teachers design lessons that are personal and meaningful for each student.
- Harvard's **Project Zero Thinking Routine Toolbox (https://pz.harvard.edu/thinking-routines)** is a collection of helpful scaffolds for use in lesson design that provide ways to make students' thinking visible, revealing that thinking both to teachers and to students themselves.

Reflection and Action: 3-2-1 Format

Directions: After completing chapter 5 on planning and lesson design with co-teaching in mind, answer the following questions.

What are three things you have learned from this chapter?

What are two questions you have after reading this chapter?

How do you plan on integrating co-teaching strategies into your planning and lesson design?

Effective co-teachers collaboratively and purposefully plan with the four universal design points: (1) diverse learner characteristics with an emphasis on strengths, (2) differentiation of content and materials, (3) differentiated product and assessment options, (4) differentiated process options with an emphasis on peer-mediated instruction and student discourse in mind. Additionally, effective co-teachers collaboratively and purposefully monitor for student engagement and outcomes.

—J. Thousand, researcher and expert in co-teaching,
personal communication, January 21, 2024

CHAPTER 6

Integrating Instructional Strategies With Co-Teaching Strategies

Like electricity powering an electric car, the instructional strategies co-teachers select to integrate with their co-teaching strategies power their instruction. Let's zoom in so we can see this in play. Think of the instructional strategies as the overarching model. Imagine that co-teachers want to use the instructional strategies of explicit direct instruction and modeling. These are evidence-based strategies that allow students to consume information and directions to complete a task (Hughes, Morris, Therrien, & Benson, 2017; Rathvon, 2008). To implement a formative assessment, the co-teachers choose to use the co-teaching strategy one teach, one assist. During this instructional sequence, one educator will explain the assessment's directions through explicit direct instruction and model how the assessment may be completed. Then, both educators will work simultaneously to deploy the assessment. Deployment may occur through the LMS or through a paper handout. Both teachers assist students in accessing the assessment and answer any immediate questions. Then, as the assessment commences, both educators monitor the students and the assessment. If it is a digital assessment, both educators will be attuned to analyzing student progress as well as monitoring the room. If the assessment is on paper, monitoring occurs as one or both teachers walk throughout the room. In some cases, one or both educators deploy an alternative assessment and implement accommodations and modifications to students. It's evident that there's quite a lot occurring during this time.

Referring to Thousand's quote in this chapter's epigraph, sometimes co-teachers focus more on content, product, and process design points and less on the important first design point of getting to know their learners deeply in multiple ways, including building genuine relationships with them within a community of learning. As we move ahead and begin digging into how to instruct using the eleven co-teaching strategies, it is important to continually reflect on how teachers build classroom community through these interactive, engaging lessons.

Belinda recalls a teaching experience in which she and her co-teacher integrated several instructional and co-teaching strategies over a period of months:

> *As a co-teacher, selecting instructional strategies was key to the planning and implementation of our lessons. We took our standards, content, and student needs into*

> consideration while building out the general design of our lessons as well as deciding which co-teaching and instructional strategies we would integrate into our lesson plan to best meet students' needs. While teaching world history, we wanted to use modeling and explicit direct instruction (Hughes et al., 2017) to begin each lesson followed by formative assessment (Spady & Karge, 2022) to gauge student knowledge. After our formative assessment, we used guided instruction and gradual release (Fisher & Frey, 2013) to build content knowledge before gradually releasing students to station rotation. Last, we used formative assessment or student reflection to summarize their major takeaways from the lesson.
>
> What I describe here is an example of what took a few months to devise. We selected the strategies because we had to build prior knowledge and skills and provide quite a bit of differentiated instruction for our diverse set of learners. We selected formative assessment at the beginning and end of our lessons to determine whether students had prior knowledge about what we'd previously covered as well as whether they were able to have a beginner's understanding of the content and skills we covered after the end of the lesson. We were able to review the data and see how our students performed and then monitor and adjust future lessons. We selected explicit direct instruction, modeling, and scaffolding to display information and tasks. We chunked instruction and task completion, and we used demonstrations to share how to access and complete assigned tasks.
>
> Our goal was to build understanding and clarify as we went so that students could practice tasks with minimal assistance. Then, to further differentiate the practice and help students receive additional one-on-one or small-group instruction, we used station rotation so students could complete tasks associated with what we covered previously. Students rotated to various stations in small groups as they practiced various skills. If we saw patterns that needed correction, we stopped the stations and gave whole-class feedback or specific feedback to one station of students. Encompassing all of these instructional strategies were the co-teaching strategies of one teach, one assist, one teach, one support, parallel teaching, and station teaching.

Based on the strategies Belinda discusses in the previous two paragraphs, can you guess during which part of the lesson they used these co-teaching strategies based on the instructional strategies they employed? The goal of this chapter is to help you identify instructional strategies that you can pair with co-teaching strategies throughout a lesson sequence. In addition, we share various examples of what these strategies look like in action within various contexts so you can ideate and think about opportunities for your co-teaching classroom to implement.

Key Themes and Ideas
- ☐ Review of co-teaching strategies
- ☐ Guided instruction and gradual release of responsibility
- ☐ Instructional strategies and instructional design
- ☐ Instructional strategies in action: putting strategies together with co-teaching

Review of Co-Teaching Strategies

Before jumping into instructional strategies, let's review the co-teaching strategies, as they are one of the overarching components we incorporate our instructional strategies into while co-teaching a lesson. We recommend referring to table 2.1 (the Co-Teaching Strategy Quick-Reference Guide, page 31) and downloading the reproducible version from **go.SolutionTree.com/instruction** to have handy while you read this chapter. Recall that each of these co-teaching strategies can be used throughout a co-taught lesson and that they are interchangeable as the lesson progresses. You can use many co-teaching strategies throughout a lesson. One co-teaching strategy may only last for a few minutes but recur only minutes later as the lesson progresses or if a student needs it. This also applies to co-teaching strategies that may last for much longer parts of a lesson. However, as we will discuss, co-teachers will want to provide a sequence within their lessons that provides more teacher guidance initially and then gives students more responsibility to complete tasks through gradual release as they progress throughout the lesson. Keep that in mind as we move through this discussion, as it's important to focus on when selecting instructional strategies to implement during your lessons.

Guided Instruction and Gradual Release of Responsibility

Gradual release means providing students more responsibility and ownership of their learning over the course of a lesson (Fisher & Frey, 2013). Generally, it means a teacher front-loads much of the instruction by guiding, modeling, and providing explicit direct instruction and scaffolding until the learner is doing the task independently (Pearson & Gallagher, 1983). This then leads to students completing a task with partial support by their teacher and then receiving feedback. Thereafter, the following similar tasks result in less and less support from their teacher until the student can complete the task independently. Ultimately, cognitive load shifts from the teacher to the student over time (Pearson & Gallagher, 1983). The I do, we do, and you do instructional sequence sums up how the increase in student responsibility occurs during gradual release through guided practice and scaffolding (Archer & Hughes, 2010).

Within the co-teaching classroom, co-teachers align their co-teaching strategies with gradual release. Then, they can select instructional strategies that fit what students are learning and how they want to teach it. For example, during a mathematics lesson, after the first formative assessment as the lesson begins, the co-teachers may want to use shared teaching as both may want to go over the lesson's objectives, activating prior knowledge and beginning to guide students into the skills and content of the lesson. Then, to further activate prior knowledge, they use the thinking routine strategy of notice and wonder because they want their students to recognize various schemas. They follow this by modeling how to complete a similar type of mathematics problem on the front board (Rumack & Huinker, 2019). Co-teachers can then use not only modeling but also a think-aloud strategy to discuss their thoughts and processes for solving a problem together, relating how to do various steps of the problem as students follow along (Nazari & Hatami, 2023;

Rosenzweig, Krawec, & Montague, 2011). Sometimes, within this sequence, you may observe the shared teaching co-teaching strategy turn into one teach, one assist, as well as one teach, one observe as students may need support during the guided modeling.

Another example might be co-teachers who are teaching a writing lesson focused on writing the main idea in the form of a conclusion. To begin the lesson, both co-teachers start with shared teaching and conversation teaching as they review the lesson's objective. They also display an initial mentor text as a side-by-side example to demonstrate two very different conclusions. Through a formative assessment using Pear Deck, an interactive slide add-on to Google Slides, they ask students to identify which paragraph within the conclusion has a statement illustrating the main idea (Oded & Oded, 2022). While this short formative assessment takes place, co-teachers move between one teach, one observe and one teach, one assist while they analyze the student answers coming in real time. Once they have completed the formative assessment, both co-teachers use interactive teaching as teacher 1 discusses the differences between the two conclusions while teacher 2 digitally underlines and annotates what teacher 1 is discussing. Once co-teachers have shared differences, the shift between one teach, one observe and one teach, one assist and interactive teaching may continue as the lesson's slideshow has yet another formative assessment of the same manner to see what trends in student learning occur to then make modeling corrections.

The examples share how gradual release works within the context of co-teaching as well as how dynamically the co-teaching and instructional strategies co-teachers select can shift throughout an instructional sequence. As a lesson progresses, the shifts in gradual release may take more or less time than other lessons. Additionally, the dynamic instructional changes we see in these examples may take place more slowly or even more quickly, depending on the lesson and student needs. Therefore, there are many variabilities to this and much that can happen.

Instructional Strategies and Instructional Design

As illustrated by the examples in the previous section, co-teaching strategies and instructional strategies can shift and change continually during a lesson sequence. What makes co-teaching such a dynamic form of teaching is that it can shift as the lesson progresses and in response to the evolving needs of students as co-teachers monitor and adjust their instruction. Luckily, with the flexibility provided by co-teaching instructional strategies, co-teachers can integrate a wide range of instructional strategies to support student learning. Several key instructional strategies work within the context of co-teaching strategies and gradual release.

Before diving into specific instructional strategies to use, let's focus on instructional design. *Instructional design* consists of employing various strategies, a curriculum, and technology to create and implement learning experiences for students (Gagné, Wager, Golas, Keller, & Russell, 2005). Through the development of lesson plans, educators can sequence the instruction by using various strategies to meet instructional goals. They can structure and design lessons using instructional strategies that relate to areas of engagement, collaboration, assessment, and feedback (Karge, 2023b). Additionally, strategies can fall into categories such as direct and explicit instruction.

Refer back to figure 5.6 (page 93) for an outline of various elements of instructional design, defining and providing examples of them in practice.

As discussed earlier, the overarching plan includes the co-teaching and instructional strategies that we decide to incorporate into our lessons. For example, to begin a mathematics lesson, the plan of the lesson integrates the team teaching co-teaching strategy along with formative assessment as both teachers go over the agenda, review two practice problems, and provide an interactive and informal formative assessment on adding fractions using interactive whiteboards. In this sequence, the team teaching co-teaching strategy is the first strategy encompassing the actions of the co-teachers followed by implementing formative assessment as an embedded strategy to see where students perform on the content area before jumping into the next segment of the lesson.

With this in mind, we also recommend that teachers include gradual release throughout their lessons to provide the necessary scaffolds and supports for students to eventually give them the opportunity to practice without teacher support over time (Fisher & Frey, 2013). Therefore, be sure to plan and design your lessons with the co-teaching strategies in mind and with gradual release as the driving force behind them.

The following sections include a series of instructional strategies that co-teachers can incorporate within co-teaching strategies. We illustrate how to do this as well as how to synthesize gradual release into lesson design by providing examples of this process across preK–12 co-teaching classroom contexts. After these initial examples, we provide even more detailed examples of this within elementary and secondary classroom contexts.

Modeling and Explicit Instruction

Modeling and explicit instruction are two instructional strategies that teachers usually conduct simultaneously by demonstrating a task or skill to show students how to do it (Archer & Hughes, 2010). Through a step-by-step demonstration, a teacher shares how to complete the task or illustrates how to use a skill to solve a problem. Explicit instruction relates to an organized and focused instructional routine, which relates to gradual release. It is essentially putting *I do, we do, you do* into practice, and it can be done throughout an instructional sequence and even throughout an entire lesson.

As an example of this strategy in a co-teaching context, in a high school algebra 1 lesson focusing on solving multistep equations, two co-teachers collaborate to facilitate the lesson using both modeling and explicit instruction. The first co-teacher begins by projecting an equation, $3x + 5 = 20$, onto the digital whiteboard and demonstrates each step required to solve it as a worked example: subtracting 5 from both sides, followed by dividing by 3. As this co-teacher verbalizes the rationale behind each step, the second co-teacher circulates around the classroom, offering individual guidance and answering students' questions in real time through the one teach, one support co-teaching strategy.

Next, the co-teachers engage the class together through a team teaching co-teaching strategy by solving a similar equation, $4x - 3 = 13$, during the *we do* phase of explicit instruction. Here, students suggest each step during a whole-class discussion, and one co-teacher performs it on the digital whiteboard while the other continues to provide support by roving the class as well as reviewing each student's mini whiteboard, ensuring that all students are actively participating and understanding the process.

For the *you do* phase, each co-teacher supervises a section of the classroom as students independently tackle equations like 2x + 7 = 17. The co-teachers monitor progress, provide feedback individually to students as well as in small groups, and assist students who need additional support. This gradual release of responsibility ensures that students internalize the problem-solving process and gain confidence in their ability to solve similar problems on their own as they progress through this instructional sequence.

Retrieval Practice

Retrieval practice is when students recall information verbally or through writing down information without having it placed in front of them (Roediger & Butler, 2011). Examples of retrieval practice involve formative assessments, brain dumps, the use of flash cards, and the recall of key facts and main ideas at the beginning and the end of a lesson. Bruna Fernanda Tolentino Moreira, Tatiana Salazar Silva Pinto, Daniela Siqueira Veloso Starling, and Antônio Jaeger (2019) purport that the practice of learning restudied information enhances student long-term memory.

In a third-grade classroom in which students are working on a science unit on birds, two co-teachers use retrieval practice along with gradual release of responsibility to help students begin learning vocabulary words to deepen their understanding and retention of key terms in the unit. To begin, the first co-teacher begins with the *I do* phase by introducing words such as *habitat*, *migration*, and *species* to the class. This teacher uses visual aids like pictures of different birds and their environments to model the words as they are displayed on a Google Slides presentation during whole-class instruction. The co-teachers go back and forth explaining each word, using it in a sentence and associating it with relevant visuals, and they engage students by using a choral chant to pronounce the word as well as repeating how to use the word in a sentence.

During the *we do* phase, both co-teachers team teach to introduce students to a matching activity handout where students pair vocabulary words with their corresponding pictures and definitions. Both teachers first explain and model the activity. Then, one co-teacher circulates the room, guiding discussions, correcting misconceptions, and encouraging students to use the vocabulary words in their own sentences. Then, the other co-teacher can take a small group of students to work together for further explicit instruction, modeling, and support, while the other co-teacher supports the remainder of the class.

In the *you do* phase, students independently create simple flash cards, writing the vocabulary word on one side and its definition or a drawing on the other. The co-teachers oversee this activity, providing support and feedback as needed, ensuring that each student can accurately recall and use the vocabulary words. As students finish, one co-teacher focuses on transitioning students to vocabulary practice by modeling to individual students as well as the small group of students from the previous phase.

The lesson concludes with a retrieval practice session led by both co-teachers. Using Quizizz, students practice recalling the vocabulary words through an engaging formative assessment, in which they must match words and images of the vocabulary words to their definitions. During this assessment, each teacher monitors the student responses on the Quizizz assessment platform to determine next steps, such as reteaching and reassessment. Both co-teachers use team teaching, one teach, one support, and one teach, one observe as the formative assessment progresses.

Interleaving and Spaced Practice

Interleaving and spaced practice help students better remember information over time. *Interleaving* involves the mixture of different types of problems within a practice set, which allows for higher levels of retention after practice (Rohrer, 2012). *Spaced practice* involves practicing and studying over time, often when teachers present a concept or skill and then give students two or more additional exposures as time goes by (Carpenter, 2014). They front-load the work, and then fade out practice up to the day before the assessment (Kim & Webb, 2022). For example, students may study and practice a topic for two hours a day the first week. Then, as they move into the next week leading up to the assessment, they spend thirty minutes less per day on the topic. Teachers can use a powerful combination of interleaving and spaced practice to help their students retain and recall the skills and content they are learning. We encourage teachers to use both strategies together in tandem to help students practice skills and content to build higher levels of retention.

In a seventh-grade mathematics lesson on reviewing fractions, both co-teachers want to prepare students for an upcoming summative assessment. With students using mini whiteboards, both co-teachers begin the lesson by introducing a problem set with six addition and subtraction problems along with one multiplication and division problem from the previous lesson. Then, for the next set of four problems, one co-teacher revisits the concepts of fraction simplification and conversion between improper fractions and mixed numbers. While teaching these initial problem sets, both co-teachers switch between team teaching and one teach, one support co-teaching strategies. As the class progresses, both teachers shift to parallel teaching to guide two groups of students through a series of mixed practice problems that incorporate both current and past fraction topics (including addition, subtraction, multiplication, division, and improper fractions). After parallel teaching, they release the class for independent practice on a worksheet with mixed problems from the unit. During this time, each co-teacher provides one-on-one support to students as they practice problem solving. Throughout this lesson, interleaving different fraction operations and spacing the revision of earlier fraction concepts in the lesson such as addition and subtraction help students practice and develop further understanding of fractions before their upcoming summative assessment.

Formative Assessment

Formative assessment is essentially a low-stakes assessment where teachers can evaluate student performance data to monitor and adjust their instruction to support student learning needs (Widiastuti, Mukminatien, Prayogo, & Irawati, 2020). Typically, teachers can implement these assessments throughout the lesson as well as at its beginning and end. This helps teachers determine instruction during and after their lesson to support planning, differentiation, and learning extensions. Formative self-assessment occurs when students self-monitor and evaluate how they learn (Spady & Karge, 2022). For example, teachers can ask students to evaluate their knowledge on a lesson by indicating 1, 2, or 3; 1 means *I can teach this to someone else*, 2 means *I have learned something*, and 3 means *I need some more information on this topic*.

In a preK classroom focusing on a lesson involving identifying and grouping shapes, both co-teachers model through team teaching during the *I do* phase by placing various shapes into the correct bin. For example, one says, "Here is a circle; we place circles into the bin that has a circle shape, because it is round all the way around." The co-teacher then places a circle into the circle bin. As the lesson progresses, one co-teacher leads students into a group activity in which students sort into the correct bin circles, triangles, and squares that have been scattered onto the carpet. As this occurs, both teachers rove the classroom together and, through alternative teaching, provide prompts and corrections such as "Let's find where the square goes—remember, it has four sides." Alongside these prompts and corrections, the co-teachers observe how well students can move the shapes into the correct bins to determine whether reteaching needs to occur to the whole class or individual students. Both co-teachers then introduce a handout via interactive teaching that asks students to circle groups of shapes. Before handing it out, both co-teachers model together how to do so using the role-play teaching strategy. Then, as students work on the handouts independently, one co-teacher works with a small group of students on the task, and the other co-teacher monitors and provides support to the rest of the class.

Cooperative Learning Strategies

Cooperative learning strategies involve group instruction in which teachers structure various prompts and roles so students can work collaboratively within parameters, which can help them work together more effectively to complete a task (Kagan, 1989; Kagan & Kagan, 2009). The structural approach to cooperative learning strategies includes three elements: (1) organization of instruction, (2) repeatability, and (3) inclusion of cooperative learning principles in the strategy in use. Examples of cooperative learning strategies include jigsaw (Aronson, 2021), inside and outside circle (Tiwery & Souisa, 2019), mix, pair, share (Kamarudin, 2021), think, write, pair, share (Karge 2023a), numbered heads (Leasa & Corebima, 2017), and team, pair, and solo (Karge, 2016).

During a ninth-grade English lesson on crafting thesis statements, two co-teachers implement the cooperative learning strategy think, write, pair, share (see Karge, 2023a) at the beginning of their lesson to practice writing thesis statements. Before the strategy protocol begins, both co-teachers showcase a model thesis on the board and break down each of its components. Each co-teacher team teaches and provides insights for each part of a thesis. Then, as the lesson transitions, they ask students to think about the main argument of a text they read earlier in the week. Students receive about a minute to think before the co-teachers ask them to articulate the main argument of the text and then craft it as thesis statement (using a Pear Deck digital interactive slideshow on their Chromebooks). For this task, students get about eight minutes. While this occurs, both co-teachers rove around the class supporting students one on one and monitoring student progress in real time using Pear Deck.

Before moving to the pair-share stage, co-teachers facilitate a whole-group discussion by encouraging students to provide each other constructive feedback, refining their statements based on the discussion. They model how this discussion should take place by conducting a short example conversation for students. Students then team up in pairs to discuss their written thesis statements. Students get three minutes to engage in peer-to-peer conversations and revisions. As they did before, both co-teachers monitor each pair and the revisions they make on their digital slides.

After the pair phase, the co-teachers cold call two pairs of students and display their thesis statements to the class. Each co-teacher provides feedback and explains strengths and areas of improvement. This takes place on a digital whiteboard, meaning the co-teachers can provide written feedback directly onto the student's slide. As this takes place, students who were not called reflect and review their thesis statements, as they will be using them later in the lesson for further practice.

Thinking Routines

A *thinking routine* is a scaffolded set of procedures and questions that can help students' thinking and learning (Ritchhart et al., 2011). Students use a graphic organizer in tandem with a set of questions and procedures that let them think deeply about a scenario or question, which can help them build skills in a multitude of different areas, such as critical thinking, problem solving, prediction, and questioning (Manurung, Masitoh, & Arianto, 2022). These sets of strategies can be integrated through guided practice and work well with the gradual release of responsibility (Fisher & Frey, 2021), since there are fewer scaffolds as students activate prior knowledge throughout the thinking routine before they generate conclusions from the work they have conducted. Strategies such as notice and wonder; see, think, and wonder; connect, extend, and challenge; and I used to think . . . and now I think . . . all fall under thinking-routine protocols.

In a second-grade classroom lesson introducing the book *Summer Vacation, Here I Come* by D. J. Steinberg (2023), both co-teachers integrate the notice-and-wonder thinking routine to engage students in predicting and connecting with the text. As they introduce the story, the co-teachers display the book cover via a digital projector. Then, they team teach, asking students to observe the book's cover and think about what they notice, such as characters, setting, and activities. One co-teacher provides and models an example before giving students a few minutes to think and analyze the cover.

After a few minutes of observation, the co-teachers pair students up to share their observations. Then, they cold call students to share what they notice about the cover to the entire class. Each co-teacher facilitates this sharing by writing down students' observations in the first column of a graphic organizer displayed on the board as a Google Slide, ensuring students' ideas are voiced and visualized. Following the notice phase, the wonder phase begins when the co-teachers prompt the students to think about questions they might have about the story based on the cover and their visualized illustrations. Each co-teacher writes down several question stems on the next Google Slide, such as "Why do you think _____ is doing _____?" and "What do you predict will happen after _____ and why?" Again, after a few minutes of thinking, co-teachers ask students to share what they wonder with a partner during a pair-share. Upon completing the pair-share, the co-teachers call on various students and write their questions on the graphic organizer in the second column beside their initial observations.

Students begin guided reading of the book with the co-teachers. The co-teachers stop after each page to add new items that students notice or wonder about to the graphic organizer. This ongoing interaction between the students and the text, facilitated by the teachers, exemplifies the gradual release of responsibility, starting from heavily guided noticing and wondering to more independent engagement with the text. As students become more comfortable and adept at the thinking routine, they connect their initial predictions and questions to the actual story content as they progress through the story.

Scaffolding

Scaffolding is a step-by-step process in which a teacher provides support to enhance students' learning while teaching them a skill or content (Karge, 2014). The goal is to prepare students over time through scaffolded gradual release so they can complete the task with minimal teacher supports (Bliss, Askew, & Macrae, 1996; Smagorinksy, 2018; Verenikina, 2004). Scaffolding can take many forms, such as modeling, think-alouds, clarifying questions, and graphics and visuals for support. Teachers can use these scaffolds throughout an instructional sequence to enhance student learning.

In a fifth-grade coding lesson, using a platform such as Code.org, both co-teachers can scaffold to build student understanding and independence in the basics of coding. To begin the lesson, the content expert co-teacher introduces the concept of coding through a think-aloud strategy by walking students through logging into and navigating Code.org using their Chromebooks. The initial modeling provides a set of scaffolds to help students start a coding task and a clear example of what to expect. During this time, the other co-teacher can do the same modeling in a small group or rove around the class to ensure students are on task as well as determine which students may be lost or confused.

As the lesson progresses, the co-teachers provide and model a second set of scaffolds on the digital classroom display. They display three lines of HTML, which they break down into various parts on an accompanying slideshow to help students identify patterns in the code and its logic. They use guided practice as they identify each part of the code; then they encourage students to ask questions about how changing parts of the code may affect its overall outcome. Just as during the opening sequence, the other co-teacher can model the same way in a small group or move around the class to monitor whether students are on task or need support. The co-teachers can use this set of scaffolded sequences as guided practice and repeat it with new lines of code. Co-teachers can decide on what actions to take depending on which co-teaching strategies may work best, such as team teaching, parallel teaching in one large group and one small group, or one teach, one support.

Station Rotation

Station rotation represents physical or digital stations where teachers ask students to complete a task within a set time. After the time has elapsed, students move from station to station until the rotations are completed for the lesson (Ayob, Halim, Zulkifli, Zaid, & Mokhtar, 2020). Teachers can create several stations to develop a skill or set of skills as well as focus on different content segments over the course of a lesson. Stations can include opportunities to work with a teacher for small-group instruction, front-loading content through video or an article review, an adaptive practice using a tool such as i-Ready, independent practice, collaborative group work, and formative assessment.

In a sixth-grade dual-language classroom focused on a lesson about writing conventions in English and Spanish, co-teachers implement station rotation and station co-teaching to support students practicing these skills in both languages. Stations in this lesson focus on writing claims, using details and evidence, and grammar and punctuation. Before moving students into stations, both co-teachers use team teaching to model and explain each station. Then, they release students to each station in ten-minute increments.

One co-teacher leads the first station, which focuses on writing claims. The co-teacher uses direct instruction and modeling to lead students through writing claims in both English and Spanish. After the modeling, students practice formulating claims using mini whiteboards, allowing for immediate feedback in real time. At the second station, which the other co-teacher leads, students delve into finding details and evidence within a text they have recently read. This station emphasizes critical reading and analytical skills as students learn to discern relevant information. After initial modeling by the co-teacher, students receive mini whiteboards to write down important details they find in the text. The co-teacher provides feedback one on one to students as they find details. With both co-teachers actively leading the first two stations, the third station asks students to work independently on a worksheet that provides worked examples to illustrate correct usage of grammar and punctuation conventions before students practice them.

After students have completed the stations, their next task is to take the written claims and details and formulate a short paragraph. Co-teachers provide time for them to write the paragraph in English. However, for a lesson the next day, the goal is to then write that same paragraph in Spanish. Students get opportunities within the stations to prepare for combining the skills they focused on with teacher-led instruction as they are gradually released for additional practice and feedback.

Instructional Strategies in Action: Putting Strategies Together With Co-Teaching

The previous section summarized a wide variety of popular instructional strategies; now we look at how they fall into various categories within instructional domains. Figure 6.1 (page 112) provides an organizer to sort strategies into domains, which can help teachers when designing their final co-taught lesson plans. This reiterates the instructional design work we discussed in chapter 5 (figure 5.7, page 95). Placing strategies within domains is a useful way to think about when and where in a co-taught lesson to integrate them. It also may help when selecting ed tech to integrate with the strategies to further amplify them and make them accessible anywhere inside and outside the classroom.

Engagement	Collaboration	Assessment	Feedback
Notice and wonder: Students receive an image, video, 3-D representation, or written statement to view and to think about. After time to process, students write out three to four observations of what they notice. Then, teachers prompt students to write down one to two questions on what they wonder about that particular phenomenon and what they may want to learn more about. According to preference, teachers weave student-to-student conversations and whole-class discussions into this strategy (Rumack & Huinker, 2019).	**Think, write, pair, share:** Teachers present students with a prompt or problem and ask them to think. After providing wait time, teachers allow them to write an answer or solve the problem at hand. Once the time has elapsed, they pair with a partner. During the group discussion, teachers prompt them to outline the steps they used to solve the problem and to discuss their answer. Last, pairs share with the class each partner's methodology and answer (Kagan & Kagan, 2009; Karge, 2023b).	**Retrieval practice as a formative assessment:** Students receive physical or digital flash cards or slides that ask them to problem solve or recall information from a previous class session. This methodology can help boost long-term memory and retention (Roediger & Butler, 2011). This can occur anytime within the scope of the lesson but often takes place at the beginning and end of the lesson to gauge student performance and understanding.	**Whole-class and small-group feedback:** Teachers provide positive and reinforcing feedback to the entire class with major trends in two to three bullet points. Then, they give specific and actionable feedback, including steps to help students see where they are going and how to get there during small-group instruction.

FIGURE 6.1: Instructional strategy organizer.

*Visit **go.SolutionTree.com/instruction** for a free reproducible version of this figure.*

Now, let's see the strategies discussed previously together with co-teaching strategies. After outlining how to incorporate instructional strategies into our lessons, we'll provide two examples of how they look in action along with co-teaching strategies as the overarching umbrella. As you read these examples, think about what we covered in chapter 5 (page 81) and so far in this chapter regarding planning co-teaching lessons and instructional strategies. Additionally, to make these concepts come together, review figure 6.2, which encapsulates co-teaching strategies, instructional strategies, and the gradual release of responsibility.

Co-Teaching Strategies	Instructional Strategies Used			
Conversation teaching	Scaffolding	Thinking routines: notice and wonder	Cooperative learning strategies: think, write, pair, share	Gradual release of responsibility ↓
Parallel teaching	Explicit instruction and modeling	Retrieval practice: digital flash cards	Formative assessment: interactive slideshow practice problems	

FIGURE 6.2: Co-teaching strategies followed by instructional strategies.

Recall, as discussed earlier in the chapter, co-teaching and teaching in general are dynamic. In the examples we provide, it is evident how co-teaching and instructional strategies change throughout the lesson. The gradual release of responsibility is also noticeable because students will receive more independence and autonomy as the lesson and unit progress. We provide two examples to illustrate these shifts in action—elementary and secondary—in which we identify strategies.

Example 1: Elementary STEM Lesson on Measurement

Two co-teachers implement a science, technology, engineering, and mathematics (STEM) lesson in which students build a catapult and then measure how far the projectiles go. The learning objective is the ability to measure the distance from one object to another using a measuring tool. In a two-hour block, the co-teachers implement a lesson that helps students reactivate prior knowledge on measurement and includes formative assessment to gauge students' knowledge. For guided practice and independent practice, the co-teachers devise measurement stations using multiple classroom objects. The group collaboration activity on building the catapult and measurement stations commences after the stations. Following this, another formative assessment on measurement takes place.

With the stage set for the trajectory of the lesson, let's discuss the integrated co-teaching and instructional strategies. First, to activate prior knowledge using conversation teaching, the co-teachers provide the objective and focus of the lesson along with an opportunity to implement a thinking routine that asks students to use a notice-and-wonder protocol related to a series of measurements. The co-teachers ask students to outline what they notice about the measurements and then discuss what they wonder about the measurements. The co-teachers note major observations on the board and jot down the questions that will remain for the rest of the lesson. Co-teachers generally preplan various roles related to a lesson like this, such as who jots down major observations on the board. However, seasoned co-teacher partnerships may be more spontaneous, with both co-teachers writing observations on the board using the team teaching co-teaching strategy.

Students receive a formative assessment using Pear Deck for interactive slides, which ask them to complete four measurement questions. These questions use retrieval practice to determine whether students can complete a task as well as recall how to measure the distance between two objects. As students complete the formative assessment, each co-teacher moves between one teach, one observe and one teach, one support as they determine real-time trends in the assessment results and support students with questions. When students complete the assessment, the co-teachers give them a review document that focuses on the types of measurements they have worked on and what they will practice in today's lesson.

Once students have completed the formative assessment, guided instruction begins with each teacher modeling several measurement examples using one teach, one support. Each student has a ruler and objects to measure so they can mimic and practice measuring as they go through a series of three examples. While one teacher models at the front of the classroom using a document camera to project for the whole class, the other teacher assists students following along. After the guided practice sequence, the co-teachers give directions for a series of stations in which students will measure several objects for practice and record the measurements. The co-teachers form students into groups assigned to four curated stations with eight-minute intervals. The co-teachers both place themselves at a station, where they use alternative teaching to monitor and provide feedback based on student performance.

After stations are complete, students assemble on the carpet for a brain break followed by directions for the catapult activity, in which they create a catapult and receive five bean projectiles, which they will use later to compete with their classmates. After providing directions, the co-teachers divide the class into groups of three. Shifting between conversation and interactive co-teaching, the co-teachers show students how to create the catapult and measure the distance the objects travel using a tape measure. Students receive a handout on which to document their measurements. As students disperse to various workstations around the classroom, both co-teachers implement the one teach, one support strategy as they go to each group of students in turn to assist and provide feedback while students build their catapults.

As students complete the catapults, the co-teachers merge the small groups into two larger groups in which groups of three students compete against each other as they test their catapults and measure the distance of their projectiles. Parallel teaching takes place as each co-teacher facilitates and monitors one of the two groups. After the top team for each group is finalized, the class meets as a whole group, and the finalist groups of three compete against each other in a quick final round. After the competition ends, co-teachers ask students to complete a very similar formative assessment on the interactive slides once again as their exit slip before moving into their prelunch routine. As students complete the assessment, the co-teachers use one teach, one support by roving around the room teaching and supporting students who have questions and observing and analyzing the trends of the assessment results.

Example 2: Secondary English Lesson

In a middle school classroom, two co-teachers have designed a writing lesson focused on crafting body paragraphs and integrating evidence. As the lesson begins, the slideshow projected on the board illustrates the learning objectives and agenda for the class period, including a focus on writing body paragraphs and embedding evidence. Both co-teachers use the conversation co-teaching strategy as they begin the class by outlining the learning objectives and agenda. Then, as a formative writing activity, students receive an informational text about the Statue of Liberty along with the task of identifying evidence and writing a body paragraph. Both co-teachers move between one teach, one observe and one teach, one support as they provide the directions, hand out the documents, and give students ten minutes to complete the task. Covertly, one of the teachers provides several of the students with a modified text at a lower reading level along with supports such as embedded sentence frames for their paragraphs.

After students have finished the formative writing activity, each co-teacher works together through interactive co-teaching to explain and annotate the text, find evidence, call on students to provide insight, and then write a short paragraph. One teacher is at the computer, highlighting the text and controlling the presentation, while the other teacher is at the front of the classroom, providing direct instruction to the class. Sometimes, the teachers trade places and use conversation co-teaching as they further explain how to write the paragraph using the identified evidence. Additionally, using a randomizer app to cold call students, the co-teacher on the device asks members of the class to demonstrate a worked example to model this skill.

Following the formative assessment, the co-teachers outline a series of three stations to work on writing body paragraphs. Each station focuses on the following elements: (1) identifying evidence, (2) citing evidence, and (3) incorporating evidence into a paragraph by writing one. This station-rotation strategy takes place using elements of blended learning in the physical classroom. Students do not physically move through stations 1 and 2. They stay stationary, working through the stations of identifying and then citing evidence, practicing specific skills as outlined in the lesson's objectives. Co-teachers move students of various ability levels to two sections of the class and use parallel teaching to teach and support students as they progress through the station tasks.

After the first two stations are complete, both teachers move to the front of the classroom and model, once again, through interactive and conversation teaching, students' responsibilities during their group work to write a paragraph based on the evidence they have found and cited. The co-teachers provide a model paragraph that they display on the board, using direct instruction and modeling. Only when students get to the final station will they move into groups of three to collaborate on writing the paragraph. The co-teachers organize the two large sections of the class into groups of three for this final station. Both co-teachers observe and provide support to the groups. Co-teachers may stop the entire class and provide feedback if groups are off task or trends among the groups demonstrate that reteaching needs to take place. Each student turns in their paragraph on the LMS, but for now, each group submits one student's work to share with the rest of the class.

Co-teachers project a few submitted paragraphs anonymously on the board and provide feedback. They switch between conversation co-teaching and one teach, one observe as they call on students to provide feedback about the draft. One of the co-teachers highlights these areas of feedback and then jots down brief notes. Students then complete a short Google Form summarizing everything they have covered and reflecting on how they did. After class, co-teachers check the LMS to review student feedback from the form to reveal key positive and reinforcement feedback to the class for next time and then quickly review individual students' Google Form responses to help prepare for their next class session.

Conclusion

Throughout this chapter, we provided examples of how to take instructional strategies along with the gradual release of responsibility and incorporate them directly into co-teaching strategies. The co-teaching strategies act as an umbrella under which to integrate various instructional strategies throughout the lesson. Additionally, with the gradual release of responsibility in mind, the hope is to provide less and less support and fewer scaffolds so students can grow more independent as the lesson progresses. An element of dynamic change allows for fluctuation between co-teaching strategies and instructional strategies throughout. Additionally, co-teachers should monitor and adjust instruction based on student needs. Therefore, having a clear set of co-teaching strategies and instructional strategies you are comfortable with is a huge factor in your success. Accepting change and, further, being proactive to enact change are key factors to consider as you design and implement your lessons and integrate the co-teaching and instructional strategies.

> **ADDITIONAL RESOURCES TO CONSIDER AFTER READING THIS CHAPTER**
> - The article **"The Essential 5" (https://bit.ly/4c4oksY)** is a great starting point for using cooperative learning strategies designed by the professional development company and publisher Kagan.
> - The book *How Teaching Happens: Seminal Works in Teaching and Teacher Effectiveness and What They Mean in Practice* by Paul Kirschner, Carl Hendrick, and Jim Heal (2022) synthesizes research about teaching and explains how it can be used in teachers' daily instructional practice.
> - *Engage 11* by Belinda Dunnick Karge (2014) provides engagement strategies geared toward co-teachers in inclusive, diverse classrooms.
> - *Making Thinking Visible: How to Promote Engagement, Understanding, and Independence for All Learners* by Ron Ritchhart, Mark Church, and Karin Morrison (2011) offers a collection of practices that will help teachers ensure their instructional strategies are engaging students.

Reflection and Action: Square, Circle, and Triangle

Directions: After reading chapter 6, write down your thoughts on the chapter's content in each shape. First, what is one thing that squared with your thinking? Second, what is one question still circling your mind about the chapter? Third, what are three points you'll remember and then put into action?

The use of AI for initial planning has opened lots of conversation around our co-teachers. They appreciate seeing how AI can build the first draft of a lesson plan, giving them time to individualize and reflect on how the components will work with their own students. Editing and revising is not as time consuming as initial drafting. I see quality in the lessons my co-teachers are implementing—lots of inquiry and depth of knowledge.

—T. Willis, high school principal, personal communication, February 2, 2024

CHAPTER 7

Co-Teaching in Classrooms Without Boundaries

Co-teaching has been around for a long time. It has even been conducted within online classroom settings for years (Kim, Woodruff, Klein, & Vaughn, 2006). As co-teaching becomes more mainstream, ever-improving ed tech tools, the COVID-19 pandemic, and the advent of generative AI have paved the way to further practice and improve on instructional settings and modalities on in ways we could not have previously imagined, both in preK–12 and higher education (Eriksson, Jaskari, & Kinnunen, 2020; Kim & Pratt, 2023). As a result, we have seen co-teaching classrooms move between in-person, online, and blended learning classroom settings, which opens the door for further innovation.

Co-teachers have the opportunity, with the alignment of instructional strategies and ed tech tools, to use co-teaching within any classroom setting. The following narrative summarizes our experience with these shifts:

> *During the beginning of the pandemic, our co-teaching class went from fully in person to online. Throughout March 2020 and since, across the world, co-teachers have had to navigate teaching in person, fully online, and in blended classroom settings supporting a wide array of students. Co-teaching within multiple classroom settings meant creating systems and strategies that worked within each. We focused on UDL within the combination of two LMSs (Seesaw and Google Classroom), the use of think, write, pair, share for gradual release, station rotation with breakout rooms, interactive slides, and formative assessment through Pear Deck, Google Forms, or the Formative tool for various assessments. Additionally, over time, we had support from the implementation of Paper, which provided opportunities for students to receive one-on-one tutoring. Combined, these instructional practices and ed tech integrations created many opportunities for learning and direct support for students that were not possible before 2020.*
>
> *Ultimately, what we did as co-teachers is determine how to provide support and monitor student progress within these digital spaces. We learned that this was possible. While not ideal for all students, we learned that each of these strategies can transcend digital*

> *and physical realms and be implemented within each. As a result, we learned that we can harness many aspects we did well while moving between various classroom settings and implementing them within our in-person co-teaching classrooms.*

Co-teachers can exist in multiple places and spheres at once. A co-teacher can be in person with students while another can be online and physically not in the same classroom space. Co-teachers can be in person and online simultaneously with one co-teacher teaching and the other one reviewing student responses and providing feedback. An interactive slideshow using Pear Deck or Nearpod makes this possible. Students might engage in formative assessment, cooperative learning, or thinking routines. As one teacher provides the scaffolds, prompts, and monitors the physical room, the other co-teacher sees the students' responses and provides feedback as individual messages or stops the class and provides whole-class feedback. Additionally, co-teachers can use AI within many education applications to make learning accessible, differentiated, and personalized. On top of this, teachers can build content and materials quickly and efficiently to meet their diverse learners' needs within a co-teaching class. The possibilities are endless! With the strategies and tools available, co-teachers can systematically respond to the diverse needs of their students in a student-centered way.

This chapter aims to conceptualize and illustrate how to use co-teaching strategies within any classroom setting. We provide examples of how co-teaching can shift from one classroom setting to another as well as how the roles of the co-teachers may change when settings change, such as certain instructional strategies they select and ed tech tools to help deliver this instruction. Last, we discuss how generative AI can act as each co-teacher's copilot in classrooms without instructional boundaries. We illustrate how this looks for co-teachers in the "new normal" and provide examples of how to put it into practice.

> **Key Themes and Ideas**
> ☐ Instruction without boundaries
> ☐ Co-teaching with formative assessment to support differentiation and equity in physical and digital realms
> ☐ Generative AI and ed tech support in classrooms without boundaries

Instruction Without Boundaries

Instruction without boundaries represents classrooms that inhabit both physical and digital realms and can exist anywhere within the physical world and online digital spaces where we provide instruction and interact with students (Rhoads, McLaughlin, & Moore, 2022). This is all possible because of ed tech tools and instructional strategies that teachers can implement for effective instruction within in-person, online, and blended classroom settings. With the appropriate infrastructure in place—such as an LMS, ed tech tools for engagement, assessment, and collaboration, and students with devices and reliable connections—teachers and students can teach and learn from everywhere. The implications allow schools and teachers to be creative with how instruction can manifest as well as support diverse learners through formative assessment, differentiation, and equitable instructional practices that provide for deeper learning and student-centered learning opportunities.

Before moving through this chapter, review table 7.1. It outlines many of the ed tech and AI tools that are mentioned throughout this chapter. Each co-teaching strategy integrated with one of more of these tools can create physical and digital spaces for co-teaching classrooms without instructional boundaries.

TABLE 7.1: Key Ed Tech and AI Tools

Types of Ed Tech Tools	Sample Applications and Websites	Instructional Uses
AI tools	<ul><li>ChatGPT (https://chat.openai.com)</li><li>Google Gemini (https://gemini.google.com)</li><li>Claude (https://claude.ai)</li><li>Khanmigo (www.khanacademy.org/khan-labs)</li></ul>	Differentiating instruction, UDL, content creation, idea generation, student work assessment, and AI tutoring
LMSs	<ul><li>Canvas (www.instructure.com/canvas)</li><li>Schoology (www.powerschool.com/personalized-learning-cloud/schoology-learning)</li><li>Google Classroom (https://classroom.google.com)</li></ul>	Content delivery, feedback, document and data tracking
Interactive slides and video	<ul><li>Pear Deck (www.peardeck.com)</li><li>Curipod (https://curipod.com)</li><li>Nearpod (https://nearpod.com)</li><li>Edpuzzle (https://edpuzzle.com)</li></ul>	Anticipatory set, formative assessment, guided practice
Assessment tools	<ul><li>Formative (www.formative.com)</li><li>Quizizz (https://quizizz.com)</li><li>iReady (adaptive assessment; www.curriculumassociates.com)</li><li>Quizalize (adaptive assessment; www.quizalize.com)</li><li>MobyMax (adaptive assessment; www.mobymax.com)</li><li>ReadTheory (adaptive assessment; https://readtheory.org)</li></ul>	Formative and summative assessment
Content creation tools	<ul><li>Canva (www.canva.com)</li><li>Padlet (https://padlet.com)</li><li>Google Workspace (https://workspace.google.com; that is, Docs, Slides, Drawings, Sites, and Sheets)</li></ul>	Formative assessment and content creation

In the following sections, we discuss co-teaching in a world without instructional boundaries and provide examples of what co-teaching without instructional boundaries looks like.

Co-Teaching in a World Without Instructional Boundaries

The instructional world has opened significantly in preK–12 education. Even if the class is designated only to be in person, it contains physical and digital realms that co-teachers must navigate. As a result, the co-teaching instructional strategies we have discussed throughout this book must and can be adapted to classrooms that have both instructional realms present. Table 7.2 provides ways to adapt and modify co-teaching strategies to in-person, online, or blended classroom settings. These examples give insight as to how both co-teachers can be present in both realms and effectively serve their students in each.

TABLE 7.2: Overview of Co-Teaching Instructional Strategies Without Boundaries

Co-Teaching Instructional Strategies	Traditional Definition	Example of Use in a World Without Instructional Boundaries
One teach, one assist	One educator teaches and another assists. The educator who is teaching typically shares the instructional information to students.	One teacher monitors real-time data and student work products on various formative digital assessment tools, strategically providing whole-class and individualized feedback and support, while the other teacher engages the class in direct explicit instruction through an interactive slideshow.
One teach, one observe	One educator takes the lead and imparts the knowledge or leads a discussion. The second educator observes.	While one teacher provides guided practice with embedded formative assessment questions, the other teacher observes and monitors real-time student data and work products through one or more ed tech tools to then determine trends within the class to provide feedback, differentiate instruction, or design future lessons.
One teach, one support	One educator provides the instruction, and the other "does something to enhance and support the instruction" (Karge, 2015, p. 6). The supporting educator might create a visual, paraphrase the instructional content, or take notes on a whiteboard or computer.	One teacher teaches the class synchronously in person or online while the other supports students within one or more breakout rooms. After instruction, both co-teachers teach or support students in physical or digital stations that students rotate through.
Graze-and-tag teaching	One educator teaches while the other educator "grazes" (that is, strolls the room viewing what students are working on and how they understand the concepts); the shifting of roles occurs when the other educator adds or teaches another concept.	Both teachers monitor student responses on the interactive slides while students are in different groups at tables. Each co-teacher then provides different levels of support based on student responses they see within specific groups in real time as well as monitor and adjust their instruction.
Parallel teaching	Each teacher teaches simultaneously the same lesson to half the class (that is, to different groups of students). Typically, the teachers are in the same room at the same time. If there is an open area outside or a neighboring classroom, sometimes one group will move to another location.	During the lesson, one co-teacher is teaching part of the class in person while the other is teaching the other half of the class synchronously online. Both teachers monitor similar formative assessments that provide real-time data, which they can see simultaneously. After the synchronous instruction, co-teachers meet briefly to discuss patterns in student performance and adjust for the second portion of class.

Station teaching	Prior to class, the educators plan the goals and objectives for the lesson. Sometimes they develop a generic plan, and then the educator working at a specific station spends more time developing their individual station. The students are divided into heterogeneous groups. Teacher 1 is assigned to teach one group, and teacher 2 is assigned to work with an additional group. Sometimes, there are additional independent groups. The students rotate from one station to another. Every student participates in every station.	Co-teachers have students in the classroom rotate to various stations where they do physical and digital tasks (each student has a device). Co-teachers monitor the digital and physical student work products. Additionally, co-teachers can be present within an in-person set of stations, while another group of students are present within online synchronous stations, where one co-teacher guides them in a similar fashion to the in-person students.
Alternative teaching	As educators plan, they consider how students will be divided into groups. Teacher 1 works with the enrichment group, while teacher 2 reteaches a concept.	Teachers support students within in-person groups or online groups simultaneously. Additionally, teachers can switch to and from online and in-person stations as needed or as the class moves between being in person, synchronously online together, or in open office hours.
Conversation teaching	Both teachers are the "stars" of their own reality show. The co-teachers preplan the content and then have an educational conversation in front of the students.	Both teachers, whether synchronously in person, online, or in a recorded video, provide direct instruction to students. This can occur through each modality over the course of the year.
Role-play teaching	Role-play teaching allows the co-teaching team to plan and share a think-aloud, characterization, or debate in skit format with the entire class.	Whether together or individually, co-teachers synchronously role-play in person, online, or in a recording for students to view asynchronously. Additionally, one teacher can role-play in person while the other co-teacher role-plays to students who are online.
Interactive teaching	Villa and colleagues (2013) refer to interactive teaching as complementary co-teaching. They describe the practice as one where co-teachers do something to enhance the instruction provided by the other teacher.	One teacher interacts with students synchronously on an interactive slideshow or whiteboard, while the other co-teacher reviews data, moves students into breakout rooms or small groups for review and reteaching, or provides instruction simultaneously with the entire class while monitoring student progress.
Shared teaching	Collaborative teaching teams of educators fully share all responsibilities for the classroom, doing what traditionally one teacher has done (plan, teach, assess, and reflect) and taking full responsibility for every aspect of the classroom.	Regardless of where the class setting may be and what modality of instruction is occurring, both co-teachers share the planning, instruction, and assessment of students.

Source: Karge, 2015; Rhoads et al., 2022.

After reviewing the co-teaching strategies and how they can adapt to classrooms without instructional boundaries, consider further how to implement them within your co-teaching classroom. We would like you to think about three questions that can help you assess how you can implement instructional strategies within the physical and digital spaces where students and teachers interact within your classroom.

> 1. What instructional strategies in your tool kit can be integrated with the ed tech tools you have available?
> 2. What ed tech tools do you have available to utilize?
> 3. What content and skills are you trying to teach your students?

Once you have analyzed these questions, you can begin planning and testing these adaptations. You can determine the effectiveness of these strategies and integrations within your classroom setting based on how they can adapt to your students and instructional learning objectives.

Examples of Co-Teaching Without Instructional Boundaries

After reviewing how co-teaching and instructional strategies can manifest within classrooms without instructional boundaries, let's dive into lesson examples of what this may look like in primary and secondary co-teaching classroom. The goal is to illustrate what various lessons, teacher actions, and co-teaching and instructional strategies look like integrated together within physical and digital classroom spaces.

PRIMARY CLASSROOM: PROJECT-BASED LEARNING WITH PHYSICAL AND DIGITAL CENTERS

In a third-grade classroom, two co-teachers plan a unit to work on reading, writing, and research skills. Both decide to use the topic of animal habitats and determine their lessons will involve various stations to receive direct instruction, have opportunities to read curated research, and practice skills through adaptive assessment and practice tools. There are physical and digital stations after students receive primary instruction together as a class.

To begin the lesson, both co-teachers use interactive and conversation teaching to introduce the topic of animal habitats. They describe them with a whole-class notice-and-wonder protocol, in which they show various animal habitats on the overhead projector using 3-D visuals. Through the notice-and-wonder protocol, the co-teachers connect prior knowledge with opportunities to think and discuss characteristics associated with each habitat. While students are collaborating and writing down thoughts in pairs, both teachers graze the room to support them. After they review each habitat, the co-teachers place a collaboratively created digital anchor chart both on the front board and the students' LMS, Seesaw, as evidence for the students to use when they are learning more about each habitat. The teachers are team teaching as they collaborate on the digital anchor chart.

After the first part of the lesson, the co-teachers outline four stations, two physical and two digital. The physical stations involve direct instruction provided by each co-teacher to support students improving their reading and taking notes on passages involving each habitat. At the third station, students work on i-Ready to practice reading, phonics, and vocabulary at their own level. Students at the fourth station watch an Edpuzzle video on various habitats that asks them formative assessment questions. Groups of five to seven students can move from their seats to the tables where co-teachers provid instruction and then back to their original seats to work on the digital content.

Each station is designed to last ten to fifteen minutes with a three-to-five-minute rotation time, getting students out of their seats and moving. Students can work on the digital stations during class time and resume them before or after school. Both co-teachers use quantitative and qualitative measures to determine student progress by monitoring how they respond to their direct instruction and feedback while reviewing their Edpuzzle and i-Ready scores during each station rotation.

Once the stations are complete, the co-teachers ask students to summarize in writing or through an audio recording on Seesaw what they remember about each animal habitat they read about and researched throughout the stations. After the ten-minute summarization activity, each co-teacher asks students to choose their favorite habitat and then walk to the corner of the room designated as that habitat to do a quick pair-share with their classmates on why that specific animal habitat was their favorite.

SECONDARY CLASSROOM: PARALLEL TEACHING STATION ROTATION

In an eleventh-grade English class during a two-hour block period, both co-teachers are teaching the novel *The Great Gatsby*. In addition to the novel, they are teaching important writing skills, such as constructing a thesis statement that includes a main argument and providing evidence and analysis to back it up. The co-teachers are using excerpts from the novel as an instructional vehicle to build these skills.

As the class begins, one member of the co-teaching team employs a formative assessment using a Quizizz multiple-choice quiz as both co-teachers ask students several questions to activate their prior knowledge about the various parts of a thesis statement. Additionally, the quiz includes questions about how they would support various statements with evidence and pieces of analysis. Based on the results displayed in a data dashboard, both co-teachers know going into the lesson likely areas of growth and those likely needing less attention.

Once the assessment is over, the co-teachers cover the agenda and unveil stations for three skills: (1) thesis statement arguments, (2) thesis statement evidence statements, and (3) finding evidence within several text excerpts to support newly created thesis statements. Before moving into the stations, co-teachers team teach together to discuss each station, modeling the skills through direct instruction and worked examples and using the front interactive SMART Board and Google Slides to depict examples. While this guided practice and modeling is taking place, the co-teachers screencast their team teaching experiences to upload to the LMS for student review and for students who are not present.

After the co-teachers review the stations and skills for about fifteen minutes, the stations begin. The co-teachers divide the class in half; each takes a half. They use parallel teaching, meaning both halves of the class receive the same instruction; in this case, it also means the whole class begins with station 1. Each station is designed to last twenty minutes. Both co-teachers instruct and support their half of the class as they complete a short asynchronous interactive slideshow on Pear Deck to front-load the skill. This is followed by a practice activity, after which co-teachers ask students to provide each part of their work (that is, thesis statement argument, evidence statement, and analysis) after each station on a Padlet board. The co-teachers then use this work as examples to provide whole-class feedback on writing strengths and areas of growth for each skill during the rotations.

As students complete each station, both co-teachers work with their parallel student groups to collect data in real time to support them in building each of these skills. To support each student in their work, both co-teachers use their iPad and computer to provide feedback as students practice each form of writing.

After the third station, students receive a Quizizz formative assessment that is similar to the one they completed at the beginning of class. Question order differs, and one additional question appears at the end that asks students to write a complete thesis statement that contains both the argument and evidence statement. The co-teachers assess these skills in comparison to the previous formative assessment to see if students can take what they practiced and perform well when asked to put the skills they are learning into action. After the formative assessment, co-teachers open all the activities to students to work on asynchronously outside of class for practice; they are also available to any students who may have missed class that day.

SECONDARY CLASSROOM: TWO CO-TEACHERS TEACHING SYNCHRONOUSLY ONLINE

In a twelfth-grade English class, two co-teachers teach synchronously online through Zoom. An interactive slideshow using Google Slides and Pear Deck is active, which allows for both co-teachers to monitor students' progress as they integrate various formative assessment and cooperative learning strategies. They begin class by using think, write, pair, share to activate prior knowledge and act as a formative assessment. Students receive a prompt to think, write a response, discuss, and share with the entire class. Being synchronously online allows for consistent monitoring of student thinking by each co-teacher, as the edits on each individual student slideshow are visible. As the strategy progresses after the writing sequence, the co-teachers break the class into pairs using breakout rooms. Both co-teachers check on pairs of students as they meet to discuss their answers along with the additional prompt to synthesize the responses they have created so they can then share with the class. As students generate their responses in the breakout rooms, both co-teachers review and discuss within a backchannel chat how they will formulate follow-up questions and what they may need to reteach.

After students have come back to the main meeting to share, the lesson plan calls for an online station rotation using station teaching; both co-teachers teach two interrelated topics that will converge after the guided practice portion of the lesson. The co-teachers use two breakout rooms and generate two Padlet boards related to the two topics. For two fifteen-minute segments, the co-teachers use brainstorming, direct instruction, and concept mapping to teach the two topics. They have two options during this time: (1) they move throughout the two groups, or (2) one or both stations are teacher led, depending on the lesson, student needs, and so on. Since both co-teachers have access to both Padlets, they can see trends related to student thinking. After each fifteen-minute rotation of the two groups, they all converge in the main meeting room. Here, they discuss independent practice tasks, and a final concept-mapping exercise occurs where students draw on their breakout sessions with their teachers.

The next phase is for students to work in breakout rooms in groups of three to discuss, summarize, and link their current research to the topics discussed in class using the two original Padlets, which all groups of three can access. Breakout rooms run for five minutes total, and both co-teachers move to each breakout room to facilitate. This might look like both co-teachers checking in on each room, or each room might receive a check-in from one or the other. Once the breakout room time has elapsed, co-teachers facilitate a digital gallery walk and final discussion. During the final discussion, one of the co-teachers creates a final Padlet and places the link to it on the LMS. Once the discussion is final, the co-teachers assign students a task playlist that asks them to first independently review three resources in the form of a text, podcast, and slideshow, which they do asynchronously outside of class time to extend their learning.

Co-Teaching With Formative Assessment to Support Differentiation and Equity in Physical and Digital Realms

As we've emphasized throughout this chapter, instruction has no boundaries; it does not have to be face to face. It can be in a variety of formats, including but not limited to online modules, asynchronous viewing of a teacher or student presentation, or synchronous instruction online. With the emergence of AI, learning could even occur solely from a computer, tablet, or mobile device, with co-teachers providing interventions when students need additional support and reteaching (Fitzpatrick et al., 2023; Rhoads et al., 2022). Underpinning this notion are the possibilities offered by real-time formative assessment (Spady & Karge, 2022).

Co-teachers can deploy learning opportunities driven by student performance in real time. Students can quickly take a formative assessment on a skill or content area and then receive a series of lessons that focus on continued practice or refinement of that skill. On the other hand, if a student excels in this skill, lessons can extend and become more difficult, which expands on already learned skills and content areas. Tools such as iReady, Quizalize, and ReadTheory provide these types of opportunities. Student data appear on dashboards that co-teachers can review and use to make real-time, data-driven instructional decisions to optimize their instruction. As a result, co-teachers can differentiate instruction on the spot, monitor and adjust, and personalize and create student-centered instructional opportunities within the sequence of their lessons. Along with formative assessment and differentiation and support possibilities, the real-time nature of this instruction provides opportunities for students to receive access to equitable content and instruction at any time.

Formative Assessment

Teachers have an arsenal of formative assessment tools from which they can draw real-time data on student performance at any moment within a lesson (Stiggins, 2017; Spady & Karge, 2022). Easily deployable from an LMS, link, or QR code, a wide variety of digital tools allow teachers to see and analyze student thinking and performance related to the concepts and skills they are teaching. Co-teachers who can access the data can both monitor and adjust the strategies they are using for the entire class, groups of students, or individual students. Additionally, teachers can use adaptive ed tech tools formatively and for ongoing practice to cater lessons to students based on their ability level; these tools further allow co-teachers to monitor the data produced during these activities. As a result, co-teachers monitoring formative assessment and adaptive practice data can be extremely data-driven and use these data to plan in real time and, accordingly, longitudinally in their lesson and unit design to meet the needs of their students.

Differentiation and Support Possibilities

With the advent of formative assessment, adaptive practice and assessment tools, and digital tools, there are many ways to differentiate through a data-driven approach in which students can receive additional support within physical and digital learning spaces. Co-teachers can see student performance daily, which can then inform instruction in real time, support, and short- and long-term planning. Co-assessing can occur frequently since the teachers are together (Guise, Hegg, Hoellwarth, & O'Shea, 2022). Co-teachers can also embed supports into almost every task they ask their students to complete. And scaffolded choice and differentiation, such as students performing tasks that meet them where they are, is possible and scalable with ed tech. The examples in this section illustrate each of these differentiations and supports within the classroom without instructional boundaries and what they look like within co-taught classes.

As we've seen, formative assessment allows co-teachers to see student performance and thinking in real time, which allows them to make data-driven instructional decisions (Guise et al., 2022). The data teachers collect helps inform the differentiations and supports they plan to provide their students. It is a critical bridge they will always have to cross before building in further differentiations and supports for students. With two teachers working together, seeing students complete a digital formative assessment can allow them to see trends. They can also distribute various types of formative assessments to the wide range of learners they have in their class. Examples of this include tools such as i-Ready, MobyMax, and Quizalize, along with the likes of Quizzizz and Kahoot!, to create adaptive assessments that meet learners' ability for individualized practice as well as fun and engaging opportunities for retrieval practice and data collection. Teachers can use these formative assessments and adaptive assessments and practice anytime and anywhere within a lesson sequence. Now, let's focus on supports and differentiations that come from the opportunities that digital and anytime formative assessment allow.

DIFFERENTIATIONS

Digital templates with embedded supports that teachers can differentiate for various students and groups of students are key. For example, a playlist template (figure 7.1) allows students to all complete three distinct tasks that require them to passively take in information that they later use to complete a culminating assessment. Students choose one of three tasks they already know how to complete to put the information they have processed into action. Examples of these tasks could include a student podcast or video response, a *sketchnote* (a style of note taking that incorporates writing and visual elements), a three-paragraph essay, an infographic, and more. There are many possibilities, depending on what co-teachers have taught their students to complete to demonstrate they have met their learning targets and standards.

Step	Task Directions	Standards and Skills Assessed
1	Watch a video on the main characters of *The Great Gatsby*. Answer several comprehension questions and summarize each character's role in the story.	Understanding of key concepts and the ability to identify main characters' impact on the plot of a story
2	Read two articles from *The New York Times* published in the 1920s that provide overarching key details about the setting and societal themes of the time. Paraphrase the articles, answer questions, and develop a timeline related to important events that took place during the 1920s and discuss how they may impact character motivations of *The Great Gatsby*.	Reading comprehension, summarization, and how multiple texts interact with each other
3	Complete a digital timeline on a Google Slides presentation that provides five key events that happened in *The Great Gatsby* as well as the historical context and the impact of the main characters on each of the plot points you provide.	Synthesis of information from outside articles, a novel, and digital content to develop a digital work product that can sequentially outline a series of events
Culminating Assessment	Develop a video, podcast, or sketchnote that represents key characters, events, or themes from *The Great Gatsby*. Develop the product based on a rubric measuring your ability to apply your knowledge of the story, outside resources, and digital literacy. You will present your content to the class by recording a short three-minute presentation, which will be posted to Canvas for your classmates to view.	Creative expression and application of knowledge and communicating ideas in various formats

FIGURE 7.1: Playlist template example.

*Visit **go.SolutionTree.com/instruction** for a free reproducible version of this figure.*

SUPPORTS

Students have never before had so many supports to support accessibility for learning skills and content; many options are available that co-teachers can embed into learning experiences through the digital devices and ed tech tools they use in their classrooms (American Institutes for Research, 2018; Crossland et al., 2017; U.S. Department of Education Office of Educational Technology, 2017). These supports include immersive readers, translators, closed captions, video, audio, dyslexia reading tools, and many more; teachers can include them if students receive the appropriate modeling and consistency to regularly use them within the course of instruction. Co-teachers can also combine physical tools to support students, which can create a powerful combination of opportunities to meet students where they are in their learning. Examples of these supports include three instructional scenarios we will briefly explore in third-, seventh-, and eleventh-grade co-taught classes.

In a third-grade classroom, students are working on a reading comprehension activity on their tablets. As an automated reader reads the story aloud, students who struggle with certain words can use a built-in dyslexia aid such as Google Read&Write to highlight and separate syllables, making reading smoother. Meanwhile, multilingual learners use an immersive reader to translate challenging words into their native language, ensuring comprehension. One co-teacher uses physical flash cards with images to reinforce vocabulary in a small group that rotates throughout the lesson, while the other co-teacher guides students through the digital tools and roves around the classroom supporting students with just-in-time direct instruction.

Jump to a seventh-grade science class, where students are learning about photosynthesis through a video to front-load content before diving deeper into specific details related to the processes of photosynthesis. Closed captions on the video may improve accessibility for students who are deaf or hard of hearing, and a translator assists multilingual learners who have access to the video on their own devices to watch again later in the lesson. The class then breaks into groups, with one creating a physical model of the photosynthesis process steps with craft supplies, overseen by one co-teacher while the other co-teacher guides the other group in using a digital interactive diagram to explore each step.

Last, in an eleventh-grade history class, students are researching World War I. They watch interviews with historians and use audio tools to slow down or speed up the playback. One co-teacher offers a workshop on using the digital dyslexia tools and immersive readers for those who find the old texts challenging, while the other co-teacher sets up a station with physical copies of primary source documents, magnifiers, and reading guides to help students dive deeper.

A summary of available tools and their uses in the classroom is available in table 7.3.

TABLE 7.3: Digital Ed Tech Tool Supports Integrated Into Classroom Instruction

Support Type	Digital or External Tools	Implementation in Classroom
Reading comprehension	Automated readers, dyslexia aids (for example, Google Read&Write), and immersive readers	Automated reading aloud, highlighting and separating syllables, translating challenging words
Scientific processes	Closed captions, translators, and digital interactive diagrams	Accessibility for students who are deaf or hard of hearing, language support for multilingual learners, and interactive exploration of scientific processes
History research	Audio tools, digital dyslexia tools, immersive readers, and physical resources (such as primary sources, magnifiers, reading guides)	Playback adjustment for audio, reading support for challenging texts, and hands-on analysis of primary sources

Equitable Instruction

Co-teachers have many opportunities to provide equitable learning to their students (Karten & Murawski, 2020). Instruction that takes place within physical and digital classroom environments can provide ample opportunities for all students to access instruction and the curriculum. Co-teachers can not only cover content in real time but also create content that helps students learn the content and skills beyond the lesson and unit they designed. For example, co-teachers can record and screencast all direct instruction and modeling moments of a lesson and place them on the class's LMS. Additionally, co-teachers can integrate the day's slideshow to go right next to that same content. They can even use tools such as Edpuzzle or Nearpod to place formative assessment questions within the screencast, which can also include closed captions translated into each student's first language.

The notion of interactive content availability on the LMS while collecting data is transformative. Students can continue to practice and extend their learning while both co-teachers can review the data available and then plan small-group or one-on-one instruction and supports for specific students. For example, teachers can place Quizlet digital flash cards within the LMS for students to practice with. They can include the very same flash card content on an asynchronous Quizizz where students can self-test and practice retrieval. Ultimately, both co-teachers can see over time and across multiple opportunities how much each student is practicing, what they are doing well, and any areas of growth.

Another element of creating equitable learning environments is that both teachers can be in physical and digital spaces at the same time. This means that while there may be physical stations present throughout the room with different tasks, each co-teacher can see students' progress in real time if most of the tasks require a digital work product. Using the various co-teaching strategies with this element in play provides opportunities to monitor and adjust instruction in that very moment as well as throughout the planning process. This provides an environment that ensures all students have access to high-quality instruction with the same opportunities. Accommodations can be made in real time for multilingual learners or students with disabilities. The supports are placed such that all students can learn at the same level as their peers. For example, co-teachers can embed supports within spaces where students are interacting with digital content. Additionally, since teachers can see student progress and performance in real time, they can use each student's accommodations by reviewing their work and providing necessary just-in-time direct instruction, reteaching, and other accommodations and modifications that may be placed in a student's IEP or 504 plan.

Generative AI and Ed Tech Support in Classrooms Without Boundaries

Generative AI has completely changed how teachers can approach lesson planning, differentiation and personalization, and adaptive ed tech to meet learner needs in physical and digital classroom spaces. We discuss planning with generative AI in chapter 5 (page 81). In this section, we build on this discussion to address creating content and materials for classroom instruction, using adaptive ed tech for assessment and personalized instruction, assessing students, and using AI to provide students with support 24/7. We also briefly discuss the ethical considerations of using AI.

Content Workflow for Classroom Instruction

Co-teachers can use generative AI to support them in their planning. Here, we want to touch on workflow, going beyond the prompts and planning of a lesson.

Let's jump into an example of workflow in action. For example, in a third-grade class, co-teachers want to differentiate a text the class is going to read, dissect, and then write about. In the planning process, both co-teachers also decide they will team teach the dissection of the text and then model the writing task through the one teach, one support strategy. Once that's been selected, co-teachers decide on the text they would like students to read. Then they can develop a prompt to change the text's reading level. After the generative AI creates the differentiated texts, co-teachers place them into a document or slides for students, uploading the content to the LMS and providing printouts to students. Co-teachers place the slides with the grade-level text into the slideshow that they will display and then teach from for the lesson, which is also uploaded to the LMS. The content is ready to be integrated into the lesson.

This workflow demonstrates the backend tasks necessary to prepare for a lesson in which co-teachers need to generate, differentiate, and then place content on multiple media for the lesson. This process does not take long with two co-teachers dividing the labor, especially with the support of AI as their copilot. Once this type of workflow becomes the norm, it takes drastically less time than it would without the help of AI.

Adaptive Assessment and Learning Tools to Personalize Instruction

Since approximately 2010, classrooms have seen a variety of ed tech tools adapt their assessments and lessons in response to student progress and performance. For example, a student may be taking an assessment on a tool like i-Ready, MobyMax, ReadTheory, or even a Smarter Balanced state assessment, in which a student's correct or incorrect response ultimately changes the difficulty of the next question. Now, these tools and many more do this while also taking data from a preassessment so that a teacher has input to generate assessments and lessons to teach or reteach a student a concept or skill, meeting the student where they currently are and taking into account how they have historically performed in that concept or skill.

With these tools, co-teachers can see student performance in real time as well as differentiate and personalize students' paths to learn concepts and skills. Independent practice is the ideal time to use these adaptive tools in co-taught classrooms. Assigning students short assessments and then follow-up lessons to provide opportunities for additional practice, reteaching, or extending their learning gives co-teachers a multitude of options to support all their students. Seeing student performance data in real time also allows them to strategically make decisions for further individualized one-on-one or small-group instruction. Therefore, during independent practice time, students may work independently on their lessons, but co-teachers may also work with students one on one and within small groups.

24/7 Tutors

With generative AI, there are a number of text-based tutors students can use to support their learning. One example is Khan Academy's Khanmigo tutor. Khan Academy's vast library of videos, lessons, and practice problems offers a twenty-four-hour tutor that uses the Socratic method to support student conceptual understanding. Instead of giving an answer and an explanation like ChatGPT, Claude, or Google Gemini, Khanmigo provides feedback one step at a time followed by a question students will need to answer to move forward.

We expect more resources like Khanmigo to appear and become viable options for co-teachers. Accessibility resources such as speech-to-text and the opportunity for an AI to visualize and model problems will be more available. However, like any tool, co-teachers must build routines for how they use it in their classes to support students. Without intentional digital routines and integrating the AI tutor into daily instruction, students will not engage to a high degree.

Student Assessment and Visible Learning in an AI World

With AI present in our lives, teachers must rethink assessment. We believe co-teachers should harness formative assessment and opportunities to see student thinking in real time to assess and provide feedback. Seeing this real-time performance gives co-teachers the ability to provide necessary individualized and whole-class support based on trends. Co-teachers can use AI to create formative assessments based on this capability in moments. For example, if co-teachers are assessing students on a problem, and the trend illustrates over half of the students in class are struggling with the distributive property, they can use a generative AI tool to produce subsequent problems that focus directly on the distributive property. On top of this, the AI tools can provide teachers with content in the form of notes and feedback to aid them in reteaching as they progress through the new set of problems. Using ed tech tools to see students' responses and problem solving in real time is critical. The low-tech solution is mini whiteboards, but the ed tech options are numerous. Tools such as Google Slides, Canva, Pear Deck, Nearpod, Padlet, and many more allow teachers to see progress for all their students in class. On top of these tools, adaptive AI-integrated tools use student data in real time to provide differentiated problem sets for students that co-teachers can see in the present and over time.

Even though assessment may change when co-teachers see student performance in real time, we can still use summative assessments as a mechanism for encouraging students to use AI to augment and amplify their work products. Co-teachers can scaffold projects so that students generate ideas and then need knowledge of the content and skills along with digital literacy skills to integrate them with the AI tool to create their final product. Teachers can integrate design thinking to scaffold projects (Hasso Plattner Institute of Design at Stanford, 2016), which will lead students on a journey of creating numerous final products they will revise before completing. At the end of the summative assessment, they can discuss and reflect on their step-by-step approach to creating this summative work product.

Ethical Considerations

There are many ethical considerations for co-teachers to consider when students use AI tools in their classrooms, the first of which is student data privacy. Whenever students use an AI tool, the data they input could be used for a wide variety of purposes that are not necessarily disclosed openly. Additionally, teachers need to consider that the more a student engages with an AI, the more the AI can learn about that student's behavior and tendencies. When interacting with an AI tool, co-teachers need to be aware that all data they input into an AI tool to generate content and reports should be anonymous. Avoid inputting names or associations related to data into an AI tool unless an agreement regarding student data privacy has been reached between the school, district, or educational organization with the company behind the AI tool being utilized. Third, co-teachers must understand the world of AI is ever-changing. We encourage teams to do ongoing research and ask questions about using AI and student privacy before thinking about implementing it within your classroom practice.

Cheating is another concern with AI tools. As with the advent of the internet and sites like Wikipedia, we must adjust how we assess students to prevent cheating. Co-teachers should focus their assessment on real-time formative assessment with summative assessments taking place in class. For project-based assignments, co-teachers should specify how students can or cannot use AI tools for the project. The project instructions should explicitly state this. On top of this, during project-based assessments, if AI is allowed for parts of the project, students should discuss, as part of the project, how they employed AI and outline their methodologies and workflow. Examples of these opportunities include student-recorded reflections and self-reflection surveys outlining AI usage for the assignment. With a balanced approach to assessment, co-teachers can avoid the pitfalls of AI while supporting students in learning to use it responsibly so they can be prepared for a world where this knowledge will be essential.

Conclusion

Instruction beyond boundaries with co-teachers inhabiting both physical and digital learning spaces is a recipe for inclusive, equitable, data-driven, and effective classrooms. Co-teachers can use co-teaching strategies as the basis for research-based instructional strategies implemented within physical and digital learning spaces. This is powerful practice, as co-teachers can see student progress in real time and monitor and adjust throughout the course of their lessons. Two teachers can do this much more easily and efficiently, as is evident in the examples we provided. Additionally, co-teachers can further differentiate and individualize instruction with strategy planning and the use of adaptive tools and supports. Last, intentional design and ed tech tools can help instruction be truly data driven, which can help stakeholders track student progress and support them in reaching their academic goals.

> **ADDITIONAL RESOURCES TO CONSIDER AFTER READING THIS CHAPTER**
> ▶ The **Technology Integration Matrix (https://fcit.usf.edu/matrix)** from the Florida Center for Instructional Technology is a framework of instructional strategies and ed tech tool integrations that teachers can use in the classroom. It provides lesson examples and videos of these ed tech integrations in action within K–12 classrooms. It can also be utilized as a rubric for the degree of ed tech integration taking place within a classroom.
> ▶ *Instruction Without Boundaries: Enhance Your Teaching Strategies With Technology Tools for Any Setting* by **Matthew Rhoads, Janelle McLaughlin, and Shannon Moore (2022)** is a book that focuses on integrating a wide range of instructional strategies with ed tech tools for in-person, online, and blended learning classrooms that include topics such as digital classroom routines, engagement, collaborating, critical thinking, innovation, and formative assessment.
> ▶ *Amplify Learning: A Global Collaborative Series* by **Matthew Rhoads and Becky Lim (https://ampglobaledu.com)** is a four-book series on integrating ed tech tools with instructional strategies by showcasing examples of K–12 teachers from around the world and their classrooms that focus on topics including instructional design, reading, writing, mathematics, computer science, robotics, STEAM (science, technology, engineering, the arts, and mathematics), multilingual learners, special education, and personalized learning.

Reflection and Action: Pause, Ponder, and Wonder

Directions: After reading chapter 7 on co-teaching in classrooms without boundaries, first, write down your initial thoughts immediately after reading the chapter (pause and ponder). Then, wait a day or so and then write down a few questions or statements you want to further explore and investigate in your co-teaching practice (wonder).

Pause and Ponder	Wonder

A powerful opportunity for student learning emerges when IEP team members collaborate to develop standards-based IEP goals. These goals provide increased opportunities for students to receive meaningful instruction in inclusive settings. Additionally, there are often more frequent and more varied opportunities for progress monitoring. It's a win-win situation for students and educators!

—M. Jenkins, professor of special education and expert in inclusive practices, personal communication, February 1, 2024

CHAPTER 8

Integrating Specialists Into Co-Teaching

Co-teaching usually consists of a general educator and another licensed professional, including but not limited to a learning support teacher, instructional coach, special education teacher, psychologist, speech and language specialist, English language specialist, or language specialist, to plan and deliver substantive instruction to a diverse or blended group of students in a single physical space (Karge, 2023b). Dual-immersion bilingual teachers have also seen the value of second-language instructional support in general education classes, thus leading to co-teaching partnerships (Daley, 2021; DeVoss 2023). In places where gifted education teachers are providing instruction, they, too, are spending more time in co-taught environments. For example, co-teachers from science classes share that their students outperformed peers who were not in co-taught classes (Lenard & Townsend, 2017). The integration of these specialists working alongside general education teachers provides exemplary co-teaching.

Throughout this chapter, we explore the integration of various specialists, including special education teachers, bilingual educators, speech and language pathologists, and other related services personnel within dynamic co-teaching environments. Emphasizing the need for all co-teachers to hold a solid understanding of special education, this chapter elaborates on the nuances of implementing accommodations and participating in IEP meetings. The narrative broadens to encompass bilingual education, recognizing all students as multilingual learners and underscoring the need for language development strategies in various contexts. A focus on the integration of speech and language pathologists and other related services workers highlights their crucial role in this multidisciplinary approach.

Belinda recalls an experience from her work in Finland that illustrates efficient integration of specialists:

> *At an international school in Finland, it is commonplace to see an integration of specialists into a co-teaching setting. Sometimes there are two and other times three or more specialists in one classroom. I was able to observe a first-grade classroom implementing station teaching. At one station, the first-grade teacher was working with a small group on a vocabulary lesson. At the second station, the English language specialist was facilitating phonetic development with a small group, and at a third station, a parent volunteer was*

> *overseeing independent work for a decoding activity. Every student had the chance to participate in each station, with rotations every twenty-five minutes within the seventy-five-minute language arts period twice a week. Across campus at the secondary school, a similar session was taking place in a ninth-grade English class. The class read a chapter in a novel aloud together as a group, and then broke into three stations. At one station, the English teacher was teaching a vocabulary lesson. At another station, the language specialist was checking for understanding by asking various comprehension questions. The final station was an independent reading station where students were reading the chapter for the following day.*

Key Themes and Ideas
- ☐ Special education and general education co-teaching
- ☐ Dual-immersion bilingual education co-teaching
- ☐ Co-teaching with speech and language pathologists and other related services personnel
- ☐ AI copilots and ed tech tools for specialists
- ☐ A case study

Special Education and General Education Co-Teaching

When the general education teacher co-teaches with the special education specialist, the co-teachers need to have a solid foundation in special education and understand how to implement various services, provide accommodations, collect data on goals and current levels, and attend IEP meetings. Regardless of whether the co-teacher is considered the "special education teacher," both teachers need to be well versed in the world of special education, as they will be supporting each student and implementing their IEPs.

Co-teachers can employ the eleven strategies of co-teaching when supporting students who need special education services and who are receiving those services in general education classrooms. This form of co-teaching blends two types professional expertise: (1) a teacher who is an expert in curriculum, pacing, classroom management, and large-group instruction with (2) a teacher who specializes in individualization, assessment strategies, accommodation, modifications, and technical information about special education. When co-teaching is successful between general education and special education, both planning and delivering instruction are collaborative and a shared responsibility (Alsarawi, 2019; Karge, 2023b).

In 1997, Naomi Zigmond shared seminal words to the field of special education. She states:

> First and foremost, instruction focused on individual need that is carefully planned . . . is intensive, urgent, relentless, and goal directed . . . is empirically supported practice, drawn from research . . . monitoring each student's progress . . . changing instruction when monitoring data indicate that sufficient progress is not being made. (Zigmond, 1997, pp. 384–385)

This quote reinforces the importance of individualized instruction, a premise on which special education services are based. When these individualized instruction services are implemented in the general education co-taught classroom, student progress can be tremendous. We have evidence that this intensive, goal-directed instruction combined with research-based instructional strategies yields faster rates of student growth than do segregated, self-contained special education classrooms (Karge, 2023b). When implemented correctly, evidence shows that co-teaching can greatly enhance the success of students with disabilities in general education classrooms (Dieker, 2007). Part of implementing co-teaching correctly is ensuring the explicit instruction Zigmond (1997) discusses is provided in the general education classroom. We have seen co-teaching teams fail when they do not address the explicit instruction of individual needs.

Students with disabilities have the right to an exemplary education that meets their individual needs and gives them access to their peers without disabilities and the curriculum these peers are learning (Anderson, 2021; Cosier, Sandoval-Gomez, Cardinal, & Brophy, 2020; Krämer, Möller, & Zimmermann, 2021; Taub & Foster, 2020). Co-teaching between general education and special education is a viable solution to supporting strong inclusive education globally (Coviello & DeMatthews, 2021; Karge, 2023b). Students with disabilities included in general education classes are absent fewer days and exhibit higher test scores in reading and mathematics than their peers in segregated settings (Anderson, 2021; Cole, Murphy, Frisby, Grossi, & Bolte, 2021).

A key element of successful co-teaching is that the students within the class build successful relationships with their peers. In diverse classrooms, we want our students to communicate and collaborate with their peers. By emphasizing students building relationships with all students, the classroom environment can be inclusionary for all students. One way to develop relationships is to use engagement strategies (see chapter 6, page 101) and assign group roles, such as speaker, recorder, timekeeper, and so on. Allowing students with disabilities to serve in leadership roles where they can be successful helps all students see value in their peers. Additionally, the interactive group work scaffolds pragmatic language-building social interactions and collaborative relationships for all involved (Lin, Chen, Justice, & Sawyer, 2019).

Another idea is to assign peer supporters or helpers to students with disabilities in the co-teaching classroom. Seat these students near their peer and instruct them how to support and encourage their assigned partner. Encourage peers, rather than adults, to provide any needed assistance to build relationships among students.

In many schools, a paraeducator (teacher aide) is assigned to work with the specialist. Many co-teacher teams find that once the specialist has spent time in the classroom and established routines and teaching sequences, they can give direct supervision to a paraeducator, who can also spend time in the classroom to work alongside the general education teacher when the co-teacher is not present. This provides more time for explicit instruction and relationship building in small groups. Delivering specialized academic instruction to students with disabilities through co-teaching in general education is the primary way many schools meet least restrictive environment requirements (Hackett, Kruzich, Goulter, & Battista, 2021).

Cook and Friend (1995) write, "Collaboration is a style for direct interaction between at least two co-equal parties voluntarily engaged in shared decision making as they work toward a common goal" (p. 25). They stress this should be two certified (co-equal) educators. We are willing to open this definition up a bit because we believe co-teachers can be any teacher or assistant willing to put in the effort and time to learn and share instructional responsibilities as well as collaborate within a shared space to maximize student learning. This may mean a paraeducator co-teaching as described previously (with direct supervision of the certified staff they are assigned to). It might be teachers with different requirements, as we often see in early childhood settings, where a child development specialist may not have an advanced degree.

In addition to establishing and maintaining strategies for classroom routines and lesson planning, as discussed in chapter 5 (see figures 5.5–5.7, pages 91–95), many specialists find it necessary to go a step farther. We recommend using the co-teaching lesson plan form in figure 8.1 to lay out how to meet the lesson objective and goals with co-teaching strategies and accommodations or modifications, behavioral interventions, and assessments you plan to use. This form is also good documentation to keep for IEP meetings to verify the use of these strategies.

Lesson Objective or Goal	Co-Teaching Strategy	Accommodation or Modification	Behavioral Intervention	Assessment
Students will use a seven-step process to produce a three-paragraph written response.	Graze-and-tag teaching: Each teacher shares a step of the writing process back and forth until they cover all seven steps.	Accommodation: Student writes the seven steps on paper and fills the content in as co-teachers present. Modification: Student draws pictures and writes a sentence to explain each picture.	Have Juan write the seven steps on the board as the teachers give the explanations (helping him focus). Suzy will use a self-monitoring checklist three times during the lesson.	Formative assessment as co-teachers are teaching the steps: The students get time to work on each step with both teachers circling class and viewing writing in progress. Summative assessment: All students will write a three-paragraph written response.

FIGURE 8.1: Co-teaching lesson planning form with accommodation and modification considerations.

Visit **go.SolutionTree.com/instruction** *for a free reproducible version of this figure.*

At an inclusive school in Austin, Texas, that Belinda worked with, several co-teaching teams used figure 8.1 combined with figure 8.2. These teachers had been trained using pyramid lesson planning—some, most, all: What will all students learn? What will most students learn?

Date: _____ Class Period: _____ Unit: _____	
Lesson Objectives: • • •	
Student Learning Pyramid	**Agenda**
What some students will learn (Top)	
What most students will learn (Middle; Tier 2 supports)	
What all students should learn (Bottom; Tier 1 and 2 supports)	

Source: Vaughn et al., 2023.

FIGURE 8.2: Pyramid lesson planning—Some, most, all.

*Visit **go.SolutionTree.com/instruction** for a free reproducible version of this figure.*

And what will some students learn (Vaughn, Bos, & Schumm, 2023)? This system provides Tier 1 and Tier 2 interventions and supports that co-teachers can build into the agenda of their lessons.

Another excellent suggestion from the same school in Texas is to make sure parents or caregivers are aware of the co-taught classroom by sending out a family letter (figure 8.3). This way, right from day one, parents or caregivers are aware that their child has two teachers to support them.

> Dear families,
>
> We would like to share our excitement with you as we look forward to a brand-new school year! Your child has been placed in our co-taught combination classroom. In this collaborative environment, two certified teachers will work together to plan, deliver, assess, and reflect on teaching and providing formative and summative assessments to support your child's growth academically, emotionally, socially, and physically. This inclusive classroom welcomes students with gifts and various abilities, fully reflecting the world we live in. In a few weeks, you will receive an invitation to parent-teacher conferences. At the conference, you will meet with both of us, and we will explain how we work collaboratively using eleven co-teaching strategies to give every child in the class individualized attention.
>
> Sincerely,
> [Both co-teachers and the principal]

FIGURE 8.3: Sample family letter.

We have found it beneficial to share various forms and graphics with the co-teaching teams we consult with. Belinda created figure 8.4 as a quick and simple way to look at an IEP and share details between co-teachers. The special education specialist can share specific goals that are beneficial for the co-teaching setting. In the example, the teachers can quickly see that Johnny has two organization and time-management goals, and Missy has goals related to attention and focus.

Student: Johnny Smith **Grade:** 8	By the end of the school year, when given assignments, Johnny will use a planner or digital tool to record homework and due dates accurately for 80 percent of assignments. Johnny will independently prioritize tasks and manage time effectively to complete assignments on time in at least three out of five instances.
Student: Missy Gonzalez **Grade:** 8	During classroom instruction, Missy will maintain attention on the teacher or task for at least fifteen minutes without becoming distracted, as measured by teacher observation, in four out of five instances. When Missy is given multistep tasks or assignments, she will use self-monitoring strategies such as breaking down tasks into smaller parts to sustain attention and focus until completion. She will demonstrate this in 80 percent of opportunities.
Student: **Grade:**	
Student: **Grade:**	
Student: **Grade:**	
Student: **Grade:**	

FIGURE 8.4: A quick look at the IEP.

*Visit **go.SolutionTree.com/instruction** for a free reproducible version of this figure.*

Belinda created figure 8.5 as a simple co-teaching lesson plan outline while at a school in Arizona. The teachers were using a Madeline Hunter (2004) lesson plan format and wanted to know how to integrate co-teaching. Putting the Hunter areas in the first column, then deciding which of the eleven co-teaching strategies to use and each co-teacher's responsibilities, became a simple way for the co-teachers to plan. There is no right or wrong way for co-teaching teams to work together. As you use any of the forms we provide or gather forms from other field experts, we recommend keeping electronic copies for use the following year.

Co-teachers:			
Content:			
Time, room, materials needed:			
Details	**Co-Teaching Strategy**	**Co-Teacher 1**	**Co-Teacher 2**
Opening	Team teaching	Welcomes students at door and ensures orderly entrance	Welcomes students and takes attendance
Goal of Lesson	One teach, one support	Reads the objective	Roves around the room to ensure all students' materials are out
Main Content of Lesson	Team teaching, graze and tag, and one teach, one support	Models the first problem set; supports student problem solving for the second and third problem sets (left side of classroom)	Explains step by step the problem modeled by co-teacher 1; supports student problem solving for the second and third problem sets (right side of the classroom)
Guided Practice			
Independent Work or Homework			
Closure			
Reflection after lesson is taught:			

FIGURE 8.5: Simple co-teaching lesson plan outline.

*Visit **go.SolutionTree.com/instruction** for a free reproducible version of this figure.*

Dual-Immersion Bilingual Education Co-Teaching

All students are multilingual learners. By this we mean that language learning can include learning a language to communicate, a new problem-solving methodology, or a software user interface. As a result, co-teachers must be aware of strategies furthering language development within a variety of contexts and settings. In many co-teaching environments, students may learn academics in two languages, receiving part of their day's instruction in English, while during the other part of the day, they may receive instruction in another language. In this situation, the essential components of integrated, collaborative bilingual co-teaching promote student growth. Multilingual learners need guided oral practice to enhance academic discourse. The strategies in chapters 5–7 provide wonderful instructional techniques for co-teaching with strong student and instructor engagement and discourse.

Access a video example of a dual-immersion co-teaching lesson:

https://bit.ly/3P44u8b

A general education and dual-immersion co-teaching team Belinda worked with in New Mexico explained they appreciated all the engagement and grouping strategies; however, to ensure their multilingual learners participated, they had to go back and actually teach academic discourse. They created a poster resembling the one in figure 8.6 to visually support their lesson.

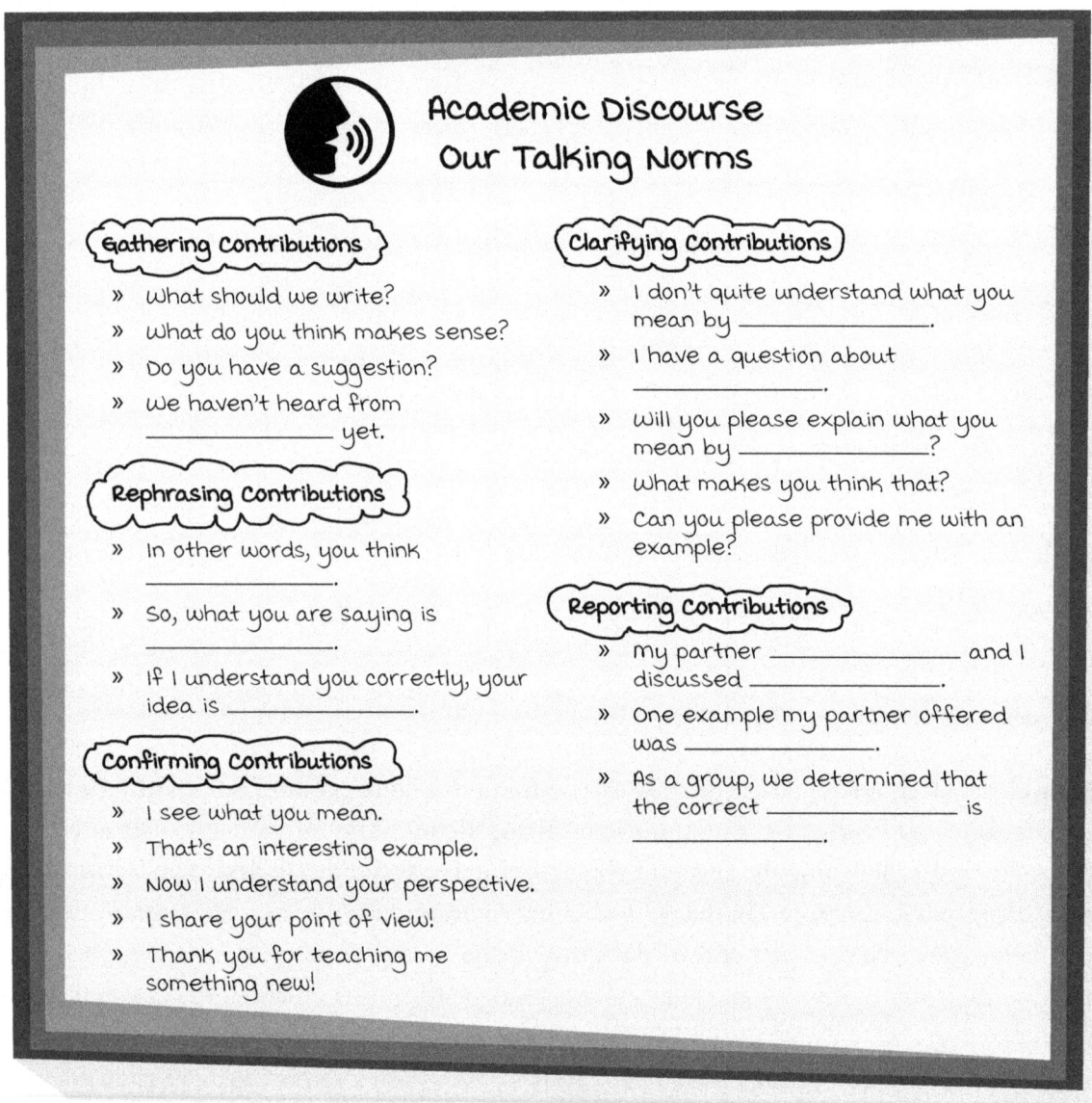

FIGURE 8.6: Visual support for a co-teaching lesson on academic discourse.

As Megan DeVoss (2023) notes, close to five million multilingual learners in U.S. schools need instruction that leads to "equal access to content standards through language diversification" (p. 4). She discusses the utility and effectiveness of co-teaching that provides content instruction and language assistance in one classroom. Maria Dove and Andrea Honigsfeld (2010) discuss how co-teaching completely replaced multilingual learner pullout services in a large Minnesota school district. Differentiated instruction enriches multilingual learners' and their classmates' learning in co-taught classrooms. Dove and Honigsfeld (2010) give the example of a fourth-grade classroom where the general education co-teacher conducts a shared reading lesson, and the multilingual learner specialist co-teacher uses computer-generated photographs of the same material to build understanding. This is an example of the co-teaching strategy alternative co-teaching, using differentiated materials with a small group to teach the same content.

Co-Teaching With Speech and Language Pathologists and Other Related Services Personnel

Many speech and language pathologists spend time in general education classrooms as teachers. In these environments, they can have targeted students working in groups with their peers while the speech pathologist models the language. Life-skills instruction offers another possibility for a co-teaching variation with an occupational therapist and special education teacher doing the co-teaching (Cerdenio, 2023). And when describing the co-teaching between physical education teachers and their teachers in training, Jeanne L. Mullican (2021) discusses the use of many co-teaching strategies that would work beautifully with recreation therapists or physical therapists. Related services personnel have traditionally provided services in segregated settings. Bringing their practices into the classroom with other educators allows students to experience inclusive conversations and experiences and for generalization to take place quickly.

AI Copilots and Ed Tech Tools for Specialists

Just like other co-teachers, specialists of all kinds can use AI to augment and amplify their work. Many specialists assess, develop, and compose reports, attend meetings, and meet with students to conduct services. As discussed in chapter 7 (page 119), they can design initial paperwork with the assistance of AI tools. And many of the technology tools in general can make the co-teaching colleague's life easier. Areas where specialists may save time with AI and ed tech tools include assessing and collecting data and report writing.

Assessing and Collecting Data

Beyond using Google Docs to design lessons, there are many tools that co-teachers can use for formative and summative assessments and overall data monitoring. Creating forms for report writing as well as lesson planning can save time and enhance collaborations.

Belinda worked with a high school English general education and special education co-teaching team that collects work samples and uses AI to analyze basic grammar and sentence structure.

The co-teachers work together to paste each essay into the free version of ChatGPT and ask the program to analyze for basic grammatical and structural formatting. They then skim each paper and add their own notes related to content. This saves them so much time that they are able to differentiate individually in each paper and give specific writing strategies for moving each student forward. The next day, they share the details with the students using the co-teaching strategy of station teaching. Both co-teachers have their own station; one focuses on grammar and the other on content, with a third independent workstation where students can review and edit on their own. The depth of learning that the teachers at this priority school were able to achieve within a single lesson greatly excited them as they watched their struggling student writers making real, substantial progress on their writing skills.

Another general education and special education co-teaching team Belinda worked with shared that they purchased clickers to track behavior. As a student exhibits a certain behavior they're tracking for their IEP, they use the clicker to tally. Both co-teachers, along with the instruction aide, use the clickers as well. Each time they provide a tally, they enter it in a behavior spreadsheet to data share over time. Both teachers, along with the instructional aide, are responsible for the behavior clicker as each has access to the shared digital spreadsheet for the student. Importantly, each time they provide a tally, they note on the spreadsheet which educator created the tally.

Keeping track of IEP goals can be confusing for co-teachers when their classroom includes many students with IEPs. Another general education and special education team Belinda worked with used index cards as reminders. Then, after they heard Matt speak at a professional learning session, they realized they could create a digital chart to not only share the IEP goals but track each student's progress. They used an interactive Google Sheet, which included the IEP goals, dates, data input, and stakeholder notes. Co-teachers can do this chronologically and collaboratively so each stakeholder in the student's IEP can see current and past progress.

Report Writing

For developing reports related to student progress for IEPs, specialists can have AI analyze the data they have collected and then transform them into narratives, which they can in turn place into reports. They can use student data (removing all identifying information) within a prompt and ask the AI to analyze them and generate reports aligned with each area of the IEP. A social worker and general education co-teaching team that Belinda worked with uses this method when they collaborate once a month. The same general education teacher also works with the school's speech and language pathologist, who also has access and uses the same report-writing tools. These specialists share a secure Google Drive for this documentation where they can access information together as stakeholders and collaborators. The shared drive can include past IEP documentation, student assessment and IEP goal data, psychological assessment reports, and other service provider notes and logs.

A Case Study

This case study demonstrates how specialists may work with more than one teacher during the school day to enhance the co-teaching partnerships at a school with limited resources. At a small school in Eastern Africa, a talented intervention specialist with special education and bilingual certification, Abeba, co-teaches with two different teachers, a general education literacy teacher and a general education mathematics teacher; both classrooms are dual immersion. Abeba believes the key to her success with each of these teachers is the preplanning and ongoing continual planning that she does.

Preplanning

Before the co-teaching team begins working together, Abeba spends a significant amount of time with each co-teacher on initial planning: typically, two full days. During this time, the co-teachers review all student files and go over IEP and language goals. If there are specific accommodations or modifications indicated together, they plan how to reflect these in the co-teaching process. The IEP or language development plan often indicates specific behaviors or instructional needs; in these cases, they talk about how the co-teaching team will deal with these behavior issues or instructional needs during co-teaching. Another question they ask each other is whether they'll share the process of grading or if each teacher will grade their assigned caseload. In other words, will the general education teacher grade general education students and the special education teacher grade special education students? The co-teachers also talk through how they anticipate lesson planning. Will they meet once a month? Once a week? Then, they book their calendars for one semester.

The co-teachers take the time to think and talk about how they will introduce themselves to the class on the first day. Setting the stage right away so students see that they have two teachers is critical. Abeba said she always suggests placing both names on the door to the classroom. In combined caseloads or classrooms, the students may not know each other. Abeba indicates it is important to plan for icebreaker activities to help students get to know each other and for co-teachers to have some fun working together. Finally, Abeba notes how the last conversation of her co-teaching planning days is about how the co-teachers will determine if the work together is successful. We summarize Abeba's suggestions in figure 8.7.

- How will we plan lessons?
- How will we introduce ourselves on the first day?
- Do we want both our names on the classroom door?
- Do we want to plan an icebreaker or some other activity to get acquainted with the class?
- How will we determine if our co-teaching is successful?
- What knowledge or skills should all students gain from this subject or grade level?
- What teaching units—in teaching order—will we use in this semester or trimester?
- Are there specific accommodations or modifications indicated on the IEP?
- Are there specific behaviors noted on the IEP that we need to proactively plan for?
- Are there specific instructional strategies indicated on an IEP that we might want to incorporate?
- Who will do the grading? Will we share grading?

FIGURE 8.7: Questions for preplanning day.

*Visit **go.SolutionTree.com/instruction** for a free reproducible version of this figure.*

Continual Planning

Abeba continued discussing her co-teaching success by expressing the importance of scheduling time to consult on a regular basis. She admitted it is sometimes difficult to schedule legitimate time to consult and collaborate. Figure 8.8 provides some ideas. Also see chapter 5 (page 81) for additional suggestions.

- Administrator assigns time each week for staff collaboration.
- Once a month during an early release for students, co-teachers earmark collaboration time.
- One day a week per grading period, bring in two roving substitutes to cover one-hour sessions for co-teachers to specifically plan.
- On a rotating basis, special education teachers attend department or grade-level meetings.
- Establish various forms of communication including but not limited to online journals, Google Docs, and other types of online exchanges to allow planning and reflective communication. Consider dividing the initial lesson planning work by using ChatGPT to write the first draft.
- Attend a professional learning conference with co-teacher. This provides time for collaborative conversation and rapport building.

FIGURE 8.8: Finding time to plan.

Conclusion

The chapter uniquely addressed the structure and components of integrated, collaborative co-teaching and explored the complexities and richness of a co-teaching environment that embraces and integrates a variety of specialist roles for the benefit of all students. A case study from Africa exhibited planning more deeply for students with disabilities, as did examples from many schools Belinda has worked with in the United States.

> **ADDITIONAL RESOURCES TO CONSIDER AFTER READING THIS CHAPTER**
> - The **American Speech-Language-Hearing Association (www.asha.org)** is a national professional organization that credentials speech language pathologists.
> - The **Co-Teaching Connection (https://coteach.com)** is the website for the work of Marilyn Friend, one of the foremost experts on co-teaching and collaboration, including with specialists.

Reflection and Action: Reflection and Goal Setting

Directions: After reading chapter 8, reflect on how specialists and service providers in your school can support your co-teaching lessons. How can you collaborate with them? What types of lessons can you plan? Can this be a regular occurrence? Then, set goals related to integrating specialists in your classroom. An example of a goal may be to try to incorporate them into your co-teaching lessons at least once every two weeks.

Reflection

Goal Setting

Co-Teaching Evolved © 2025 Solution Tree Press • SolutionTree.com
Visit **go.SolutionTree.com/instruction** to download this free reproducible.

Critical components for successful co-teaching include frequent open communication, collaborative planning, mutual understanding of the roles of each teacher at different times during the lessons, consistent data collection on student progress, an inclusive mindset in addressing student needs and behaviors, and showing students that the two teachers are equal by presenting a united front.

—S. Raybold, early childhood special education program administrator, personal communication, January 30, 2024

CHAPTER 9

Co-Teaching in PreK and Early Childhood Settings

High-quality early childhood programs should be accessible to all families to help every young child achieve their full potential. Educators working in early childhood programs co-teach and collaborate and build systems within their schools to support all learners. As many school districts add universal preschool and transition kindergarten classrooms, it is important to implement co-teaching immediately. When students with disabilities and students with language challenges are included at an early age and experience co-teaching, it sets the stage for their K–12 experience. Neurotypical young children learn to accept classmates who may appear or sound different or who may learn differently, and this early acceptance remains as they enter school together. This chapter discusses inclusion in early childhood programs, the challenge of working in an environment where the adults have different levels of formal education and expertise, and lessons using observation to build creative systems of inclusive education.

Belinda observed a preK classroom with a fabulous flow for co-teaching in the preschool program sponsored by the Shasta County Office of Education in Northern California:

The twenty young children entered the classroom, put their lunch pails in cubbies, and sat in a circle on the floor. At 9:00 a.m., Miss M. (the preschool teacher) sang, "Here we sit like birds in the wilderness, waiting to begin." Mr. H. (the early childhood special education teacher) asked each member of the class, "Are you ready to begin?" He called on each three-year-old by name, and they responded, "Yes, I am ready to begin." This was excellent reinforcement of both full sentences for language and patience in waiting while each name is called. When every child had responded, Miss M. again sang, "Here we sit like birds in the wilderness, waiting to begin." Mr. H. asked, "Are you ready to begin?" and everyone shouted "Yes, we are ready to begin!" This co-teaching team was using the co-teaching strategy of interactive teaching to begin their day. They shared co-teaching responsibilities throughout the day (the co-teaching strategy of shared teaching).

> Miss M. said, "The color of the week is red, and the letter of the week is A; can anyone think of something that is red and begins with an A?" Miss Y. (the classroom assistant) walked into the room carrying a basket of red apples. Some of the students raised their hands, and Miss M. called on a student who stated, "Red apples," to which Mr. H. replied, "You are correct, José; apples are red, and they begin with an A." The discussion continued as Miss M. and Mr. H. used the advanced co-teaching strategy of interactive teaching to introduce and explain the concepts they were teaching.
>
> Miss Y. then read a picture book about apples to the students while Miss M. and Mr. H. prepared for the co-teaching strategy of station teaching. They placed the basket of apples at one station where students would create a painting (using the basket as a visual). They set up another station where students would practice the letter A both verbally and in writing. And finally, they set up a station for the students to put together a storybook about a red apple. When Miss Y. finished reading the book, she moved to the storybook station, where she invited a third of the students in the class to join her. Mr. H. called a third of the students over to put on paint aprons for the painting station, and Miss M. was ready at the letter A station for the remaining third of the students. The teachers spent the next twenty minutes using the station teaching strategy. There were three stations, so the teachers rotated three times, and all students had the opportunity to learn from each adult. With very small groups, each station moved quickly, and everyone had an individualized conversation with the teacher at the station.
>
> When it was time to transition, Miss Y. turned on some music. The students knew this was their clue to move to the next activity. Each student found their name and sat at one of two tables. Mr. H. and Miss M. each had a table group. Miss Y. took the basket of apples and put five in front of Mr. H. and five in front of Miss M. Each of the teachers counted the apples and conducted a similar lesson related to numbers using the co-teaching strategy of parallel teaching.
>
> The music sounded again, and the students moved to the rug. The co-teachers role-played an addition game by picking up a card (it read 1 + 2 =). Miss M. asked one student to stand and come to the front, then Mr. H. brought two other students to the front. Together they counted 1, 2, 3. They turned over and role-played several similar cards before it was time for morning recess: the advanced co-teaching strategy of role-play teaching was a hit!

This example from Northern California demonstrates how a preK setting can seamlessly incorporate many co-teaching strategies in a relatively short time. In K–12 education, it is typical to see one teacher in a classroom with a large group of students for most of the day. However, many early childhood classrooms have more than one adult throughout the day. This opens the door for continual collaboration and co-teaching.

> **Key Themes and Ideas**
> ☐ Inclusion in early childhood programs
> ☐ Adults with different expertise
> ☐ Lessons based on observation
> ☐ Creative systems of inclusive support

Inclusion in Early Childhood Programs

Early childhood programs may be facilitated within a school district, a county office of education, a local planning area, or a consortium of state or federally funded programs, or they may be privately funded through a nonprofit or for-profit agency. Some programs are in private homes and childcare facilities. Federal government, state, and local systems work together to build capacity and support early learning.

Close to forty-five million adults in the United States have disabilities (Barton & Smith, 2015). These adults live in society, shop at stores, eat at restaurants, work out at fitness centers, attend family gatherings at the local park, and use banks, just as others do. However, data indicate little progress toward increasing attendance of young children with disabilities in inclusive early childhood programs (Barton & Smith, 2015). Therefore, it is urgent that, at a very young age, the one out of six children with developmental delays are included in early childhood programs (U.S. Department of Health and Human Services & U.S. Department of Education, 2023). Head Start and Early Head Start programs are required to have 10 percent enrollment available to young children with disabilities (Head Start Act, 2017). However, for many programs, the decision to include students with disabilities is an upper-level management or school board decision.

The exclusionary practices that have persisted across educational ecosystems lead to "learning access disparities that are the crux of educational inequalities" (Cruz, Firestone, & Love, 2023, p. 1). We strongly believe that this must stop. A quote many use in the field resonates with us: Vanderbilt University professor of special education Erik W. Carter (2015) says, "Early segregation does not merely predict later segregation; it almost ensures it" (p. 16). This is why it is crucial to break down the various barriers to access that families of young children with disabilities face. We must integrate early childhood education programs and ensure that programs include young children with disabilities.

The trajectory for lifelong inclusion is set at birth and continues as students are accepted and supported in elementary school and through college. Inclusion is a mindset, an attitude shift. It is a philosophy of acceptance. The adults who provide childcare and education to young children set the stage. The research is clear: inclusion in early childhood is beneficial to young children with and without disabilities (Grisham-Brown, Cox, Gravil, & Missall, 2010; Odom et al., 2004). Kimberly Maich and colleagues (2019) purport that the sooner interventions are implemented within inclusive education, the stronger the outcomes are. Individualized evidence-based strategies are effective in inclusive settings where the adults work collaboratively and co-teach (Grisham-Brown, Pretti-Frontczak, Hawkins, & Winchell, 2009; Strain, 2017). The goal of special education is to individualize learning for every student. We argue that this individualization must happen for every student (with or without disabilities) to succeed. When two or more adults work together to provide that individualization in the form of evidence-based instructional strategies, every student in the classroom setting benefits.

Adults With Different Expertise

Affirmations and interactions with adults shape young children's developmental progression and social skills. Depending on the program, the adults in the classroom may have different expertise areas.

Regardless of the level of professional education, variability in the level of training and support often deters the progression of co-teaching and inclusion in general in early childhood settings. These support features for staff are usually based on funding streams (Center for the Study of Child Care Employment, 2021; Child Trends, 2019; Urban Institute, 2021). Sometimes the level of education differs in the preK classroom. For example, Belinda visited a co-taught classroom in Maine where one co-teacher holds a master's degree in education and the other an associate of arts degree in child development; these educators work together, and each shares their gifts and knowledge. One co-teacher is talented in lesson planning and behavior supports, while the other excels with child development stages and learning systems for young children. They value each other and what they bring to the co-taught classroom. This type of collaboration is necessary when two adults with different education paths find themselves working together. It is a matter of identifying the skill set of each and amplifying the teaching components to enhance instruction and ultimately ensure the needs of every young child in the classroom are met.

Belinda also visited a co-taught class in Vermont that was housed in a Head Start–sponsored program. One co-teacher is funded by Head Start and the other co-teacher by the local school district. They shared that this is problematic, as Head Start and the school district both hold trainings, sometimes on the same day, and they are not able to attend with each other. The district teacher is not able to attend other training since they are not technically employed by Head Start (even though the co-teacher works in the same class with the Head Start teacher every day). The type of training and professional learning a co-teacher receives can have a viable impact on inclusive programs; opportunities for professional improvement need to be available to all providers, not just those with formal education (Coleman, Hestenes, & Ozdemir, 2021; Hebbeler & Spiker, 2016). When only one co-teacher can receive training and must impart that knowledge or those directives to the other, communication is vital. These co-teachers learned quickly that the employment systems (Head Start and the school district) do not always allow for them to be together, so they have to increase their time for planning and sharing training information.

Lessons Based on Observation

As indicated in chapter 2 (page 29), the co-teaching strategy one teach, one observe is one of the basic strategies in the supportive stage of co-teaching. In the early childhood classroom, this strategy often sees use to build lessons and encourage deeper student thinking. Dawn Petitpas and Teresa Buchanan (2023) suggest using observation to guide lesson development for teaching and to build out and adjust early learning teaching strategies. Petitpas and Buchanan (2023) are staff assessors for the National Association for the Education of Young Children (NAEYC) early learning programs team. They visit early childhood programs across the United States and assess their co-teaching, co-assessing, and co-implementation skills. In their article, "Using Observation to Guide Your Teaching," they discuss how co-teachers complement each other and can add value to teaching (Petitpas & Buchanan, 2023). For example, they share the scenario of co-teachers observing students during outdoor play as they use blocks to create a tower. Because they put the smaller blocks on the bottom, as the students add the larger blocks, the tower falls over. One co-teacher suggests the students put the larger blocks on the bottom; however, the students do not use the suggestion, and they continue to watch the tower crash down. It is not until the other co-teacher asks the students, "I remember when you were building a tower inside the other day. What happened to that tower? . . . Hmm, I wonder what else you could try?" (Petitpas & Buchanan, 2023, p. 5). This prompts the students to push the smaller pieces of wood together to create a studier base, and they succeed in building the tower. The decision to ask questions of the students was based on the teacher's previous observation, and it led to a developmentally appropriate strategy that guided the students to complete the task. In this case, the co-teacher who was observing saw it was advantageous to accommodate and assist her co-teacher by taking another approach and asking more questions based on the observation. Ultimately, they both felt the activity was successful (Petitpas & Buchanan, 2023).

In the scenario at the beginning of the chapter, Miss M. and Mr. H. role-play based on the recommendation of Mr. H., who had observed the students while Miss M. taught a lesson on addition the day before. The students were confused and unable to count the items on their worksheet. During reflection and planning, he had suggested they use role-play to teach the skill. When both educators respect each other and honor shared views, it adds strength to the co-teaching partnership. Instead of blaming Miss M. for the student confusion, Mr. H. came up with a suggested alternative (the role-play). Miss M. and Mr. H. provide an example of how expertise can be complementary in the co-teaching environment.

Let's jump into three examples of how co-teachers can implement the strategies of one teach, one observe, one teach, one support, and station teaching within their classrooms in a wide array of content areas. Following that, there are two video examples to review. After the examples, we provide some questions to consider in your future observations.

One Teach, One Observe in a PreK Phonics Lesson

In a preK class, Mrs. Lee leads a phonics lesson focusing on letter sounds. She first projects a slideshow while leading students in a choral chant of each sound. Then, for practice and assessment, Mrs. Lee shows a YouTube video with the sounds that uses music. While she engages students with the lively song about letter sounds, encouraging them to sing along in a choral chant for each sequence of sounds displayed in the video, her co-teacher, Mr. Jones, observes the students, taking notes on their engagement and pronunciation. He quietly moves around the room, making mental notes and jotting down specific data notes on which students are struggling with specific sounds. This strategy allows them to later plan targeted interventions for students who need extra help and further reteaching and practice for future lessons.

One Teach, One Support in a Kindergarten Social-Emotional Learning Lesson

During a lesson on sharing and empathy, Ms. Patel introduces a story about friendship and empathy called "The Cat and the Mouse" to her kindergarten class. She generated the story through her favorite storybook AI generator (Storybookai.app). Before she reads the story, Ms. Patel front-loads the vocabulary on two slides that illustrate what friendship and empathy mean. As she reads and displays the pictures with her projector while her students are on the rug, she pauses to ask questions such as "How do we think the cat made the mouse feel when it was chasing it across the house?" prompting her students to think about how the characters feel during that sequence of the story and share their thoughts with a partner sitting next to them. Meanwhile, her co-teacher, Mr. Garcia, circulates around the rug, offering support by rephrasing questions for better understanding, helping various pairs of students articulate their thoughts, and ensuring that all students are engaged and understanding each part of the story and how it aligns to friendship and empathy.

Station Teaching in PreK Collaborative Play

Ms. O'Connor and Mr. Kim have set up different play stations around their preK classroom. Each station focuses on a specific aspect of collaborative play, like building structures with blocks, role-playing, or puzzle solving. Before students are sent to each of the stations, both co-teachers use team teaching to model each station and its expectations and rules for their students. This ensures their students and the other support staff and classroom volunteers understand the expectations. Following this sequence, they divide students into groups of four, and each station lead (either a paraprofessional or a classroom family volunteer) escorts them to their stations. After students arrive at each station, Ms. O'Connor and Mr. Kim rotate among the stations, facilitating play and guiding interactions through their feedback to each group as well as the adult leading the station. This lesson and co-teaching strategy of station teaching allows students to explore various activities while learning key skills like teamwork, problem solving, and communication in a structured yet playful environment.

Video Examples to Analyze

Besides analyzing the previous examples, take a moment to watch two distinct lesson plans of co-teaching at the kindergarten and preschool level. In this section, we invite you to delve into practical examples. Through the provided QR codes, you will access video case studies that illuminate the richness and complexity of these co-teaching classroom environments. As you analyze each video, pay close attention to how each student and the whole class respond to the way the co-teachers are using a wide array of strategies to support student learning. Look specifically at the dynamics between teachers and students and evaluate the subtle cues that may reveal student learning and social interactions.

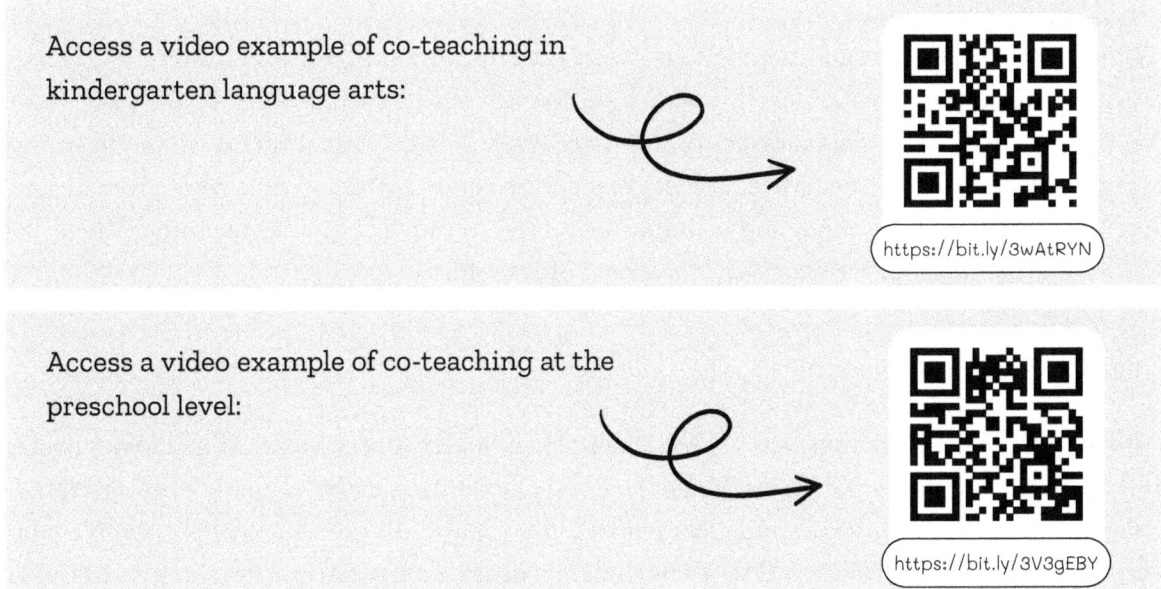

Access a video example of co-teaching in kindergarten language arts:
https://bit.ly/3wAtRYN

Access a video example of co-teaching at the preschool level:
https://bit.ly/3V3gEBY

As you engage in these examples, reflect on the effectiveness of the co-teaching strategies you observe. Additionally, evaluate the interactions between the students and teachers and consider how the observations can better inform teaching in classroom environments serving preschool and kindergarten students.

Questions to Consider

When observing young children, consider some of Petitpas and Buchanan's (2023) suggested questions.

- What activities and materials does each child respond to (positively or negatively)?
- What are some questions and statements each child has said that stand out to you?
- What does each child talk about?
- How does each child play?
- Who does each child enjoy playing with?

- When is each child most successful?
- When does each child smile and laugh? (p. 5)

We add the following.

- Is every student following directions?
- Does one student ask more questions than others?
- Is there one co-teacher that a certain student goes to consistently and not the other?
- How do students respond when the co-teachers use the eleven co-teaching strategies?

Intentionally watching and listening to students is a critical skill in every classroom. It becomes easier with the implementation of the co-teaching strategy one teach, one observe. The co-teachers can then use the observational evidence to guide future lessons while individualizing learning opportunities for all students. The educators can ensure equity by taking time to notice and support students with backgrounds and identities that differ from the classroom majority. When two educators are present, they expand equal learning opportunities.

Creative Systems of Inclusive Support

As indicated in the opening vignette, co-teaching can use creative systems of inclusive support as they implement the eleven co-teaching strategies. One of the benefits of many early childhood programs is the adult-to-student ratio (most states, like California, mandate a one-to-twelve ratio for preK programs; Thornton, 2024). Typically, this means a paraeducator (teaching assistant) is available in every co-taught classroom. In the opening vignette, the co-teachers use the element of surprise by having Miss Y. walk in with the basket of apples. The co-teachers then have Miss Y. read a book so the co-teachers are free to quickly set up their stations. Finally, once the stations move forward, Miss Y. turns on music to signal transition time. All three instances are creative uses of the third adult in the classroom. Miss Y. was working with this co-teaching team for the first time and had no college training. However, the ways she was integrated into the lesson gave her credibility with the students and teachers. Paraeducators can enhance support for unique learning needs. There are many tasks they can perform. Figure 9.1 gives an example of the added value tasks paraeducators can perform.

- ☐ Reinforcing skills using materials and activities as directed by the teacher
- ☐ Explaining and reteaching a lesson (after watching the teacher provide the instruction)
- ☐ Coaching students through a sequence of tasks
- ☐ Checking homework or work completion
- ☐ Monitoring students during seatwork or group activities
- ☐ Providing daily assignment support

> - ☐ Reading a book to a student or listening to a student read a book
> - ☐ Checking backpacks or assisting with the organization of backpacks or desks
> - ☐ Lifting, rotating, or supporting students with physical needs
> - ☐ Taking data for monitoring or charting behavior
> - ☐ Conducting a small-group lesson using the lesson plan provided by the certified teacher
> - ☐ Accompanying students to a therapy session, a classroom, the bus, lunch, the bathroom, recess, or passing period
> - ☐ Assisting with implementation of IEP goals under the direction of the certified educator
> - ☐ Implementing behavior plans developed by the certified educator
> - ☐ Supervising students at lunch, passing periods, recess, study hall, bus arrivals and departures, or various activities (field trips, assemblies, and so on)
> - ☐ Performing clerical duties such as operating media, maintaining daily logs, or photocopying (Clerical duties should be kept to a minimum, and school leaders should tell the teacher and paraeducators their main purpose is to work with students.)

Source: Karge, 2023b, p. 89.

FIGURE 9.1: Tasks paraeducators can perform.

Creative systems of inclusive support include analysis of the environment. This is especially true in early childhood programs, where often there are open learning spaces both inside and outside.

> **Different Places, Different Needs**
> Following is a list of considerations for teachers when establishing a classroom environment to meet the needs of all students. Are there places for students to be part of a group and places to be alone? Use the following list to assess the classroom environments in your school.
>
> | | |
> |---|---|
> | Places to be part of a group | Places to be quiet |
> | Places to be alone | Places to be messy |
> | Places to be taken care of | Places to have one's own things |
> | Places to be on one's own | Places to share with others |
> | Places to be free and move | Places to be creative |
> | Places to be noisy | |
>
> What is your environment like?
>
> *Source: Karge, 2023b, p. 160.*

Creative systems of inclusive support mean consistently thinking about inclusion every time a young child is placed and receives services. Districts, county offices, and local education agencies make placement and setting decisions within the public school systems or in community-based early childhood programs. Regardless of the location, having the opportunity to play, interact, and communicate with typically developing peers is important for every young child. This is often a lot of work, as all entities need to work together and develop relationships; public schools collaborate with Head Start programs, childcare centers, and private preschools. Understanding the policy and federal law that requires the least restrictive environment paves the way for adequate infrastructure and collaboration to occur (Barton & Smith, 2015).

There are many examples of successful inclusive programs. San Diego State University (SDSU) and San Diego Unified School District (SDUSD) collaborate by having an employee of SDUSD with training in special education work full time at the SDSU Campus Children's Center and co-teach with one of the child development specialists at the center. The reverse happens in Brea School District in Southern California. It opened a fee-based early childhood program within the school district and hired a district child development specialist with certification and a special education specialist with credentials to co-teach. In both examples, all partners had to be innovative in how they created, evaluated, and established for longevity classes with typically and atypically developing students. The adults in these early childhood settings ensure every student has access, and they work to foster active strategies leading to friendships between students with and without disabilities (Barton & Smith, 2015). For example, the co-teachers role-play examples of how to be a friend, ask for a toy, participate in a game, and other simple strategies that build relationships and, ultimately, friendships. Sometimes these classrooms include students whose second language is English, making it even more critical for the educators to use active engagement strategies like station co-teaching, where students can be in smaller groups with more adult attention.

Lack of funding should never be a reason to limit access. Creative systems of inclusive practices include memoranda of understanding developed between agencies to share teachers or paraeducators (SDUSD and SDSU did this), setting up tuition-based programs for typically developing peers (as Brea School District did), providing free transportation for typically developing peers to attend inclusive classrooms (this is what the school in the vignette did), or giving parents the funds to send their children to community programs. Coordinating across programs can be complex. Siloed programs (that is, independent programs that provide childcare, early care, health care, or special education) are the norm in education. In Brea School District in Southern California, prior to co-teaching, there were three siloed programs on the same campus for Early Head Start, Head Start, and independent preschool, and none of these programs coordinated services.

Due to the nature of where schools are located, many of the rural areas of the world do a better job sharing funds and collaborating on personnel, space, and material resources. In the Black Hills of South Dakota, families were very vocal in saying that they did not want their three- and four-year-olds riding the bus long distances to school (in snow five months out of the year!). Therefore, educators had to be creative and share resources within the environments supporting the home school of the young children—sometimes they received education in a public school and other times in a community partnership (private preschool). A *home school* is the neighborhood school—the school closest to where the student resides. Typically, a home school is walking distance from a family home. It comes down to supporting students and their families and ensuring they can achieve continual, steady growth.

Talk to your fiscal experts to find out how funds are distributed and can (or cannot) be shared. In the United States, compliance with Individuals With Disabilities Education Act (IDEA) mandates allow states to be eligible for funds from the federal government. The funding formula includes the number of students with disabilities and the severity of their needs (Rothstein & Johnson, 2021). Early childhood educators must be able to advocate for their students in this way.

Creative systems of inclusion mean transparency. Belinda attended a parent meeting in London where the public was invited to see the research from over thirty years on early childhood inclusion. The speakers shared examples of how young children with and without disabilities make significant progress in inclusive settings in academic, social, emotional, physical, developmental, and communication goals (Grisham-Brown et al., 2010; Warren, Martinez, & Sortino, 2016). A panel of parents from neighboring cities where children had been included shared their perspectives and knowledge on not only their own children but all the children in their communities. They then broke into stations where each of six co-teachers gave more specifics on each of the areas (academic, social, emotional, physical, developmental, and communication). Then, when the group came back together, the head of schools (superintendent) explained that the families had just participated in a form of co-teaching (station teaching) and continued to give details, including their commitment to every early childhood program being co-taught. Any school can emulate this model of parent participation. When parents experience the small-group interaction while at the stations, they can see firsthand how their own children would receive instruction in a smaller group with the co-teaching model. If you need to "sell" the families on implementation of co-teaching, this type of parent night is a useful tool.

Conclusion

This chapter made the point that the eleven co-teaching strategies are effective at all levels. Early childhood co-teachers often flow from one strategy to another. Most early childhood co-teaching teams spend at least three hours a day teaching together, so their planning and reflection time weaves into their implementation and data collection. While all the co-teaching strategies are useful in early childhood, we especially emphasize the strategy of one teach, one observe, as observation is key to play and other activities evident in early childhood environments. The variety of programs and staffing in early childhood programs means that teachers and leaders in early childhood education must be creative in implementing co-teaching in settings where inclusion is the norm.

> **ADDITIONAL RESOURCES TO CONSIDER AFTER READING THIS CHAPTER**
> - The **Head Start Early Childhood Learning and Knowledge Center (https://eclkc.ohs.acf.hhs.gov)** provides resources and information to support the development and education of young children in Head Start programs.
> - The **Center of Excellence for Infant and Early Childhood Mental Health Consultation (www.iecmhc.org)** offers teachers resources and consultation to promote the social, emotional, and mental well-being of young children.
> - The **American Academy of Pediatrics Council on Children With Disabilities (https://bit.ly/3XaSvKR)** is full of information and resources to help teachers support students with disabilities and health needs in inclusive classrooms.

- The **Division for Early Childhood (www.dec-sped.org)** focuses on evidence-based practices and resources to improve the development and education of young children with disabilities or who need support for developmental delays.
- **Help Me Grow National Center (https://helpmegrownational.org)** connects teachers to a network of resources for supporting families and monitoring the development of their young students.
- The **National Association for the Education of Young Children (www.naeyc.org)** provides research-backed resources, professional learning opportunities, and accreditation information for early childhood educators to enhance their practice.

Reflection and Action: Challenge

Directions: After reading chapter 9, we challenge you to create a lesson that uses the same co-teaching strategies that can work with preK and kindergarten students as well as older students (late elementary or secondary). Discuss two to three co-teaching strategies that would be in each lesson and how you would have implemented them differently. Last, challenge yourself to integrate the co-teaching strategies you discuss here in an upcoming lesson with your current students.

Challenge

The benefits of co-teaching cannot be overstated. Both our students and educators benefit from the collective expertise and collaboration that co-teaching offers. We become so much more than just colleagues; we become lifelong friends and genuine supporters of the greater good for our entire community.

—M. Smith, inclusion expert and assistant principal, personal communication, February 1, 2024

CHAPTER 10

Cultivating a Culture of Co-Teaching

The implementation of co-teaching is a massive instructional shift for a school. It can be a huge cultural change. When co-teaching is implemented, it is a new form of teaching and a new set of inclusionary practices for a school to take on as it begins its co-teaching journey. This chapter discusses how teachers and school leaders can make the cultural changes necessary for successful co-teaching, including focused direction, a strategic plan and timeline, accountability, a collaborative culture, and deepened learning. It also touches on the leadership necessary to build and sustain successful co-teaching programs.

Before diving in, let's see Matt's recollections of the cultural change that co-teaching had at a large comprehensive high school over time:

> *In my first year of co-teaching, when my school site had recently adopted the practice, students and general education teachers alike made it seem like special education teachers were instructional aides. Several teachers were co-teaching only one period per day and had no planning time with their general education co-teacher. One special education co-teacher in our department co-taught with three different general education co-teachers in one school year and had shared planning time with only one of them.*
>
> *Even though the school used the PLC process, our collaborative team meetings were more about special education policy and IEP writing instead of teaching and learning—let alone co-teaching. Co-teaching partnerships typically lasted one year, with only a few teams working together for consecutive years. Co-teaching classrooms only amounted to about 30 percent of our special education student placements. In co-taught classrooms, the percentage of students with disabilities regularly came to over 40 percent of all students in the classroom.*
>
> *There was an overall attitude that general education teachers did not want to participate in co-teaching partnerships. Many general education teachers who participated were brand-new teachers or teachers early in their careers. Veteran general education teachers participated in co-teaching only rarely. The sense was that participating in co-teaching diminished standing among general education teachers. They did not want to navigate the additional challenges they thought co-teaching would bring to their teaching practice.*

> *Five years later, special education teachers across the school felt more like equals among their co-teaching general education counterparts and students in their co-taught classes. Collaborative team meetings focused much more on teaching best practices versus special education policy and IEP writing and compliance discussions. Co-teaching partnerships between special education and general education teachers were lasting multiple years. Co-teaching partnerships were at least two periods per day, and some partnerships had four dedicated periods together per day.*
>
> *In addition, school leaders worked planning time for co-teachers into the master schedule for all co-teaching partnerships. Co-teaching amounted to nearly 75 percent of special education student placements. Within co-taught classrooms, the percentage of students with disabilities remained at over 40 percent. With the growth and success of the program, many seasoned general education teachers were participating in the co-teaching program. While some hesitance was still apparent from a few general education teachers, more than ever before were willing to participate and engage in co-teaching.*

Can you see how the culture of co-teaching changed over the course of five years? What changed? Additionally, did anything stay the same from years one to five of its implementation? It's no accident that the school improved its co-teaching culture: it increased supports for facets like planning, and it took steps to maintain the consistency of co-teaching partnerships. This school took elements of the coherence framework by Michael Fullan and Joanne Quinn (2016) to make necessary changes over time.

This chapter discusses elements of how schools can use the coherence framework to support implementation of co-teaching and the necessary cultural shift. The chapter's goal is to share with teachers and school leaders how to make a positive cultural shift over time to implement and sustain co-teaching in a way that benefits students, teachers, service providers, and the school community. Before jumping into how developing a co-teaching culture can manifest from the coherence framework and the leadership necessary to move forward with great co-teaching programs, we briefly discuss school culture and how teachers and leaders from every level of a school can provide leadership in building a culture where co-teaching flourishes.

Key Themes and Ideas
☐ Leaders at every level to build school culture
☐ The coherence framework for cultural change
☐ Leadership for building and sustaining the best co-teaching programs

---

Leaders at Every Level to Build School Culture

School culture encompasses many layers. From the school's systems, personalities, vision, goals, stakeholders, programs, and community to its history and its current context, these layers make it extremely complex. Therefore, it's up to educators and stakeholders within every part of the fabric of a school to implement and sustain programs, like co-teaching, over time.

Janelle Clevenger McLaughlin (2022) argues that everyone is a leader in their own right within a school system. Each stakeholder holds the keys to making any major cultural shift. Co-teaching, like any major systematic and cultural shift, requires all stakeholders to advocate for its implementation as well as consider how they can act to create sustainability. Throughout this chapter, as we discuss the coherence framework, we outline how different stakeholders within a school can act as leaders to support co-teaching, developing and sustaining it over time. In table 10.1, we illustrate each level of stakeholder within a school and how they can act as leaders to support the systems required for co-teaching to take place sustainably.

TABLE 10.1: Leadership at Every Level for Co-Teaching Cultures

General Education Teachers	Special Education Teachers	Special Education Specialist	School and District Leaders
Advocate for inclusive classroom environments for all students. Openly collaborate with special education teachers and service providers. Provide feedback about what works and what can be improved in co-teaching. Model effective co-teaching strategies and classrooms for peers. Continually focus on improvement of co-teaching and inclusive practices.	Advocate for inclusive classroom environments for all students. Openly collaborate with general education teachers and service providers to adapt instruction and meet the needs and goals of each student. Model effective co-teaching strategies and classroom environments with peers. Advocate for time to sustainably case manage, plan, and hold meetings. Continually focus on improvement of coaching and inclusive practices.	Collaborate with all teachers and stakeholders to provide supportive services to students. Assist in creating systems that bridge the classroom and external supportive services. Advocate for resources and supports necessary for co-teaching to flourish. Provide professional learning and resources for teachers, leaders, and the community on how to best support students with disabilities.	Create systems that value and support co-teaching. Ensure resources and professional development opportunities and coaching are available for co-teaching. Incorporate co-teaching within school and district policy. Develop procedures for planning, IEP meetings, dividing work among teachers and stakeholders, and communicating what co-teaching is to the local community. Encourage open communication among all stakeholders for continual improvement of co-teaching practices. Recognize and celebrate successful co-teaching collaborations.

The Coherence Framework for Cultural Change

With the understanding that a successful co-teaching culture requires leadership from all stakeholders, let's focus on what it takes to cultivate such a culture. In a dynamic education landscape, the coherence framework developed by Fullan and Quinn (2016) has proven to be an effective tool in instigating school reform, including implementing co-teaching. The strength of this framework lies in its adaptability, since each school environment presents a distinctive, unique amalgamation of conditions and challenges. When seeking to cultivate change and implement a new instructional program such as co-teaching, it's critical to consider the specific needs and conditions of the school site, its students, and the teachers who will carry out the change. We focus on what this framework is and its critical elements of focused direction, accountability, collaborative cultures, and deepening learning, as they can propel a school site to sustainably establish co-teaching.

Focused Direction

Having a focused direction means all stakeholders within a school share a common understanding and vision for co-teaching. A focused direction foster commitment among stakeholders, and it guides how decisions are made because it provides a basis for measuring progress. Let's look at what this means at the beginning of the initiative of co-teaching and then later in its implementation. Stakeholders in a school community who may have interest in co-teaching can, for example, have a conversation to set goals. In this committee, a school leader, teachers, district representatives, and community members outline their rationale for developing a co-teaching program. They can consider why co-teaching will benefit students, the school, and the community and then develop goals that align with the inclusion of students with disabilities, short-term and long-term academic outcomes, and social-emotional development.

SMART goals that lead into a strategic plan and timeline will help schools achieve their focused direction.

SMART GOALS

We recommend using specific, measurable, achievable, relevant, and timebound (SMART) goals to build your focused direction (see figure 10.1; Conzemius & O'Neill, 2013; Doran, 1981). With these goals established and the ability to measure progress, the committee can then develop programmatic strategies for implementing these goals with the stated amount of time.

Specific: Increase the inclusion of students with disabilities in general education classrooms by implementing a co-teaching model in at least 70 percent of core classes by the end of the academic year.

Measurable: Improve the short-term academic outcomes for all students participating in co-taught classes, with a target increase of 15 percent in overall average grades and benchmark assessments in these classes within the first semester of implementation.

Achievable: Develop a co-teaching model where general education and special education teachers are effectively collaborating in planning and instruction to support social-emotional development of students, with 80 percent of teachers reporting a positive impact on student relationships and classroom communities by the end of the first semester of co-teaching.

Relevant: Expand the co-teaching model to all grade levels in the school within two years to increase inclusivity and promote academic and social-emotional development across the school community.

Time bound: Increase the long-term academic outcomes for students with disabilities by reducing the achievement gap by 20 percent within three years as a result of consistent co-teaching practices.

Source: *Conzemius & O'Neill, 2013; Doran, 1981.*

FIGURE 10.1: SMART goals for co-teaching based on focused direction.

For any program with goals to measure its success, the school needs to illustrate this progress over time. Co-teaching and special education both strive to create the least restrictive environment for students; schools can measure this in several ways. For example, an inclusionary rate of students with disabilities within the general education setting is one way, as co-teaching makes inclusion possible. Figure 10.2 provides a chart for measuring the SMART goals we developed for figure 10.1, and figure 10.3 (page 170) provides a template for input over time.

Metrics of the SMART Goal	Baseline (Percentage)	Target (Percentage)	End of Semester 1 (Percentage)	End of Year 1 (Percentage)	Year 2 Target (Percentage)	Year 3 Target (Percentage)	Notes
Inclusion of students with disabilities in general education classrooms	40	70	60	70	100	100	Incremental increases expected; full implementation by year 2
Improvement in academic outcomes for all students in co-taught classes	–	+15	+10	+15	+20	+25	Measured by average grades and benchmark assessments
Teachers reporting positive impact on student relationships	–	80	70	80	90	95	Measured by teacher feedback surveys
Reduction in achievement gap for students with disabilities	–	-20	-10	-15	-18	-20	Long-term academic outcomes improvement

Note: The baseline percentage indicates the starting point before the implementation of co-teaching. The target percentage relates to the metrics according to the SMART goal. The end-of-semester percentage columns show expected progress at various intervals, tracking progress toward the ultimate goals after three years.

FIGURE 10.2: SMART goal–tracking chart example.

SMART goal:

School Year	Number of Students Enrolled in Special Education	Number in General Education Classrooms	Inclusionary Rate (Percentage)
2022–2023			
2023–2024			

Academic Outcomes of Students: Measure short-term academic outcomes by tracking either test scores or grades across co-taught classes within each marking period.

Assessment or Grading Period	Average Assessment Score or Grade in Co-Taught Classes

Social-Emotional Impact of Co-Teaching: Use a survey developed for teachers to measure their perception of co-teaching on the social-emotional development of students.

Semester	Mean Positive Response Percentage From Survey
Fall 2023	
Spring 2024	

Co-Teaching Implementation: Keep track of the number of co-teaching classes

School Year	Total Number of Classes	Number of Co-Taught Classes	Co-Teaching Implementation Rate
2022–2023			
2023–2024			

Achievement Gap: Through the use of state or district test scores, the achievement gap can be measured between students with special needs and their general education peers. Measure these data to see the long-term impact of the co-teaching model on student achievement.

School Year	Average Standardized Score—General Education Students	Average Standardized Score—Students With Disabilities	Achievement Gap
2022–2023			
2023–2024			

FIGURE 10.3: Data sheet template for co-teaching SMART goals.

Visit **go.SolutionTree.com/instruction** *for a free reproducible version of this figure.*

As you can see, each of the facets of this figure interrelate with the goals developed as a result of having a focused direction. Now, with the background of knowing what to measure, the next step in this framework is to ensure the focused direction is strategic and has a timeline for when and where certain events will need to unfold.

STRATEGIC PLAN AND TIMELINE

Part of having a focused direction is a strategic plan and timeline that lay out the direction the school is going. With progress-monitoring steps in place, your school can focus on creating this plan, what its implementation will look like, and when steps will take place.

School and districts leaders need to build the strategic plan and timeline in collaboration with stakeholders within the school community (Northouse, 2021), including the voices of everyone from teachers to service providers (Murawski & Lochner, 2018). The trajectory we generally recommend for developing the plan and timeline is to hold initial information-gathering focus groups followed by forming a strategic implementation team. Stakeholders should gather feedback throughout the process through surveys, reviews of the draft plan, and formalized discussion. We provide a sample strategic plan and timeline in figure 10.4 that presents key events and times. Following this, we provide a summarized sample strategic plan for a high school looking to implement co-teaching over the next three years (see figure 10.5, page 172).

Year 1: Planning and Pilot of Co-Teaching Program

Summer Year 1: Initiate co-teaching professional learning for teachers. Conduct professional development workshops focused on the principles and practices of co-teaching. Involve both general education and special education teachers in these sessions.

Fall Year 1: Pilot co-teaching. Implement a co-teaching model in a select number of core classes. Teachers with early buy-in form initial partnerships.

Spring Year 1: Evaluate pilot program. Analyze data from the pilot program to assess its effectiveness, identify areas of improvement, and revise the model accordingly. Celebrate successes and communicate them to the wider school community.

Year 2: Full-Scale Implementation and Refinement of Co-Teaching Program

Summer and Fall Year 2: Deploy full-scale implementation. Roll out the refined co-teaching model across 70 percent of core classes. Continue data collection on student outcomes and teacher feedback.

Spring Year 2: Refine. Analyze data from full-scale implementation to determine areas that need refinement. Implement changes to improve co-teaching effectiveness for teachers and students.

Year 3: Schoolwide Implementation and Long-Term Evaluation of Co-Teaching Program

Fall Year 3: Deploy schoolwide implementation. Expand the co-teaching model to all grade levels and classes within the school. Continually collect data on student outcomes and teacher feedback.

Spring Year 3: Engage in long-term evaluation. Analyze data to evaluate the impact of the co-teaching model on student academic outcomes and social-emotional development. Look specifically at the achievement gap reduction for students with disabilities. Continue refinement and improvement of co-teaching model based on data.

FIGURE 10.4: Strategic plan and timeline of co-teaching implementation example.

> **Co-Teaching Implementation: A Strategic Plan for Our High School**
>
> We are delighted to present a strategic plan designed to foster the effective implementation of a co-teaching program in our high school. This initiative embodies our commitment to inclusion and to the individual success of each student to support their short-term and long-term learning goals.
>
> Informed by the collective insights of our diverse school community—from teachers and service providers to administrative staff and parents—this strategic plan aims to progressively introduce co-teaching in a systematic manner to our school community. Our key stages for implementation are as follows.
>
> **Year 1: Planning and Pilot of Co-Teaching Program**
>
> The first year of this initiative is dedicated to laying a strong foundation for our co-teaching program. In the summer, we will kick-start co-teaching professional development for teachers with workshops focusing on principles and practices. Come fall, we will pilot co-teaching in a select number of core classes, leveraging the commitment of teachers who initially buy into the concept. By spring, we will evaluate this pilot program, making necessary adjustments and celebrating our accomplishments.
>
> **Year 2: Full-Scale Implementation and Refinement of Co-Teaching Program**
>
> Year 2 sees the full-scale rollout of our co-teaching model across 70 percent of core classes. Our primary focus during this period is ongoing data collection on student outcomes and teacher feedback. By spring, we will analyze these data to identify areas that need refinement, implementing necessary changes to enhance co-teaching effectiveness.
>
> **Year 3: Schoolwide Implementation and Long-Term Evaluation of Co-Teaching Program**
>
> By the third year, we anticipate a schoolwide implementation of our co-teaching model. Our aim is to embed this approach across all grades and classes. We will continue to assess student outcomes and teacher feedback with a specific focus on the reduction of the achievement gap for students with disabilities along with all students through designated formative and summative assessments. By spring, we will conduct a long-term evaluation of the co-teaching model's impact on academic outcomes and social-emotional development, implementing necessary refinements along the way.
>
> This strategic plan provides a road map for our journey toward inclusive education at our school site. As we navigate the process, we will maintain open lines of communication, ensuring that our school community remains involved, informed, and invested in the success of our co-teaching program. We look forward to the shared achievement that this initiative promises.

FIGURE 10.5: Summarized co-teaching strategic plan.

Accountability

Accountability, the second element of the coherence framework, focuses on how a school can maintain the integrity of the co-teaching program that it is implementing or maintaining. Accountability is about encouraging continual improvement, reviewing data, and ensuring the co-teaching program aligns with the school and district's broader goals of student achievement, well-being, and inclusion. Our goal is to outline several examples of what accountability would look like in schools where co-teaching programs are present.

- Maintain co-teaching partnerships for over one year.
- Establish and maintain co-teaching planning time.
- Ensure collaborative team meetings are rotating and teacher driven.
- Establish and maintain co-teacher duties and responsibilities.

MAINTAIN CO-TEACHING PARTNERSHIPS FOR OVER ONE YEAR

In many schools where co-teaching takes place, teachers do so in a voluntary manner; general education teachers sign up to be a part of the initiative. Usually, the school conducts this practice of selecting co-teachers until there is a pool of available co-teachers. Sometimes, when no volunteers are available, school leaders select teachers necessary for particular grade levels and sections. When they struggle to fill roles for several co-teaching classes, school leaders tend to shuffle co-teaching partnerships often—usually by necessity. While this may seem convenient at the time, it can harm the cultivation of co-teaching partnerships among teachers; as we establish earlier in the book, it may take more than one year before they meet their full potential. Additionally, if evaluations and student assessments show that co-teachers are effective together, leaders should not break up these partnerships. Overall, for accountability and the integrity of a co-teaching program to continue, schools must ensure they are maintaining effective co-teaching partnerships.

ESTABLISH AND MAINTAIN CO-TEACHING PLANNING TIME

School leaders and teachers must work together to first ensure weekly planning time for co-teachers and second to encourage co-teachers to take advantage of that time to plan lessons, assessments, and supports for students. Without co-teaching planning time in place throughout the week, lessons will be much less effective than if co-teachers have the time they need and the support to take advantage of it. Therefore, school leaders and teachers must emphasize planning time in the master schedule.

With available planning time, co-teaching partnerships must ensure that time is effective as possible. As we discuss earlier in this book with the strategies for effective planning, we must emphasize here again how important these strategies are. They ultimately will make or break a co-teaching partnership and the effectiveness of instruction. As a result, available planning time must also be effective planning time for co-teachers.

ENSURE COLLABORATIVE TEAM MEETINGS ARE ROTATING AND TEACHER DRIVEN

In schools functioning as PLCs, collaborative team meetings relating to co-teaching should be driven by teachers working to build capacity in developing their instructional tool kit. This breaks down to instructional strategies to support student learning, inclusion, tech integration, and equity. Special education teachers need to be included in general education teacher collaborative teams for long-term planning along with time for co-teachers at a school site to meet and discuss best practices in the areas covered previously. Many co-teachers do not have the preparation needed to implement proper strategies and supports (Chitiyo & Brinda, 2018). Participation in collaborative team meetings moves them closer to experiencing the preparation necessary for success.

ESTABLISH AND MAINTAIN CO-TEACHER DUTIES AND RESPONSIBILITIES

One of the first activities co-teachers should complete as a co-teaching partnership is a list of duties related to partnership (see chapter 5, Roles and Responsibilities in Planning and Workflow, page 90). Co-teaching is an active system that needs consistent attention (Hackett et al., 2021).

For example, list duties such as content creation during lesson planning, assessing student performance, IEP data input, goal progress, and so on. These duties can be co-assigned as well as assigned individually. This is a living document with key areas school leaders and teachers have determined as non-negotiables that must be assigned during a co-teaching partnership. Developing this list holds together a co-teaching partnership, helping ensure that duties are distributed equitably to benefit students.

Collaborative Cultures

Co-teaching by nature is a collaborative partnership, which needs to be modeled with special education and general education departments as well as those working with multilingual learners inside and outside of classrooms. The school's principle must model collaboration in administrative leadership that stems from decision making, professional development, and transparency (Darling-Hammond, Wechsler, Levin, Leung-Gagné, & Tozer, 2022).

Ultimately, collaborative cultures cultivate not only buy-in but also collaborative instructional risk taking, which allows for the instructional capacity of individuals, co-teaching partnerships, and departments to improve. In service of this, schools must implement systems that are collaborative in action and function: use the PLC process and ensure it is functioning and teacher driven, engage with rotating professional development, encourage teacher observation and feedback, support instructional coaching, and invite stakeholders' contributions to program development and improvement.

FUNCTIONING, TEACHER-DRIVEN PLC

Have you ever been in a collaborative team meeting that was mostly driven by mandates of school leadership? Where most of the meeting was about compliance versus discussing applicable instructional practices for your day-to-day work in classrooms to support student learning? These are general pitfalls we see over and over in schools. While structures are important, the notions of micromanagement and compliance are antithetical to a PLC (DuFour et al., 2024) and do not work when trying to build a collaborative culture where authentic feedback and instructional risk taking take place.

What we mean by a functioning, teacher-driven PLC is that the goals and structures of the PLC are formulated by the school and teacher leaders (Stanulis, Cooper, Dear, Johnston, & Richard-Todd, 2016). These structures include rotating teacher-driven professional development, lesson design, shared assignments, curriculum design (that is, program design), and receiving and giving feedback to colleagues regarding instructional practices. The school can distribute general essential information, but the ultimate goal of the schoolwide PLC process is to improve instruction so all students can optimize their classroom time and achieve the highest levels of learning (DuFour et al., 2024). A well-functioning PLC is critical for co-teaching partnerships, as the PLC process provides the structures they need to collaborate with other co-teaching teams and that general education and special education teachers need to develop their instructional tool kits (Lanning, 2022). This level of collaboration in co-teaching partnerships may also attract other teachers at the school to co-teaching.

ROTATING PROFESSIONAL DEVELOPMENT

Rotating professional development means that co-teaching partnerships and teachers who teach a wide variety of concepts and skills to diverse groups of students get an opportunity to share their best instructional practices during time allotted for collaborative team meetings (Karge, 2023b). Each of these best instructional practice demos can last from ten to thirty minutes and may include modeling key strategies within a lesson sequence with the group of teachers present acting as students. Another way this can occur is when a selected team of co-teachers provides the materials and partially models how these best practices look in their classroom. A third method is to record sequences of a lesson and bring the recording into the meeting for discussion and analysis. In these videos, the presenting co-teachers front-load and discuss the strategies, followed by short sequences of a lesson where they implement the strategies with students. Analysis and discussion can then take place in the meeting, followed by opportunities for co-teaching partnerships and teachers to reflect individually on how they may implement the strategy or strategies into their classroom instruction.

OBSERVATION FOR TEACHERS AND BY TEACHERS FOR FEEDBACK

Another facet of a collaborative culture is giving teachers an opportunity to observe other co-teaching classrooms (Smith, 2023). Whether it's a live observation or lesson recordings, observations provide teachers with an opportunity to see instructional strategies and co-teaching strategies in action. Observation additionally allows teachers to supply constructive feedback and reflect as teams on their own practices. In this light, recordings of the co-teaching partnership's lesson can be helpful for them to review and dissect. Methods for collecting the observation feedback can include a Google Form and then a graphic organizer with space for feedback and reflection. Co-teachers can then put what they've learned into an action plan, which can be a good method for holding teams accountable for continual instructional improvement.

INSTRUCTIONAL COACHING

Instructional coaching is one of the keys for building teachers' instructional capacity (Perret, 2023). Having an instructional coach provide co-teaching partnerships with consistent instructional feedback can be a powerful tool for reflection and improvement. On top of generalized feedback, co-teaching partnerships can benefit from the opportunity to participate in co-teaching cycles focused on an instructional strategy or co-teaching strategies. This gives co-teachers an opportunity to hone areas in which they would like to improve. Beyond focusing on instruction, the instructional coach can also uplift co-teaching partnerships by supporting them in planning, ed tech integration, and classroom management. All these facets are essential in creating effective instruction and healthy classroom environments for students.

STAKEHOLDER CONTRIBUTIONS TO PROGRAM DEVELOPMENT AND IMPROVEMENT

Stakeholders throughout a school are responsible for improving its programs. They know the ins and outs of the systems the program uses and have navigated the program in their own work as teachers, support staff, service providers, family members, students, and school leaders. For new initiatives, such as co-teaching, it is important to have these stakeholders' contributions to the decision-making and policy-creating process. When leadership makes decisions without consulting stakeholders, those decisions ultimately will not have the initial buy-in and enthusiasm to be sustainable or effective.

For a co-teaching program, even after its implementation, there should be a co-teaching leadership team at each school site that comprises important stakeholders and meets on a quarterly basis. In these meetings, team members review the same data that school leaders and teachers have access to when they work in their collaborative team meetings. Besides review and analysis of data, they discuss from a qualitative viewpoint the program's progress through the eyes of teachers, students, and families with students enrolled in the co-teaching program. Schools can use these leadership team conversations to evaluate the strategic plan, timeline, and goals of the co-teaching program with the objective of continual program improvement (Murawski & Dieker, 2013).

Deepening Learning for Teachers and Students

Each co-teaching program needs to focus on the continual process that empowers teachers to build capacity and efficacy in their co-teaching instructional practices. Along with this notion, co-teachers must focus on providing students with opportunities to learn critical content and skills to help them navigate an ever-changing world. The content and skills co-teachers provide to students should focus on four critical elements: (1) critical thinking, (2) creative thinking, (3) collaboration, and (4) communication (Fullan & Quinn, 2016). State standards related to specific content and domain knowledge, SEL skills, and digital, data, and AI literacy all encompass and interrelate together with these four major pillars of deepening learning.

Developing a set of strategies to teach deepening learning concepts with students in co-teaching classroom is essential to support all students to succeed in the future (Karten & Murawski, 2020). However, we recommend a less-is-more approach with the number of instructional and co-teaching strategies co-teaching partnerships and schools focus on, making it more feasible and sustainable to integrate concepts and skills to deepen learning in classrooms. By concentrating on a few well-chosen co-teaching strategies that teach deepening learning concepts, co-teachers can provide more consistent, thorough, and adaptable instruction that meets the varied needs of their students. Ultimately, implementing a focused approach to co-teaching strategies aligned to deepening learning concepts with a less-is-more mindset and focused direction promotes equity by ensuring all students in the class have access to the same high-quality instruction. Also, it gives both co-teachers opportunities to improve their instructional capacity to deliver these strategies more effectively, which can improve the instructional outcomes of students, thus impacting and promoting student equity.

Several key elements can help build the instructional capacity of co-teaching partnerships. Within rotating professional development, have co-teaching partnerships demo examples like the ones provided in this chapter. Additionally, offer co-teaching partners the opportunity to see these types of lessons recorded to conduct a lesson observation and analysis of the lesson and how it went with students. Finally, use instructional coaches who can provide real-time feedback to co-teachers throughout the year. Incorporate co-teaching teams in co-teaching cycles to work on instructional and co-teaching strategies. Though these elements take time, they will yield results if schools and academic and grade-level departments are consistent with them.

The big question is how teachers deliver instruction within their co-teaching classrooms to build their students' skills and knowledge. Our focus with this book is to help co-teaching partnerships do just this. Let's quickly jump into a couple examples of how we can focus on deepening learning within elementary and secondary co-teaching classes.

CO-TEACHING STRATEGIES WITH COOPERATIVE LEARNING AT THE ELEMENTARY LEVEL

In this scenario, the goal of the lesson is for students to build their collaboration and communication skills as they engage in solving addition mathematics problems in teams of two to three students. Each teacher has already delivered direct instruction related to how they would like students to solve the problems. Before this lesson occurs, both co-teachers model the cooperative learning strategy think, solve, pair, share together in front of the class through the team-teaching co-teaching strategy (Kagan, 1989; Karge, 2016, 2023a, 2023b). Once modeling is complete, the co-teachers split the class in half and assign students a partner or small team. Each student receives a mini whiteboard during the transition. Using the think, solve, pair, share cooperative learning strategy, each co-teacher gives a problem to their side of the room, implementing the parallel teaching co-teaching strategy. Students have time to think and process the problem, solve the problem individually, and then share their problem-solving technique with their partner. Then, each side of the class converges back in parallel to group instruction on their half of the room, and students get the opportunity to share their results with their half of the class so their teacher can see whether students need reteaching. Co-teachers in this instance switch sides to alternately teach each side of the room, going through the protocol three to four times over the course of about fifteen to twenty minutes. This allows students to practice and receive immediate feedback and reteaching.

CO-TEACHING STRATEGIES WITH DESIGN THINKING AT THE SECONDARY LEVEL

In a secondary science class focused on the topic of climate change, co-teachers provided prior explicit instruction through team teaching about how the climate and weather patterns are connected as well as how various gases in the atmosphere interrelate with one another as a driving factor in the change of climate over time. The project for today's unit involves how students might design a community initiative on how to mitigate the impact of harmful gases that their community emits.

Let's briefly focus on the design-thinking approach before we jump back into the example to put it into practice within a co-teaching classroom. Design thinking aims to boost student engagement by allowing them to explore the why behind their learning topics or skills. Making design thinking a structured approach to understanding why encourages students to continually develop and refine solutions to their challenges, mirroring real-world professional scenarios (Hasso Plattner Institute of Design at Stanford, 2016). Ultimately, design thinking encompasses six stages—(1) emphasize,

(2) define, (3) ideate, (4) prototype, (5) test, and (6) iterate—which can be taught in a scaffolded manner to develop a summative learning artifact.

To begin the project in the secondary science class, students use a graphic organizer about design thinking to conduct research using surveys that they deploy within their school and community. As they continue their research, part of the graphic organizer asks students to define specific challenges (such as people's overreliance on cars and coal-fired power plants for electricity) and then target specific actionable areas after collaborating with classmates. After these initial stages, students ideate; they brainstorm solutions to their well-defined challenges, such as ideas related to carpooling, electricity use reduction, and tree-planting initiatives. To prototype this next step, co-teachers ask students break into groups to design and craft detailed plans and visual campaigns that they will share with peers, teachers, and community members for feedback.

Throughout this process, co-teachers will likely move between the groups of students and assist and support them. Additionally, if the entire class needs feedback, both co-teachers will explicitly model that feedback through team teaching. In the same light, the method of team teaching can model the next steps of the design-thinking framework as students progress through the project.

Leadership for Building and Sustaining the Best Co-Teaching Programs

The coherence framework provides a flexible formula to implement and sustain a co-teaching program over time. We discussed examples of how to create a purposeful and focused direction with an emphasis on collaboration and securing accountability. We outlined how deepening learning provides an impactful and equitable instructional model. All these facets working together can support program and school improvement (Fullan & Quinn, 2016). We want to emphasize an additional three elements teachers, leaders, and schools need to focus on with this framework in mind as they look toward building and sustaining their co-teaching programs (regardless of where they are in the process). We end this chapter with these three elements: first, a focus on school and classroom structures, followed by acts of leadership and teachership that can make co-teaching successful and sustainable.

School and Classroom Structures

The structures and systems of schools and classrooms are essential for realizing the goals of implementing and sustaining a program like co-teaching. We outlined how a focused direction creates a clear vision for co-teaching and aligns with the overall mission and vision of a school. Keen co-teachers and leaders need to evaluate and see the structures within a school, such as the master schedule, instructional delivery, equity and inclusion integration in classrooms, and the combined work of teachers, students, and the community to support all students. With knowledge of these structures, leaders must also promote a collaborative culture in which all spaces in the school foster teamwork and a shared responsibility to students and the community. As a school progresses toward implementing a co-teaching program, schools can ensure accountability within their structures by designing them with embedded regular and consistent assessment and feedback such as observation, coaching, data analysis, and student and teacher feedback. The school must promote common co-teaching strategies, instructional strategies, and ed tech tool integrations, as instructional consistency among classrooms is paramount for student and school success.

Acts of Leadership to Make Co-Teaching Successful and Sustainable

Effective leadership for all stakeholders involved in implementing and sustaining a co-teaching program is imperative. All leaders must work together to ensure focused direction is the theme of the program by having clearly defined ideas of what co-teaching is, its benefits, and goals for facilitating it within their classrooms and schools. All leaders must be the collaborative torchbearers of these goals by establishing and maintaining a culture where open communication and teamwork are commonplace. To ensure this happens, all leaders must ensure individual and program accountability by evaluating the success of the co-teaching program, providing feedback, and making necessary adjustments. Even when constructive feedback may be hard to provide, leaders must be willing to provide it in an open and constructive manner. Finally, to deepen learning in the program, leaders must prioritize a multitude of professional learning opportunities embedded within the structures of the school to equip teachers, service providers, and support staff with the latest strategies to support all students.

Acts of Teachership to Make Co-Teaching Successful and Sustainable

Teachership is the embodiment of putting the coherence framework into action. Teachers aligned with the focused direction of the program can develop parallel teaching goals and outcomes for their students (Fullan & Quinn, 2016). A teacher's daily interactions within the school community should epitomize the essence of collaboration, where mutual respect, friendliness, open community, and shared planning in person and digitally are the norms. Accountability in teachership means continual self-assessment and seeking feedback with the goal of improvement of all facets of teaching and leadership. When improvement in these areas is a key daily focus, it facilitates a culture of improvement where instructional risk taking and collaboration are intertwined in daily interactions. The essence of teachership in this instance is deepening learning. To enhance instruction, co-teachers focus on three to five co-teaching strategies and then several instructional strategies that they can integrate to amplify student learning in an inclusive and equitable manner. They can synthesize ed tech and AI tools with these strategies to not only support student learning but also make that learning more accessible, inclusive, and easier to facilitate and monitor. This also provides all students equitable opportunities to access the instruction and receive multifaceted support, such as from the co-teachers themselves, AI tutors, accessibility tools, and ed tech tools. These factors, altogether, ensure teachers cater to the evolving needs of their students in a dynamic world.

Conclusion

For co-teaching programs to succeed in their implementation and sustainability, we need leaders at each level of a school to build a culture of co-teaching and to integrate co-teaching into the culture and systems of their school. It is not an easy process, but with an incremental approach, schools can implement co-teaching and see it spread as buy-in from stakeholders grows over time. We advocated for leaders building co-teaching programs *not* to take a swift approach. The two-to-five-year window of integration that we discuss in this chapter is a realistic and doable timeline, as schools have many different contexts and variables that may be more or less inclined toward co-teaching.

Co-teaching is a gateway toward increasing equity and inclusion within schools. Ultimately, it takes the dispositions we see in many mission and vision statements and puts them into action. Action is what counts, and co-teaching provides a model that puts these actions into practice. It takes leaders at all levels within a school and community to make co-teaching happen. Therefore, we hope our road map and framework that can be integrated into any school system and culture can help you take action. Whether your school has already implemented co-teaching to some degree, it's up to you and your school community to work toward building and then sustaining a co-teaching program. We know it can be done by the multitude of examples we have seen in our experience. Students around the world have benefited from the opportunities it has given them.

> **ADDITIONAL RESOURCES TO CONSIDER AFTER READING THIS CHAPTER**
> - *Watch, Listen, Ask, Learn: How School Leaders Can Create an Inclusive Environment for Students With Disabilities* by Belinda Dunnick Karge (2023) is geared toward school leaders to get them up to speed on special education and offers a step-by-step guide for implementing inclusive teaching schoolwide.
> - In this chapter, we discussed the coherence framework as our recommended model for school reform. The book *Coherence: The Right Drivers in Action for Schools, Districts, and Systems* by Michael Fullan and Joanne Quinn (2016) expands on this dynamic, customizable road map to change.

Reflection and Action: Develop an Action Plan

Directions: After reading chapter 10, develop an action plan for how you can, in your position at your school, facilitate the development of its co-teaching culture. Whether co-teaching is widespread, just starting, or in the planning stages, think about how you can impact the co-teaching culture. You can use generative AI for your rough draft by prompting it to help you brainstorm an outline of an action plan based on your current position in a school, goals for co-teaching, data you are able to collect and evaluate, and systems you must be able to navigate to make progress.

Co-Teaching Action Plan
Overarching Goal:
Measurable Goals:
Intended Outcomes:
Individual Actions:

Co-Teaching Evolved © 2025 Solution Tree Press • SolutionTree.com
Visit **go.SolutionTree.com/instruction** to download this free reproducible.

EPILOGUE
Moving Forward as a Co-Teacher

I believe that the most essential thing co-teachers must do to establish a solid co-teaching partnership is trust. With trust, there is mutual respect. With mutual respect, there is a partnership where two individuals each bring the best that they can be into the classroom in order to create the best team they can be.

—T. Olsen, curriculum specialist, personal communication, January 23, 2024

Co-teaching is the most dynamic form of teaching. It adds a layer of complexity but also yields opportunities to transform learning environments and experiences for our students. This book offers several ideas for how schools can revolutionize co-teaching to meet the needs of ever-changing classroom environments that span physical and digital spaces. Our eleven co-teaching strategies, high-impact, research-based instructional strategies, and ed tech tools and AI copilots can transform co-teaching from its historical roots to a powerful form of teaching able to meet the diverse needs of our students.

With this said, co-teaching is not easy! It is one of the most difficult forms of teaching and requires planning, experience, communication, dynamic teaching relationships, and navigation of increasingly complex classrooms and student needs. As indicated throughout this book, take it slow, and you will progress through the stages steadily.

There are three stages to effective co-teaching.

1. **Supportive stage** (one teach, one assist; one teach, one observe; one teach, one support): This is often a time of controlled communication; the

> definition of lead and assistant roles may cause teachers to be cautious as boundaries can develop. Co-teachers may get stuck at this stage.
>
> 2. **Team stage** (graze-and-tag teaching; parallel teaching; station teaching; alternative teaching): This is a time for more reciprocal communication with active and defined teaching roles. The level of trust typically increases as the co-teachers become more and more comfortable working together.
>
> 3. **Advanced stage** (conversation teaching; role-play teaching; interactive teaching; shared teaching): This stage is characterized by clear, open communication and mutual respect, which allow for a natural flow between the co-teachers.

Embracing the challenges and complexities of co-teaching is not for the faint of heart; it demands dedication, creativity, and a commitment to constant communication and collaboration. The rewards, however, are immeasurable. The journey of co-teaching we outline in this book demonstrates an evolution from traditional approaches to a vibrant and multifaceted practice that meets the needs of evolving classrooms.

Effective co-teaching can lead to enriched learning experiences, deeper student engagement and learning, and professional growth for teachers and educators. It's a journey of constant learning and adaptation, in which the combined strengths of co-teachers can significantly enhance the classroom learning experience, meeting the unique needs of every student in diverse and technologically advanced classrooms. This book aims to inspire and guide educators on this transformative path, unlocking the full potential of co-teaching and its positive impact on student learning.

Key Takeaways

We close this book with some key takeaways. We hope these takeaways provide you the opportunity to reflect and think about what your next moves are in your co-teaching journey. Whether you are a seasoned co-teacher or are just beginning, we want you to jot down the key actionable areas you are going to incorporate into your practice as a co-teacher. As a result, as you review each of our takeaways, spend time with the reproducible tool "Reflection and Action: Key Takeaways and Action Steps" (page 190) to reflect and create an action plan to take your co-teaching practice to the next level. In contrast to the co-teaching school culture action plan organizer provided in chapter 10 (page 165), this is more of a personal action plan to chart your individual journey.

No Partnership Is Perfect

No co-teaching partner is perfect. Relationships take work. They ebb and flow. However, as we discuss in this book, getting to know your co-teaching partner, how they teach, how they navigate the classroom, their education philosophies, and who they are as a colleague and person is critical for forming a strong partnership that can sustain the roller coaster of a school year. Additionally, being open to communication and feedback and taking time to celebrate go a long way and can contribute to positive and long-lasting co-teaching partnerships.

Integrate Co-Teaching Strategies With Instructional Strategies

The eleven co-teaching strategies we discuss in this book are the overarching strategies for co-teaching classrooms. They can sequence from one to another throughout a lesson. Integrated directly into these co-teaching strategies are instructional strategies such as modeling, direct instruction, assessment, guided practice, cooperative learning and thinking routines, and retrieval practice. These instructional strategies occur at the same time as the co-teaching strategies. Co-teachers can build their favored strategies into a tool kit. We recommend co-teaching partnerships use a less-is-more mindset and focus on three co-teaching strategies and five instructional strategies they would like to integrate into their lessons. As the co-teaching partnership progresses, they might include additional co-teaching strategies and instructional strategies. Keep it simple at first and then expand over time as you gain more experience using your co-teaching and instructional tool kit.

Integrate Co-Teaching Strategies With Ed Tech Tools

The co-teaching strategies and instructional strategies we integrate power our co-teaching. However, as noted throughout this book, teachers have ed tech tools that can further amplify these strategies in their lessons as well as support them in assessment, planning, and differentiating instruction. We live in a digital world where our classrooms span both digital and physical spaces. As a result, we recommend that each co-teaching classroom employ an LMS, use tools that can engage students and support ongoing formative assessment, and build routines with students around various tools that allow them to create a wide range of content using word processing, drawing and designing, and video creation. Co-teachers can use AI copilots to support them in planning instruction and building content for their lessons that can be differentiated to meet the diverse student needs in their classrooms.

Co-Teaching Includes AI Copilots

Co-teachers now have AI copilots to assist in a multitude of different tasks, including planning instruction, differentiating instruction, building classroom content, supporting data-driven decision making, and drafting communication on our behalf to teachers, students, and the greater school community. AI copilots do not replace teachers and never will. However, they can amplify the practice of teachers who know how to employ them strategically. Ultimately, co-teachers who use these AI copilots have an advantage that co-teachers in the past never had. The finite element of time applies much less pressure when co-teachers can be more efficient in planning, completing their administrative tasks, providing student feedback, and communicating progress with families and students. Now, more than ever before, co-teachers have the opportunity with AI copilots to get more time back in their hands to work more directly with students.

Co-Teaching Moves Classrooms Toward Further Equity and Inclusion

Co-teaching is a step toward the least restrictive environment for students with disabilities and a step toward acceptance for every student regardless of their race, gender identity, and so on. Co-teaching provides an environment for all students to be together in an inclusive space, which then opens similar opportunities for every student to learn the same skills and content together. When co-teaching is implemented effectively, we see opportunities to further narrow equity gaps. It also can create environments where all students can be included within the classroom culture and learning. Investment in co-teaching by creating more co-teaching sections at a school and building the capacity of co-teachers increases equity and inclusion.

Constant Communication and Collaboration Is Necessary

Co-teachers must communicate and collaborate as much as possible. This means there must be well-established channels of communication as well as places where collaboration takes place. We discussed how communication can take many forms and how collaboration can take place in physical and digital spaces. This also includes having challenging conversations. As we discuss throughout this book, at the beginning of any co-teaching partnership, build that foundation, because it is key to establishing and maintaining consistent communication and collaboration routines throughout the duration of the partnership.

Co-Teaching Must Be Sustainable

Co-teaching, as we have discussed, is not easy. We talked about how schools can make it more sustainable, such as shared preparation and planning time every day, co-teaching all day at the primary level, co-teaching within multiple class sections at the secondary level, developing systems for covering IEP meetings, and how school leaders can assist co-teachers by taking tasks off their plate. Co-teachers can use strategies and ed tech tools, including AI copilots, that make it easier for them to plan, deliver instruction, and stay on top of administrative duties.

Sustainability also hinges on the choices co-teachers make and how they interact as co-teaching partners. It's about building a partnership based on mutual respect, shared goals, and effective communication. The way co-teachers interact, resolve conflicts, share responsibilities, and support each other's professional growth plays a crucial role in sustaining the partnership. This requires ongoing reflection, adaptability, and a willingness to learn from each other. The book delves into these interpersonal aspects, offering insights and strategies to foster a strong, lasting co-teaching partnership that not only benefits the educators involved but also greatly enhances student learning experiences. We also outline how leadership and school systems can play a major part. From scheduled co-planning time, sustaining long-term co-teaching partners, and keeping teachers to one co-teaching partnership per year, to dedicating time within collaborative team meetings to focus on co-teaching strategies and instructional strategies, it takes a systemic shift to help establish and maintain a friendly and sustainable co-teaching environment.

Co-Teaching Classrooms Span Both Physical and Digital Spaces

Co-teaching provides students with instruction that spans both physical and digital classroom spaces. Lessons incorporate opportunities for students to learn the skills and content of the class in multiple spaces. As a result, co-teachers must know how to integrate co-teaching strategies and high-impact instructional strategies with and without ed tech so students can learn in blended digital and physical classroom environments. We ultimately want to teach our students how to navigate each of these spaces with what we are teaching them. Therefore, co-teachers must have the skills to plan and implement effective lessons in each of these spaces to provide equitable learning opportunities for their students.

All Can Contribute to Establishing and Maintaining Co-Teaching Cultures at Our Schools

We are all leaders. Each and every educator has the opportunity to lead, collaborate, and establish and maintain co-teaching cultures at their school. Whether it's beginning the conversation, being a stakeholder in a pilot program, developing the plan to implement the program, or building system and educator capacity within the context of co-teaching, we can all contribute to moving the needle. Good and effective co-teaching programs do not happen by accident. It takes a village within educational communities to not just make co-teaching happen but make it a pillar of school and district programs. Your work and leadership can lead to greater equity, inclusion, and student achievement for all learners, because co-teaching can lead to inclusive, equitable, and effective learning in our ever-changing world.

The Rewards

When all is said and done, co-teaching is worth it; there are so many rewards. We asked over 150 co-teaching teams we have worked with around the globe to describe the rewards. Their themed responses to the question, *What has been the most rewarding?* included the following.

- Sharing the workload between two teachers
- Reducing feelings of isolation

- Feeling friendship and collegiality with the other co-teacher
- Having a teaching partner to bounce ideas off
- Tag teaming students with challenging behaviors
- Seeing students rise to the occasion and achieve significant growth
- Seeing students experience an increased appreciation of individual differences
- Working together with struggling students and celebrating success
- Lightening the load with many hands
- Making connections with all students
- Feeling included in the school community
- Providing a different perspective for students
- Learning from each other
- Allowing students to participate in higher-level learning experiences in smaller groups with more individualization
- Learning more about the general education curriculum (special education co-teachers)
- Learning more about accommodations and UDL ideas (general education co-teachers)
- Learning more about special education strategies (general education co-teachers)
- Gaining curriculum content and instructional strategies (bilingual co-teachers)
- Realizing growth for everyone: co-teachers, students, parents, and the school community
- Trying more new things with co-teacher support
- Seeing special education students interact with peers
- Reteaching while the other teacher is teaching
- Enjoying more ease for planning for a sub; not spending all day worrying if students are behaving
- Assisting more students with more adults in the class
- Modeling positive interactions; it may be the only time that the student sees adults interact in a positive way
- Going to the restroom when you need to!

These statements affirm the rewards and value of co-teaching. Collaborating side by side with other educators to enhance the education of all students is a tall order, yet it is one that co-teaching can accomplish. Each co-teacher leverages their expertise to combine unique skills, knowledge, and experience to better meet the diverse needs of every student and to ultimately enhance student learning.

> **ADDITIONAL RESOURCE TO CONSIDER AFTER READING THIS BOOK**
> - Beyond this book, there are a wide variety of resources on co-teaching to investigate to extend your learning. As with any extended learning, we recommend a **less-is-more mindset**. Pick two to three areas you would like to further investigate and then go from there. Ultimately, we want to curate our time and review resources that we believe as educators can impact our practice. When we juggle more than a few items, this becomes difficult. Therefore, as you explore this list, remember this mindset.
> - Extend your learning with us! Visit **https://coteachingevolved.com** to access our website, blog, and videos on all things co-teaching.

Reflection and Action: Key Takeaways and Action Steps

Directions: After spending some time reflecting on your practice, take a moment to write down your key takeaways from this book. Then, write your next action steps to demonstrate how you will begin furthering and extending your learning. In your action steps, discuss how you will integrate what you have learned into your co-teaching practice.

Key Takeaways	Action Steps

REFERENCES AND RESOURCES

Alsarawi, A. (2019). A process, framework, and set of tools for facilitating co-planning among co-teachers. *International Journal of Whole Schooling, 15*(2), 1–23.

American Institutes for Research. (2018, November). *How does digital accessibility and Universal Design for Learning (UDL) impact your district's technology planning process?* Accessed at https://safesupportivelearning.ed.gov/voices-field/how-does-digital-accessibility-and-universal-design-learning-udl-impact-your-districts on November 9, 2023.

Anderson, K. P. (2021). The relationship between inclusion, absenteeism, and disciplinary outcomes for students with disabilities. *Educational Evaluation and Policy Analysis, 43*(1), 32–59. https://doi.org/10.1177/1053451220914896

Anderson, N., & Karge, B. (2020). Meaningful mentorship and its impact on the efficacy of secondary music teachers. *Chronicle of Mentoring & Coaching, 1*(13), 467–473.

Archer, A. L., & Hughes, C. A. (2010). *Explicit instruction: Effective and efficient teaching.* New York: Guilford Press.

Aronson, E. (2021). The jigsaw classroom: A personal odyssey into a systemic national problem. In N. Davidson (Ed.), *Pioneering perspectives in cooperative learning* (pp. 146–164). New York: Routledge.

Atkinson, V. S. (2021). *"For us it works": Co-teaching in a high school global history class.* Accessed at www.researchgate.net/publication/352369784_For_us_it_works_Co-teaching_in_a_High_School_Global_History_Class on March 20, 2024.

Ayob, N. S., Halim, N. D. A., Zulkifli, N. N., Zaid, N. M., & Mokhtar, M. (2020). Overview of blended learning: The effect of station rotation model on students' achievement. *Journal of Critical Reviews, 7*(6), 320–326.

Bacharach, N. L., Heck, T. W., & Dahlberg, K. (2010). *Changing the face of student teaching through co-teaching.* Accessed at https://repository.stcloudstate.edu/ed_facpubs/1 on March 29, 2023.

Bandura, A., Freeman, W. H., & Lightsey, R. (1999). *Self-efficacy: The exercise of control.* New York: Worth.

Banta, T. W., & Palomba, C. A. (2014). *Assessment essentials: Planning, implementing, and improving assessment in higher education.* Hoboken, NJ: John Wiley & Sons.

Barton, E. E., & Smith, B. J. (2015). Advancing high-quality preschool inclusion: A discussion and recommendations for the field. *Topics in Early Childhood Special Education, 35*(2), 69–78.

Beebe, S. A., Mottet, T. P., & Roach, K. D. (2013). *Training and development: Communicating for success.* Boston: Pearson.

Bliss, J., Askew, M., & Macrae, S. (1996). Effective teaching and learning: scaffolding revisited. *Oxford Review of Education, 22*(1), 37–61. https://doi.org/10.1080/0305498960220103

Brown, A., & Green, T. (2018). Issues and trends in instructional technology: Consistent growth in online learning, digital content, and the use of mobile technologies. In R. M. Branch, (Ed.), *Educational media and technology yearbook* (vol. 41, pp. 61–71). Cham, Switzerland: Springer Cham. https://doi.org/10.1007/978-3-319-67301-1_5

Carpenter, S. K. (2014). Spacing and interleaving of study and practice. In V. A. Benassi, C. E. Overson, & C. M. Hakala (Eds.), *Applying science of learning in education: Infusing psychological science into the curriculum* (pp. 131–141). Washington, DC: Society for the Teaching of Psychology.

Carrillo, E. M. (2023). *General education teacher perceptions of co-teaching settings* [Doctoral dissertation, Concordia University Irvine]. Accessed at www.proquest.com/docview/2894278257 on May 29, 2024.

Carter, E. W. (2015). What matters most: Toward a future of flourishing. *TASH Connections, 41*(3), 10–20.

CAST. (2011). *Universal design for learning guidelines.* Accessed at https://udlguidelines.cast.org/binaries/content/assets/udlguidelines/udlg-v2-0/udlg_graphicorganizer_v2-0.pdf on March 26, 2024.

Center for the Study of Child Care Employment. (2021). *Early childhood workforce index 2020.* Accessed at https://cscce.berkeley.edu/workforce-index-2020/wp-content/uploads/sites/3/2021/02/Early-Childhood-Workforce-Index-2020.pdf on March 26, 2024.

Cerdenio, R. E. (2023). *Co-teaching for life skills instruction: Expanding the role of school-based occupational therapy practitioners* [Doctoral dissertation, Boston University]. Accessed at https://open.bu.edu/handle/2144/45428 on March 25, 2024.

Chandler, G. A., & Budge, K. M. (2023). *Powerful student care: Honoring each learner as distinctive and irreplaceable*. Alexandria, VA: ASCD.

Child Trends. (2019). *Policies, initiatives, and resources to support the ECE workforce*. Accessed at www.childtrends.org/project/fcd-ece-workforce on March 26, 2024.

Chitiyo, J., & Brinda, W. (2018). Teacher preparedness in the use of co-teaching in inclusive classrooms. *Support for Learning, 33*(1), 38–51. https://doi-org.cui.idm.oclc.org/10.1111/1467-9604.12190

Clancy, T., Rosenau, P., Ferreira, C., Lock, J., & Rainsbury, J. (2015). Modeling co-teaching to inform professional practices. In A. P. Preciado Babb, M. Takeuchi, & J. Lock (Eds.), *Proceedings of the IDEAS: Designing responsive pedagogy* (pp. 72–81). Calgary, AB, Canada: Werklund School of Education, University of Calgary. Accessed at http://prism.ucalgary.ca/bitstream/1880/50861/1/8%20Modeling%20 %20Clancy%20et%20al.pdf on March 26, 2024.

Cole, S. M., Murphy, H. R., Frisby, M. B., Grossi, T. A., & Bolte, H. R. (2021). The relationship of special education placement and student academic outcomes. *Journal of Special Education, 54*(4), 217–227. https://doi.org/10.1177/0022466920925033

Coleman, H., Hestenes, L., & Ozdemir, M. K. (2021). Quality in inclusive and non-inclusive infant and toddler classrooms: What are the trends after 15 years? *Journal of Research in Childhood Education, 36*(1), 126–142.

Conzemius, A. E., & O'Neill, J. (2013). *The handbook for SMART school teams: Revitalizing best practices for collaboration*. Bloomington, IN: Solution Tree Press.

Cook, L., & Friend, M. (1995). Co-teaching: Guidelines for creating effective practices. *Focus on Exceptional Children, 28*(3), 1–17. https://doi.org/10.17161/fec.v28i3.6852

Cordie, L. A., Brecke, T., Lin, X., & Wooten, M. C. (2020). Co-teaching in higher education: Mentoring as faculty development. *International Journal of Teaching and Learning in Higher Education, 32*(1), 149–158.

Cornal, R. (2021). *The grappling arts: A handbook of professional wrestling, from the perspective of a mark*. Accessed at https://soar.suny.edu/handle/20.500.12648/12418 on May 29, 2024.

Cosier, M., Sandoval-Gomez, A., Cardinal, D. N., & Brophy, S. (2020). Placement of students with extensive support needs in California school districts: The state of inclusion and exclusion. *International Electronic Journal of Elementary Education, 12*(3), 249–255. https://doi.org/10.26822/iejee.2020358218

Coviello, J., & DeMatthews, D. E. (2021). Failure is not final: Principal's perspectives on creating inclusive schools for students with disabilities. *Journal of Educational Administration, 59*(4), 514–531.

Crossland, A., Gray, T., Reynolds, J., Wellington, D. Zhou, A., & Justo-Zavaleta, M. (2017). *Digital accessibility toolkit: What education leaders need to know* (Updated ed.). Washington, DC: American Institutes for Research, Consortium on School Networking, Center on Technology and Disability.

Cruz, R. A., Firestone, A. R., & Love, M. (2023). Beyond a seat at the table: Imagining educational equity through critical inclusion. *Educational Review, 76*(1), 69–95. doi: 10.1080/00131911.2023.2173726

Daley, K. M. (2021). Investigating co-teaching for impact on academic engagement: Best practices for English subject learners in a bilingual elementary school. *Journal of Teacher Action Research, 7*(3), 87–99.

Darling-Hammond, L., Wechsler, M. E., Levin, S., Leung-Gagné, M., & Tozer, S. (2022). *Developing effective principals: What kind of learning matters?* [Report]. https://doi.org/10.54300/641.201

DeVoss, M. (2023). Models of instruction for multilingual learners: Facets of the ESOL co-teacher role. *Georgia Journal of Literacy, 45*(2), 4–14.

Dieker, L. (2007). *The co-teaching lesson plan book* (3rd ed.). Arlington, VA: Council for Exceptional Children.

Donohoo, J., Hattie, J., & Eells, R. (2018). The power of collective efficacy. *Educational Leadership, 75*(6), 40–44.

Doran, G. T. (1981). There's a S.M.A.R.T. way to write management's goals and objectives. *Management Review, 70*(11), 35–36.

Dove, M., & Honigsfeld, A. (2010). ESL coteaching and collaboration: Opportunities to develop teacher leadership and enhance student learning. *TESOL Journal, 1*(1), 3–22.

DuFour, R., DuFour, R., Eaker, R., Many, T. W., Mattos, M., & Muhammad, A. (2024). *Learning by doing: A handbook for Professional Learning Communities at Work* (4th ed.). Bloomington, IN: Solution Tree Press.

DuFour, R., DuFour, R., Eaker, R., Mattos, M., & Muhammad, A. (2021). *Revisiting Professional Learning Communities at Work®: Proven insights for sustained, substantive school improvement* (2nd ed.). Bloomington, IN: Solution Tree Press.

Eriksson, T., Jaskari, M.-M., & Kinnunen, P. (2020). *Co-teaching is great!—But only if there is time: Teacher perspectives on online co-teaching.* Accessed at http://njb.fi/wp-content/uploads/2020/12/3_3-20_Eriksson_et_al.pdf on March 27, 2024.

Esposito, R. (2023). *The perceptions of general education and special education teachers on professional development for co-teaching, administrative support and collaborative co-teaching practices* [Unpublished doctoral dissertation, Marymount University].

Feller, T. R., Jr., Myers, E., & Smith, A. (2022). Communities of practice empower teachers to tackle thorny problems. *The Learning Professional, 43*(1), 24–29.

Fisher, D., & Frey, N. (2013, October). Gradual release of responsibility instructional framework. *IRA E-ssentials*, 1–8. doi:10.1598/e-ssentials.8037

Fisher, D., & Frey, N. (2021). *Better learning through structured teaching: A framework for the gradual release of responsibility*. Alexandria, VA: ASCD.

Fitzpatrick, D., Fox, A., & Weinstein, B. (2023). *The AI classroom: The ultimate guide to artificial intelligence in education*. Indianapolis, IN: TeacherGoals.

Friend, M. (2000). Myths and misunderstandings about professional collaboration. *Remedial and Special Education*, *21*(3), 130–132.

Friend, M. (2008). Co-teaching: A simple solution that isn't simple after all. *Journal of Curriculum and Instruction*, *2*(2), 9–19.

Friend, M. (2014, June 23). *Co-teaching: Classroom partnerships for student success*. Accessed at https://wyominginstructionalnetwork.com/wp-content/uploads/2018/05/Mon-Dr-Friend-Co-Teaching-Basic.pdf on June 6, 2024.

Friend, M. P. (2019). *Co-teach!: Building and sustaining effective classroom partnerships in inclusive schools* (3rd ed.). Washington, DC: Marilyn Friend, Inc.

Friend, M., & Barron, T. (2016). Co-teaching as a special education service: Is classroom collaboration a sustainable practice? *Education Practice and Reform, 2*. Accessed at https://journals.radford.edu/index.php/EPR/article/view/55/29 on August 28, 2024.

Friend, M., Cook, L., Hurley-Chamberlain, D., & Shamberger, C. (2010). Co-teaching: An illustration of the complexity of collaboration in special education. *Journal of Educational and Psychological Consultation*, *20*(1), 9–27. https://doi.org/10.1080/10474410903535380

Fullan, M., & Quinn, J. (2016). *Coherence: The right drivers in action for schools, districts, and systems*. Thousand Oaks, CA: Corwin Press.

Gagné, R. M., Wager, W. W., Golas, K. C., Keller, J. M., & Russell, J. D. (2005). Principles of instructional design. *Performance Improvement*, *44*, 44–46. https://doi.org/10.1002/pfi.4140440211

Garvis, S., & Pendergast, D. (Eds.). (2016). *Asia-Pacific perspectives on teacher self-efficacy*. Rotterdam, The Netherlands: Sense.

Goddard, R., Skrla, L., & Salloum, S. (2017). The role of collective efficacy in closing student achievement gaps: A mixed methods study of school leadership for excellence and equity. *Journal of Education for Students Placed at Risk*, *22*(4), 220–236. 10.1080/10824669.2017.1348900

Grant, A. (2023). *Hidden potential: the science of achieving greater things*. New York: Viking.

Grisham-Brown, J., Cox, M., Gravil, M., & Missall, K. (2010). Differences in child care quality for children with and without disabilities. *Early Education and Development*, *21*(1), 21–37.

Grisham-Brown, J., Pretti-Frontczak, K., Hawkins, S., & Winchell, B. (2009). Addressing early learning standards for all children within blended preschool classrooms. *Topics in Early Childhood Special Education*, *29*(3), 131–142.

Guise, M., Habib, M., Thiessen, K., & Robbins, A. (2017). Continuum of co-teaching implementation: Moving from traditional student teaching to co-teaching. *Teaching and Teacher Education*, *66*(1), 370–382. https://doi.org/10.1016/j.tate.2017.05.002

Guise, M., Hegg, S., Hoellwarth, C., & O'Shea, M. (2022). Support for coteaching in clinical practice: The development and use of a coassessing rubric for collaboratively analyzing student learning. *The New Educator*, *18*(1–2), 148–178.

Hackett, J., Kruzich, J., Goulter, A., & Battista, M. (2021). Tearing down the invisible walls: Designing, implementing, and theorizing psychologically safer co-teaching for inclusion. *Journal of Educational Change*, *22*(3), 103–130.

Hall, P., & Simeral, A. (2015). *Teach, reflect, learn: Building your capacity for success in the classroom*. Arlington, VA: ASCD.

Hamdan, A. R., Anuar, M. K., & Khan, A. (2016). Implementation of co-teaching approach in an inclusive classroom: Overview of the challenges, readiness, and role of special education teacher. *Asia Pacific Education Review*, *17*(2), 289–298. doi:10.1007/s12564-016-9419

Hasbrouck, J., & Tindal, G. (2017). *An update to compiled ORF norms* (Technical report no. 1702). Eugene: Behavioral Research and Teaching, University of Oregon.

Hasso Plattner Institute of Design at Stanford. (2016). *An introduction to design thinking: Process guide*. Accessed at https://web.stanford.edu/~mshanks/MichaelShanks/files/509554.pdf on March 26, 2024.

Hattie, J. (2012). *Visible learning for teachers: Maximizing impact on learning*. New York: Routledge.

Hattie, J. (2023). *Visible learning: The sequel—A synthesis of over 2,100 meta-analyses relating to achievement*. New York: Routledge.

Head Start Act [42 U.S.C. 9835] Sec. 640(d)(1) through (d)(5). (2017).

Hebbeler, K., & Spiker, D. (2016). Supporting young children with disabilities. *Future of Children*, *26*(2), 185–205.

Henriksen, D., Henderson, M., Creely, E., Carvalho, A. A., Cernochova, M., Dash, D., et al. (2021). Creativity and risk-taking in teaching and learning settings: Insights from six international narratives. *International Journal of Educational Research Open*, *2*, 100024.

Hill, T. (2020). *Perceptions of co-teaching in secondary inclusion classrooms* [Doctoral dissertation, Gardner-Webb University]. Accessed at https://digitalcommons.gardner-webb.edu/cgi/viewcontent.cgi?article=1018&context=education-dissertations on March 29, 2024.

Hoover, K. K. (2007). *The benefits of collaboration and co-teaching in the elementary grades* [Master's thesis, University of Northern Iowa]. Accessed at https://scholarworks.uni.edu/cgi/viewcontent.cgi?article=1870&context=grp on March 29, 2024.

Hughes, C. A., Morris, J. R., Therrien, W. J., & Benson, S. K. (2017). Explicit instruction: Historical and contemporary contexts. *Learning Disabilities Research & Practice, 32*(3), 140–148.

Hughes, C. E., & Murawski, W.W. (2001). Lessons from another field: Applying co-teaching strategies to gifted education. *Gifted Child Quarterly, 45*(3), 195–204.

Hunter, R. (2004). *Mastery teaching: Increasing instructional effectiveness in elementary and secondary schools.* Thousand Oaks, CA: Corwin Press.

Jenkins, M. C., & Murawski, W. W. (2024). *Connecting high-leverage practices to student success: Collaboration in inclusive classrooms.* Thousand Oaks, CA: Corwin Press.

Jeong, H., & Eggleston, L. (2021). Reflections on co-teaching and collaboration: Communication, flexibility, and congruence. In B. Yoon (Ed.), *Effective teacher collaboration for English language learners* (pp. 42–61). New York: Routledge.

Jomuad, P. D., Antiquina, L. M. M., Cericos, E. U., Bacus, J. A., Vallejo, J. H., Dionio, B. B., et al. (2021). Teachers' workload in relation to burnout and work performance. *International Journal of Educational Policy Research and Review, 8*(2), 48–53

Kagan, S. (1989). The structural approach to cooperative learning. *Educational Leadership, 47*(4), 13–16.

Kagan, S., & Kagan, S. (2009). *Cooperative learning.* San Clemente, CA: Kagan.

Kamarudin, K. (2021). The implementation of mix-pair-share strategy in teaching speaking skill at school amid Covid-19 pandemic. *Cordova Journal of Language and Culture Studies, 11*(1), 19–32.

Karge, B. D. (2014). *Engage 11: Strategies to promote student engagement in Common Core lessons.* Vista, CA: The Discovery Source.

Karge, B. D. (2015). *Engage co-teach: Eleven co-teaching strategies.* Vista, CA: Discovery Source.

Karge, B. D. (2016). *Engage eleven: Strategies to promote student engagement in Common Core lessons.* Vista, CA: Discovery Source.

Karge, B. D. (2018). Integrating special education knowledge into professional development schools. In M. Cosena & M. Buchanan (Eds.), *Visions from professional development school partners* (pp. 189–206). Charlotte, NC: Information Age.

Karge, B. D. (2023a). Using think-write-pair-share for student engagement. *TCARE National Newsletter, 15*, 16.

Karge, B. D. (2023b). *Watch, listen, ask, learn: How school leaders can create an inclusive environment for students with disabilities.* Bloomington, IN: Solution Tree Press.

Karge, B. D., Phillips, K. M., Jessee, T., & McCabe, M. (2011, December). Effective strategies for engaging adult learners. *Journal of College Teaching & Learning, 8*(12), 53–56.

Karten, T. J., & Murawski, W. W. (2020). *Co-teaching do's, don'ts, and do betters.* Alexandria, VA: ASCD.

Kellerman, A. (2014). The satisfaction of human needs in physical and virtual spaces. *The Professional Geographer, 66*(4), 538–546.

Kim, A., Woodruff, A. L., Klein, C., & Vaughn, S. (2006). Facilitating co-teaching for literacy in general education classrooms through technology: Focus on students with learning disabilities. *Reading & Writing Quarterly, 22*(3), 269–291. doi: 10.1080/10573560500455729

Kim, E., & Pratt, S. M. (2023). Co-teaching goes online: The impact of virtual co-teaching on the practices of a co-teaching partnership during COVID. *Studying Teacher Education, 20*(1), 107–127. doi: 10.1080/17425964.2023.2250361

Kim, S. K., & Webb, S. (2022). The effects of spaced practice on second language learning: A meta-analysis. *Language Learning, 72*(1), 269–319.

King-Sears, M. E., Stefanidis, A., Berkeley, S., & Strogilos, V. (2021). Does co-teaching improve academic achievement for students with disabilities? A meta-analysis. *Educational Research Review, 34.* doi.org/10.1016/j.edurev.2021.100405

Klassen, R. M., & Tze, V. M. (2014). Teachers' self-efficacy, personality, and teaching effectiveness: A meta-analysis. *Educational Research Review, 12*(4), 59–76.

Knight, J. (2011). *Unmistakable impact: A partnership approach for dramatically improving instruction.* Thousand Oaks, CA: Corwin Press.

Koehler, M. J., & Mishra, P. (2009). What is technological pedagogical content knowledge? *Contemporary Issues in Technology and Teacher Education, 9*(1), 60–70.

Krämer, S., Möller, J., & Zimmermann, F. (2021). Inclusive education of students with general learning difficulties: A meta-analysis. *Review of Educational Research, 91*(3), 432–478. https://doi.org/10.3102/0034654321998072

Krammer, M., Gastager, A., Lisa, P., Gasteiger-Klicpera, B., & Rossmann, P. (2018). Collective self-efficacy expectations in co-teaching teams—What are the influencing factors? *Educational Studies, 44*(1), 99–114.

Lanning, J. W. (2022). *Encouraging trust, collaboration, and best practices for co-teachers through a professional learning community* [Doctoral dissertation, Trident University International]. Accessed at www.proquest.com/openview/9a29feb36b3e4442d4ad41 6dedb31773/1?pq-origsite=gscholar&cbl=18750&diss=y on March 28, 2024.

Leahy, W., & Sweller, J. (2008). The imagination effect increases with an increased cognitive load. *Applied Cognitive Psychology, 22*(2), 273–283. http://dx.doi.org/10.1002/acp.1373

Leasa, M., & Corebima, A. D. (2017). The effect of numbered heads together (NHT) cooperative learning model on the cognitive achievement of students with different academic ability. *Journal of Physics: Conference Series, 795*(1), 012071.

Lenard, M., & Townsend, M. (2017). *Academically gifted co-teaching in the Wake County Public School System: Implementation, perceptions and achievement* (DRA Report No. 17.03). Accessed at https://files.eric.ed.gov/fulltext/ED606971.pdf on March 28, 2024.

Lin, T. J., Chen, J., Justice, L. M., & Sawyer, B. (2019). Peer interactions in preschool inclusive classrooms: The roles of pragmatic language and self-regulation. *Exceptional Children, 85*(4), 432–452. https://doi.org/10.1177/0014402919828364

Little, M. E., & Theker, M. (2009). Co-teaching: Two are better than one. *Principal Leadership, 9*(8), 42–60. https://doi.org/10.1177/15407966974002338

Maich, K., Davies, A. W., Penney, S. C., Butler, E., Young, G.D., & Philpott, D. (2019). Young children with autism spectrum disorder in early education and care: The earlier we begin together, the better. *Exceptionality Education International, 29*(3), 77–91.

Manurung, M. R., Masitoh, S., & Arianto, F. (2022). How thinking routines enhance critical thinking of elementary students. *International Journal of Recent Educational Research, 3*(6), 640–650.

McGuire, S. Y. (2015). *Teach students how to learn: Strategies you can incorporate into any course to improve student metacognition, study skills, and motivation.* Sterling, VA: Stylus.

McLaughlin, J. C. (2022). *Leadership at every level: Five qualities of effective classroom, school, and district leaders.* Bloomington, IN: Solution Tree Press.

Mills, J., Wiley, C., & Williams, J. (2019). *"This is what learning looks like!": Backward design and the framework in first year writing.* Accessed at https://repository.belmont.edu/libraryscholarship/1 on March 28, 2024.

Mofield, E. L. (2020). Benefits and barriers to collaboration and co-teaching: Examining perspectives of gifted education teachers and general education teachers. *Gifted Child Today, 43*(1), 20–33. doi.org/10.1177/1076217519880588

Mojavezi, A., & Tamiz, M. P. (2012). The impact of teacher self-efficacy on the students' motivation and achievement. *Theory and Practice in Language Studies, 2*(3), 483–491.

Moreira, B. F. T., Pinto, T. S. S., Starling, D. S. V., & Jaeger, A. (2019, February). Retrieval practice in classroom settings: A review of applied research. *Frontiers in Education, 4,* 5.

Mullican, J. L. (2021). *Co-teaching training and paired placements in physical education teacher education field experience* [Doctoral dissertation, The University of North Carolina at Greensboro]. Accessed at https://libres.uncg.edu/ir/listing.aspx?id=37078 on March 25, 2024.

Murawski, W. W. (2009). *Collaborative teaching in secondary schools: Making the co-teaching marriage work!* Thousand Oaks, CA: Corwin Press. https://doi.org/10.1108/09578231011015476

Murawski, W. W. (2010). *Collaborative teaching in elementary schools: Making the co-teaching marriage work!* Thousand Oaks, CA: Corwin Press.

Murawski, W., & Dieker, L. (2013). *Leading the co-teaching dance: Leadership strategies to enhance team outcomes.* Arlington, VA: Council for Exceptional Children.

Murawski, W. W., & Lochner, W. W. (2018). *Beyond co-teaching basics: A data-driven, no-fail model for continuous improvement.* Alexandria, VA: ASCD.

Murawski, W. W., & Scott, K. L. (Eds.). (2017). *What really works with exceptional learners.* Thousand Oaks, CA: Corwin Press.

Murawski, W. W., & Spencer, S. A. (2011). *Collaborate, communicate, and differentiate! How to increase student learning in today's diverse schools.* Thousand Oaks, CA: Corwin Press.

National Governors Association Center for Best Practices & Council of Chief State School Officers. (2010a). *Common Core State Standards for English language arts and literacy in history/social studies, science, and technical subjects.* Washington, DC: Authors. Accessed at www.corestandards.org/assets/CCSSI_ELA%20Standards.pdf on March 29, 2024.

National Governors Association Center for Best Practices & Council of Chief State School Officers. (2010b). *Common Core State Standards for mathematics.* Washington, DC: Authors. Accessed at www.corestandards.org/assets/CCSSI_Math%20Standards.pdf on March 29, 2024.

Nazari, R., & Hatami, J. (2023). Improving math performance using the written think-aloud strategy: Written think aloud in math learning. *International Journal of Learning spaces Studies, 1*(4), 11–20.

Nix, J.-M. L. (2021). Co-teachers' perceptions of collaborative EFL teaching: A case study in Taiwan. *Asia Pacific Education Review, 22*(4), 595–608.

Northouse, P. G. (2021). *Leadership: Theory and practice.* Thousand Oaks, CA: Sage.

Oded, I., & Oded, Y. (2022). Pear Deck. *CALICO Journal, 39*(3), 383–392. doi:10.1558/cj.18575

Odom, S. L., Vitztum, J., Wolery, R., Lieber, J., Sandall, S., Hanson, M. J., et al. (2004). Preschool inclusion in the United States: A review of research from an ecological systems perspective. *Journal of Research in Special Educational Needs, 4*(1), 17–49.

Pearson, P. D., & Gallagher, M. C. (1983). The instruction of reading comprehension. *Contemporary Educational Psychology, 8*(3), 317–344.

Pedler, M., Yeigh, T., & Hudson, S. (2020). The teachers' role in student engagement: A review. *Australian Journal of Teacher Education, 45*(3). https://doi.org/10.14221/ajte.2020v45n3.4

Perret, K. (2023, August). To avoid overload, establish priorities and focus on your goals. *The Learning Professional, 44*(4), 12–13.

Petitpas, D., & Buchanan, T. (2023). Using observation to guide your teaching. *Teaching Young Children, 16*(1), 4–7.

Rathvon, N. (2008). *Effective school interventions: Evidence-based strategies for improving student outcomes.* New York: Guilford Press.

Rhoads, M., & Lim, B. (2022). *Amplifying instructional design.* Alexandria, VA: EduMatch.

Rhoads, M., McLaughlin, J., & Moore. S. (2022). *Instruction without boundaries: Enhance your teaching strategies with technology in any setting.* Alexandria, VA: EduMatch.

Ritchhart, R., Church, M., & Morrison, K. (2011). *Making thinking visible: How to promote engagement, understanding, and independence for all learners.* Hoboken, NJ: John Wiley & Sons.

Roediger, H. L., III, & Butler, A. C. (2011). The critical role of retrieval practice in long-term retention. *Trends in Cognitive Sciences, 15*(1), 20–27.

Rohrer, D. (2012). Interleaving helps students distinguish among similar concepts. *Educational Psychology Review, 24*(3), 355–367.

Roorda, D. L., Koomen, H. M. Y., Spilt, J. L., & Oort, F. J. (2011). The influence of affective teacher–student relationships on students' school engagement and achievement: A meta-analytic approach. *Review of Educational Research*, *81*(4), 493–529. https://doi.org/10.3102/0034654311421793

Rosenzweig, C., Krawec, J., & Montague, M. (2011). Metacognitive strategy use of eighth-grade students with and without learning disabilities during mathematical problem solving: A think-aloud analysis. *Journal of Learning Disabilities*, *44*(6), 508–520.

Rothstein, L., & Johnson, S. F. (2021). *Special education law* (6th ed.). Thousand Oaks, CA: Sage.

Rumack, A. M., & Huinker, D. (2019). Capturing mathematical curiosity with notice and wonder. *Mathematics Teaching in the Middle School*, *24*(7), 394–399.

Rytivaara, A., Pulkkinen, J., & de Bruin, C. L. (2019). Committing, engaging and negotiating: Teachers' stories about creating shared spaces for co-teaching. *Teaching and Teacher Education*, *83*, 225–235.

Scruggs, T. E., Mastropieri, M. A., & McDuffie, K. A. (2007). Co-teaching in inclusive classrooms: A metasynthesis of qualitative research. *Exceptional Children*, *73*(4), 392–416.

Simon, B. D. (2017). *Successful collaboration between general education and special education teachers: A case study* [Doctoral dissertation, Northcentral University]. Accessed at www.proquest.com/docview/1966212363 on March 28, 2024.

Skaalvik, E. M., & Skaalvik, S. (2019). Teacher self-efficacy and collective teacher efficacy: Relations with perceived job resources and job demands, feeling of belonging, and teacher engagement. *Creative Education*, *10*(7), 1400–1424.

Smagorinsky, P. (2018). Deconflating the ZPD and instructional scaffolding: Retranslating and reconceiving the zone of proximal development as the zone of next development. *Learning, Culture and Social Interaction*, *16*, 70–75. https://doi.org/10.1016/j.lcsi.2017.10.009

Smith, M. (2023). *Elements that impact early childhood individualized education program teams in supporting inclusive practices* [Unpublished dissertation, Concordia University Irvine].

Spady, R., & Karge, B. D. (2022). The value of formative feedback in graduate online courses. *Distance Learning*, *19*(3), 73–82.

Stang, K. K., & Capp, G. (2004). Co-teaching: Collaboration at the middle level. *Academic Exchange Quarterly*, *8*(3), 228–232.

Stanulis, R. N., Cooper, K. S., Dear, B., Johnston, A. M., & Richard-Todd, R. R. (2016). Teacher-led reforms have a big advantage—teachers. *Phi Delta Kappan*, *97*(7), 53–57.

Steinberg, D. J. (2023). *Summer vacation, here I come!* New York: Grosset & Dunlap.

Stiggins, R. (2017). *The perfect assessment system.* Alexandria, VA: ASCD.

Stone, D., & Heen, S. (2014). *Thanks for the feedback: The science and art of receiving feedback well.* New York: Penguin.

Strain, P. S. (2017). Four-year follow-up of children in the LEAP randomized trial: Some planned and accidental findings. *Topics in Early Childhood Special Education, 37*(2), 121–126.

Sweller, J. (1988). Cognitive load during problem solving: Effects on learning. *Cognitive Science, 12*(2), 257–285.

Syrek, C., Kühnel, J., Vahle-Hinz, T., & De Bloom, J. (2022). Being an accountant, cook, entertainer and teacher—all at the same time: Changes in employees' work and work-related well-being during the coronavirus (COVID-19) pandemic. *International Journal of Psychology, 57*(1), 20–32.

Taub, D., & Foster, M. (2020). Inclusion and intellectual disabilities: A cross cultural review of descriptions. *International Electronic Journal of Elementary Education, 12*(3), 275–281. Accessed at https://iejee.com/index.php/IEJEE/article/view/1090 on March 25, 2024.

Thompson, K. W., & Dow, M. J. (2017). Co-teaching to improve control variable experiment instruction in physical sciences education. *Electronic Journal of Science Education, 21*(5), 36–52.

Thompson, M., & Schademan, A. R. (2019). Gaining fluency: Five practices that mediate effective co-teaching between pre-service and mentor teachers. *Teaching and Teacher Education, 86,* 102903. https://doi.org/10.1016/j.tate.2019.102903

Thornton, L. (2024, May 22). *TK staffing ratios are often unmet, teachers say; why some districts escape fines.* Accessed at https://edsource.org/2024/staffing-ratios-arent-being-met-teachers-say-why-are-some-districts-escaping-fines/712442 on May 29, 2024.

Tiwery, D. S., & Souisa, T. R. (2019). Inside-outside circle as the way in building students' motivation and interaction in speaking classroom activities. *International Journal of Language Education, 3*(1), 33–45.

Trust, T., & Horrocks, B. (2018). *Six key elements identified in an active and thriving blended community of practice.* Accessed at https://doiorg.libproxy.nau.edu/10.1007/s11528-018-0265-x on March 27, 2024.

Urban Institute. (2021). *Strengthening the diversity and quality of the early care and education workforce.* Accessed at www.urban.org/sites/default/files/publication/104998/strengthening-the-diversity-and-quality-of-the-early-care-and-education-workforce.pdf on March 27, 2024.

U.S. Department of Education Office of Educational Technology. (2017, January). *Reimagining the role of technology in education: 2017 national education technology plan update. Washington, DC: U.S. Department of Education.* Accessed at https://tech.ed.gov/netp on November 9, 2023.

U.S. Department of Health and Human Services & U.S. Department of Education. (2015). Policy statement on inclusion of children with disabilities in early childhood programs. *Infants & Young Children, 29*(1), 3–24.

U.S. Department of Health and Human Services & U.S. Department of Education. (2023). *Policy statement on inclusion of children with disabilities in early childhood programs.* Accessed at https://sites.ed.gov/idea/files/policy-statement-on-inclusion-11-28-2023.pdf on March 27, 2024.

Vaughn, S. R., Bos, C. S., & Schumm, J. S. (2023). *Teaching students who are exceptional, diverse, and at risk in the general educational classroom.* New York: Pearson.

Verenikina, I. (2004). From theory to practice: what does the metaphor of scaffolding mean to educators today? *Outlines: Critical Practice Studies, 6*(2), 5–16.

Viel-Ruma, K. A., Houchins, D. E., Jolivette, K., & Benson, G. (2010). Efficacy beliefs of special educators: The relationships among collective efficacy, teacher self-efficacy, and job satisfaction. *Teacher Education and Special Education, 33*(3), 225–233.

Villa, R. A., Thousand, J. S., & Nevin, A. I. (2013). *A guide to co-teaching: New lessons and strategies to facilitate student learning.* Thousand Oaks, CA: Corwin Press.

von Ahlefeld Nisser, D. (2017). Can collaborative consultation, based on communicative theory, promote an inclusive school culture? *Issues in Educational Research, 27*(4), 874–891.

Walsh, J. M. (2012). Co-teaching as a school system strategy for continuous improvement. *Preventing School Failure, 56*(1), 29–36. http://dx.doi.org/10.1080/1045988X.2011.555792

Warren, S. R., Martinez, R. S., & Sortino, L. A. (2016). Exploring the quality indicators of a successful full-inclusion preschool program. *Journal of Research in Childhood Education, 30*(4), 540–553.

Wexler, J., Kearns, D. M., Hogan, E. K., Clancy, E., & Shelton, A. (2021). Preparing to implement evidence-based literacy practices in the co-taught classroom. *Intervention in School and Clinic, 56*(4), 200–207.

Widiastuti, I. A. M. S., Mukminatien, N., Prayogo, J. A., & Irawati, E. (2020). Dissonances between teachers' beliefs and practices of formative assessment in EFL classes. *International Journal of Instruction, 13*(1), 71–84.

Wiggins, G. P., & McTighe, J. (2011). *The understanding by design guide to creating high-quality units.* Alexandria, VA: ASCD.

Wilson, G. L. (2016). *Co-planning for co-teaching: Time-saving routines that work in inclusive classrooms.* Alexandria, VA: ASCD.

Wisniewski, B., Zierer, K., & Hattie, J. (2020). The power of feedback revisited: A meta-analysis of educational feedback research. *Frontiers in Psychology, 10,* 3087.

Wray, E., Sharma, U., & Subban, P. (2022). Factors influencing teacher self-efficacy for inclusive education: A systematic literature review. *Teaching and Teacher Education, 117,* 103800.

Zigmond, N. (1997). Educating students with disabilities: The future of special education. In J. W. Lloyd, E. J. Kameenui, & D. J. Chard (Eds.), *Issues in educating students with disabilities* (pp. 377–390). New York: Routledge.

Zimmerman, K. N., Chow, J. C., Majeika, C., & Senter, R. (2023). Applying co-teaching models to enhance partnerships between teachers and speech-language pathologists. *Intervention in School and Clinic, 58*(3), 146–154.

INDEX

A

academic discourse, 143–145
accommodations and modifications
    equitable instruction and, 131
    essential agreements and, 69, 70
    example co-teaching lesson planning form with accommodations and modification considerations, 140
    integrating instructional strategies with co-teaching strategies and, 101
    preplanning and, 147
    service providers and, 18
    special education and general education co-teaching and, 138, 140
    specialists and, 137
action and expression, 5, 6. *See also* Universal Design for Learning (UDL) framework
administrative support, 67
advanced co-teaching. *See also* co-teaching strategies
    about, 39
    co-teaching strategy quick-reference guide, 31
    co-teaching strategy sequence, 30
    strategies for, 39–42
alternative teaching, 31, 37–38, 123, 145. *See also* team co-teaching
artificial intelligence (AI)
    acts of teachership and, 179
    AI copilots and ed tech tools for specialists, 145–146
    in classrooms without boundaries, 121, 131–134
    co-teaching and, 2, 8–9
    ethics and, 133–134
    key takeaways, 185–186
    for maximizing time and embodying essential agreements, 76–78
    for planning support, 63–64, 87–88

assessments, 132, 133, 145–146. *See also* formative assessments; self-assessments

B

backward planning, 84–85, 95
building and maintaining co-teaching relationships. *See* co-teaching relationships

C

Carter, E., 153
celebrations, 66
certified teachers, types of co-teaching partnerships, 18. *See also* co-teaching partnerships
classroom aides. *See* paraeducators
classroom environment
    digital and physical orientation of lesson planning and design and, 88
    dynamic co-teaching classroom environment, 17–18
classroom guest volunteers, 19
classroom management, 17, 89–90, 92, 94
coherence framework for cultural change
    about, 167–168
    accountability and, 172–174
    collaborative cultures and, 174–176
    deepening learning for teachers and students and, 176–178
    focused direction and, 168–171
collaboration
    collaborative brainstorming, 89
    collaborative community of practice, 64–65
    collaborative cultures, 174–176
    co-teaching relationships and, 50
    direct instruction and, 140
    key takeaways, 186
    role of, 42–43

collective efficacy, 60, 61. *See also* efficacy
communication
    co-teaching relationships and, 52–53
    key takeaways, 186
contemplative practice, phases of, 94
control, letting go of, 51–52
conversation teaching, 31, 39–40, 123, 124. *See also* advanced co-teaching
Cook, L., 30, 140
cooperative learning strategies, 108–109, 177
co-teachers and co-teaching. *See also* cultivating a culture of co-teaching; themes of co-teaching in changing classrooms
    acts to make co-teaching successful and sustainable, 179
    duties and responsibilities of, 91, 173–174
    generative AI copilots and, 8–9
    planning roles and, 86, 90
    potential as co-teachers, 19–22
    rewards of co-teaching, 187–189
    stages to effective co-teaching, 183–184
    who co-teachers are as teachers, 68
co-teaching in classrooms without boundaries. *See also* themes of co-teaching in changing classrooms
    about, 119–120
    additional resources for, 134
    conclusion, 134
    co-teaching with formative assessment to support differentiation and equity, 127–131
    generative AI and ed tech supports in classrooms without boundaries, 131–134
    instruction without boundaries, 120–127
    key takeaways, 187
    key themes and ideas, 120
    reproducibles for, 135
    technology and, 6–8
co-teaching in preK and early childhood settings
    about, 151–152
    additional resources for, 161–162
    adults with different expertise and, 154
    conclusion, 161
    creative systems of inclusive support and, 158–161
    inclusion in early childhood programs, 153–154
    key themes and ideas, 153
    lessons based on observation and, 155–158
    reproducibles for, 163
co-teaching partnerships. *See also* co-teaching relationships
    about, 15–16, 18
    additional resources for, 26
    basic elements and examples of, 22–25
    coherence framework for cultural change and, 173
    conclusion, 26
    co-teaching relationships and, 47
    dynamic co-teaching classroom environment, 17–18
    hidden potential of prospective co-teachers and, 19–22
    key takeaways, 184–185
    key themes and ideas, 16
    relationships and partnerships for teachers and students, 3–4
    reproducibles for, 27
    research: effective co-teaching partnerships, 22–23
    steps to cultivate, 55
    student outcomes and, 53–55
    types of, 18–19
co-teaching relationships
    about, 47–48
    additional resources for, 56
    conclusion, 55–56
    key themes and ideas, 48
    relationships and partnerships for teachers and students, 3–4
    reproducibles for, 57
    shared teaching philosophies and integration into classroom instruction and, 90
    strong partnerships for better student outcomes, 53–55
    suggestions for building and maintaining, 49–53
co-teaching strategies. *See also* instructional strategies
    about, 29–30
    additional resources for, 44
    collaboration and, 42–43
    conclusion, 43–44
    co-teaching strategy quick-reference guide, 31
    co-teaching strategy sequence, 30–31
    eleven co-teaching strategies, 32–42
    incorporation into lessons, 92–97
    key takeaways, 185
    key themes and ideas, 30
    overview of, 122–123
    reproducibles for, 45
    review of, 103
cultivating a culture of co-teaching
    about, 165–166
    additional resources for, 180
    coherence framework for cultural change, 167–178
    conclusion, 180
    key takeaways, 187
    key themes and ideas, 166
    leaders at every level to build school culture, 166–167
    leadership for building and sustaining the best co-teaching programs, 178–179
    reproducibles for, 181

D

decision making, 42, 43, 140
design thinking, 177–178
DeVoss, M., 145
differentiation
    co-teaching with formative

assessments and, 127–131
dual-immersion bilingual education co-teaching and, 145
dual-immersion bilingual education co-teaching, 143–145

E

ed tech
    acts of teachership to make co-teaching successful and sustainable, 179
    AI copilots and ed tech tools for specialists, 145–146
    classroom instruction and, 130
    in classrooms without boundaries, 121, 131–134
    key takeaways, 185
efficacy. *See also* synthesizing efficacy, attitude, and essential agreements
    about, 61
    elements impacting, 61–62
    elements of co-teaching that maximize co-teacher efficacy, 62–67
    essential agreements and, 67–78
    mindset and, 60–62
engagement, 4, 6. *See also* Universal Design for Learning (UDL) framework
epilogue
    additional resources for, 189
    key takeaways, 184–187
    reproducibles for, 190
    rewards of co-teaching, 187–189
    stages to effective co-teaching, 183–184
equity
    co-teaching with formative assessment and, 127–131
    equitable instruction, 130–131
    key takeaways, 186
essential agreements. *See also* synthesizing efficacy, attitude, and essential agreements
    about, 67
    AI and, 76–78
    co-teacher efficacy and, 67–78
    development of, 70–76
    examples of, 68–69, 70
    template for, 75
    who co-teachers are as teachers, 68
explicit instruction, 105–106

F

feedback and co-teaching relationships, 52
focused direction, 168–172
formative assessments. *See also* assessments
    about, 127–128
    co-teaching with to support differentiation and equity, 127–131
    guided instruction and gradual release of responsibility and, 103, 104
    instructional strategies and instructional design and, 107–108
    long-term plans and, 83
    technology and, 6
Friend, M., 30, 140

G

gradual release of responsibility
    guided instruction and, 103–104
    modeling and explicit instruction and, 105–106
    retrieval practice and, 106–107
    thinking routines and, 109
graze-and-tag teaching, 31, 35, 122. *See also* team co-teaching
guided instruction and gradual release of responsibility, 103–104

H

home schools, 160

I

inclusion
    creative systems of, 158–161
    in early childhood programs, 153–154
    key takeaways, 186
individual strengths and co-teaching relationships, 51
individualized education plans (IEPs)
    AI copilots and ed tech tools and, 146
    co-teaching and, 17
    digital organization and, 63, 83
    essential agreements and, 69, 70
    preplanning and, 147
    quick look at, 142
    relationships and partnerships for teachers and students and, 3
    service providers and, 18
    special education and general education co-teaching and, 138, 140
    specialists and, 137
instruction
    elements of instructional design definitions and examples, 92–93
    equitable instruction, 130–131
    instruction without boundaries, 120–127
    shared teaching philosophies and integration into, 88–90
instructional and co-teaching strategy and routine incorporation into lessons. *See also* planning and designing lessons
    about, 92
    strategies for classroom routines, 92, 94
    strategies for instructional use, 94, 96
    time to plan, 96–97
instructional coaching, 175
instructional design, 82. *See also* planning and designing lessons
instructional risk-taking culture, 67
instructional strategies

about, 101–102
additional resources for, 116
conclusion, 115–116
cooperative learning strategies, 108–109
co-teaching strategies followed by, 112
formative assessments and, 107–108
guided instruction and gradual release of
 responsibility and, 103–104
instructional strategies and instructional
 design, 104–111
instructional strategies in action: putting strategies
 together with co-teaching, 111–115
instructional strategy organizer, 112
interleaving and spaced practice, 107
key takeaways, 185
key themes and ideas, 102
modeling and explicit instruction, 105–106
reproducibles for, 117
retrieval practice, 106–107
review of co-teaching strategies, 103
scaffolding, 110
station rotation, 110–111
thinking routines, 109–110
integrating instructional strategies with co-teaching
 strategies. *See* instructional strategies
integrating specialists into co-teaching. *See* specialists
interactive teaching, 31, 41, 123.
 See also advanced co-teaching
interleaving and spaced practice, 107
intervention specialists, 33, 53–55, 147.
 See also specialists
introducing co-teaching strategies.
 See co-teaching strategies
introduction
 about co-teaching, 1–2
 guide to reading this book, 9–13
 model of co-teaching that can work for
  every teacher, 13
 underlying themes of co-teaching in changing
  classrooms, 3–9

K
Karge, B., 65

L
leadership
 acts of to make co-teaching successful and
  sustainable, 179
 for building and sustaining the best co-teaching
  programs, 178–179
 leaders at every level to build school
  culture, 166–167
Leamons, M., 97
 lessons based on observation, 155–158.
  See also planning and designing lessons
long- and short-term planning with workflow in mind.
 See also planning and designing lessons

about, 82
digital and physical orientation, 86–88
establishment of long-term plans, 83
planning roles of co-teachers, 86

M
mentoring, 65–66
mindsets and efficacy, 60–62
modeling
 alternative teaching and, 38
 differentiation and support possibilities and, 129
 explicit instruction and, 105–106
 formative assessments and, 108
 guided instruction and gradual release of
  responsibility and, 103–104
 interactive teaching and, 41
 scaffolding and, 110
 shared teaching and, 42
 station rotation and, 111
 TPACK and, 7
 UDL framework and, 5
Myers-Briggs Type Indicator, 55, 56

N
navigating co-teaching partnerships.
 See co-teaching partnerships
norms and co-teaching relationships, 51

O
observations. *See also* one teach, one observe
 lessons based on observation, 155–158
 teacher observations, 175
one teach, one assist, 31, 32, 122.
 See also supportive co-teaching
one teach, one observe. *See also* supportive co-teaching
 co-teaching strategy quick-reference guide, 31
 lessons based on observation, 155–158
 overview of co-teaching instructional strategies
  without boundaries, 122
 in a preK phonics lesson, 156
 supportive co-teaching, 33
one teach, one support, 31, 33–34, 122, 156.
 See also supportive co-teaching
open-mindedness, 52

P
paraeducators, 19, 158–159
parallel teaching. *See also* team co-teaching
 co-teaching strategy quick-reference guide, 31
 examples of co-teaching without instructional
  boundaries, 125–126
 overview of co-teaching instructional strategies
  without boundaries, 122
 team co-teaching, 35–36
parent nights, 161

personalized learning, 64, 132
planning and designing lessons. *See also* instructional and co-teaching strategy and routine incorporation into lessons
   about, 81–82
   additional resources for, 98
   coherence framework for cultural change and, 173
   conclusion, 97
   continual planning, 148
   elements of instructional design definitions and examples, 92–93
   example backward planner and strategy tool kit, 95
   example co-teaching lesson planning form with accommodations and modification considerations, 140
   example of weekly backward planner, 84–85
   example pyramid lesson planning, 141
   example simple co-teaching lesson plan outline, 143
   instructional and co-teaching strategy and routine incorporation into lessons, 92–97
   key themes and ideas, 72
   lessons based on observation and, 155–158
   long- and short-term planning with workflow in mind, 82–88
   planning roles of co-teachers, 86
   planning time, 50, 62–64, 96–97, 173
   preplanning, 147
   reproducibles for, 99
   roles and responsibilities in planning and workflow, 90–91
   shared teaching philosophies and integration into classroom instruction, 88–90
   supportive co-teaching planning template, 34
playlist template, 129
potential as co-teachers, 19–22
preK and early childhood settings inclusion, 153–154. *See also* co-teaching in preK and early childhood settings
professional development, 175
professional learning communities (PLCs), 96–97, 174
professional learning networks (PLNs), 12–13
professional relationships, 49–50. *See also* co-teaching relationships
prospective co-teachers, hidden potential of, 19–22

R

relationships and partnerships for teachers and students, 3–4. *See also* co-teaching relationships
representation, 5, 6. *See also* Universal Design for Learning (UDL) framework
reproducibles for
   reflection and action: 3-2-1 format, 99
   reflection and action: agree, argue, and inspired, 79
   reflection and action: challenge, 163
   reflection and action: develop an action plan, 181
   reflection and action: I noticed, I wondered, 45
   reflection and action: I used to think versus now I think, 57
   reflection and action: key takeaways and action steps, 190
   reflection and action: next steps, 27
   reflection and action: pause, ponder, and wonder, 135
   reflection and action: reflection and goal setting, 149
   reflection and action: square, circle, and triangle, 117
retrieval practice, 106–107
risk-taking culture, 67
role-play teaching, 31, 40, 89, 123. *See also* advanced co-teaching

S

scaffolding, 103, 110
school and classroom structure, 178–179
secondary English lesson, example instructional strategies in action, 114–115
self-assessments, 4, 107–108. *See also* assessments
self-efficacy, 60–61. *See also* efficacy
service providers, types of co-teaching partnerships, 18
shared planning time, 50, 62–64, 173. *See also* planning and designing lessons
shared teaching, 31, 41–42, 123. *See also* advanced co-teaching
SMART goals, 168–169, 170, 171
social learning, 65, 156
spaced practice, 107
special education
   general education co-teaching and, 138–143
   inclusion in early childhood programs, 154
   leadership at every level for co-teaching cultures and, 167
specialists
   about, 137–138
   additional resources for, 148
   AI copilots and ed tech tools for, 145–146
   case study for, 147–148
   conclusion, 148
   co-teaching with speech and language pathologists and other related services personnel, 145
   dual-immersion bilingual education co-teaching, 143–145
   key themes and ideas, 138
   leadership at every level for co-teaching cultures, 167
   reproducibles for, 149
   sample family letter, 141
   special education and general education co-teaching and, 138–143
speech and language pathologists and other related services personnel, 145
stages to effective co-teaching, 183–184
stakeholders
   focused direction and, 168, 171
   leaders at every level to build school culture and, 167

stakeholder contributions to program development and improvement, 175–176
station rotation, 110–111. *See also* instructional strategies
station teaching. *See also* team co-teaching
    co-teaching strategy quick-reference guide, 31
    examples of co-teaching without instructional boundaries, 125–126
    overview of co-teaching instructional strategies without boundaries, 123
    in preK collaborative play, 156
    team co-teaching, 37
STEM lesson on measurement, example instructional strategies in action, 113–114
strategic plans and timelines, 171–172
strategies, incorporating into lessons, 92, 94, 96. *See also* co-teaching strategies; instructional strategies
students with disabilities
    accommodations and, 131
    co-teaching and, 17, 186
    inclusion and, 153–154, 169
    special education and general education co-teaching and, 139
supportive co-teaching. *See also* co-teaching strategies
    about, 32
    co-teaching strategy quick-reference guide, 31
    co-teaching strategy sequence, 30
    strategies for, 32–34
supports
    creative systems of inclusive support, 158–161
    differentiation and support possibilities, 128–130
synchronous teaching, secondary classroom: two co-teachers teaching synchronously online, 126–127
synthesizing efficacy, attitude, and essential agreements
    about, 59–60
    additional resources for, 78
    conclusion, 78
    efficacy and mindset, 60–62
    elements of co-teaching that maximize co-teacher efficacy, 62–67
    essential agreements for greater co-teacher efficacy, 67–78
    key themes and ideas, 60
    reproducibles for, 79

T

teacher observations, 175

teaching philosophies, 88–90
team co-teaching. *See also* co-teaching strategies
    about, 34–35
    co-teaching strategy quick-reference guide, 31
    co-teaching strategy sequence, 30
    strategies for, 35–38
Technological Pedagogical Content Knowledge (TPACK), 6–8
themes of co-teaching in changing classrooms
    about, 3
    co-teachers and generative AI copilots, 8–9
    relationships and partnerships for teachers and students, 3–4
    TPACK and, 6–8
    UDL framework and, 4–6
thinking routines, 109–110
time
    co-teaching relationships and, 50, 53
    planning time, 50, 62–64, 96–97, 173
tutoring, 132

U

Universal Design for Learning (UDL) framework, 4–5, 8–9

V

video examples, QR codes for
    conversation teaching, 39
    co-teaching kindergarten language arts, 157
    co-teaching planning with AI, 88
    co-teaching preschool level, 157
    dual-immersion co-teaching lesson, 144
    introduction to co-teaching, 2
    one teach, one support, 33

W

weekly backward planner, example of, 84–85
workflow
    about, 63
    generative AI and ed tech supports and, 131–132
    planning and, 82–88, 90–91

Z

Zigmond, N., 138

Watch, Listen, Ask, Learn
Belinda Dunnick Karge

Written for current and aspiring administrators and teacher leaders, this book offers action items, case studies, and reproducible tools to help you stay in front of special education law, know and support your learning services team, and ensure students with disabilities receive equitable, inclusive education.

BKG080

Making the Move With Ed Tech
Troy Hicks, Jennifer Parker, and Kate Grunow

In this book, the authors help educators wade through ed-tech jargon and frameworks to learn how to employ technology tools strategically. Explore moves, or instructional strategies, both familiar and new, that facilitate student inquiry, dialogue, critical thinking, and creativity.

BKG101

Yes We Can!
Heather Friziellie, Julie A. Schmidt, and Jeanne Spiller

Utilizing PLC practices, general and special educators must develop collaborative partnerships in order to close the achievement gap and maximize learning for all. The authors encourage all educators to take collective responsibility in improving outcomes for students with special needs.

BKF653

Critical Conversations in Co-Teaching
Carrie Chapman and Cate Hart Hyatt

In this practitioner's guide to building quality collaborative relationships, the authors explain co-teaching models and how co-teaching fits within school improvement initiatives. Through practical examples and real-life stories, they present the critical conversations framework designed to foster dramatic improvements in the way co-teachers communicate.

BKF428

Meant for More
Angie Freese

Discover a team-oriented approach for building a classroom community that empowers each learner. Practical strategies and tools guide you in creating inclusive environments built on dignity, authenticity, and connection that close opportunity gaps and prepare all learners for future success.

BKF985

Solution Tree | Press

a division of Solution Tree

Visit SolutionTree.com or call 800.733.6786 to order.

"Excellent engagement in what truly matters in **assessment**.

Great examples!"

—Carol Johnson, superintendent,
Central Dauphin School District, Pennsylvania

 PD Services

Our experts draw from decades of research and their own experiences to bring you practical strategies for designing and implementing quality assessments. You can choose from a range of customizable services, from a one-day overview to a multiyear process.

Book your assessment PD today!
888.763.9045

Solution Tree